# FIGHTING FOR FOOTBALL

# FIGHTING FOR FOOTBALL

From Woolwich Arsenal to the
Western Front, the Lost Story of
Football's First Rebel

## George Myerson

First published in Great Britain
2009 by Aurum Press Ltd
7 Greenland Street
London NW1 0ND
www.aurumpress.co.uk

A catalogue record for this book is available from the British Library.

ISBN  978 1 84513 409 9

1 3 5 7 9 10 8 6 4 2
2009  2011  2013  2012  2010

Typeset by SX Composing DTP, Rayleigh, Essex
Printed by MPG Books, Bodmin, Cornwall

# Contents

**PART FOUR: THE FUTURE**

'Prior to the Final Tie, 998,568 had paid admission fees amounting to £37,339, and altogether 1,070,000 persons witnessed the various rounds of the competition . . . it has grown far beyond the dreams of anyone officially connected with the game in the eighties.'

Mr J.J. Bentley, chairman of Manchester United, on the rise of the professional game in *The Book of Football*, 1905

'I am one of those who believe that a man should be paid according to his ability, and a good few, I reckon, are worth more than four quid a week.'

Tim Coleman on life as a professional footballer, writing in the *Weekly News*, 1909

# Prologue

When the fans arrived at Goodison Park for the traditional New Year's Day game, they found something different in the programme. As usual, it was a joint Everton and Liverpool programme, surveying the week for both Merseyside clubs. There were some adverts, the team line-ups. Except that this was no ordinary 1 January, and the first item was not the words of the manager, or the League tables. On the cover, decorated with the two clubs' emblems, was the date of the occasion: 'January 1st 1916', the second New Year of the Great War, and there inside was the news that made the prospect of a football match seem ridiculous. Under the headline '"Tim" Coleman Killed', the programme said: 'He represented his country on the football field and also on the battlefield; he has done his duty both nobly and well, and those who love football are proud to think that he has gained the highest honours in his final international.'

There had been rumours since Christmas of the loss of the man whose name was usually written 'Tim', once an Everton favourite and always a national character. Everyone knew he was at the front, serving with the volunteers of the Footballers' Battalion and, though details were forbidden in the press, they were said to have 'seen action'. The announcement of his death was more of a confirmation than a total shock for many of its first readers.

The news had snaked across the country. The Northampton papers had started the story – that was where he was born, named John

George Coleman, in 1881 – and it had spread to London, where he had played for much of his football career, first for Woolwich Arsenal, before coming up north, and later for Fulham. It also got to Nottingham, where his former manager at Forest was trying to organise a benefit game for the man's wife and kids. Maybe they could do something here too.

The Goodison game went ahead, as Tim would have insisted. Not that it was a real match, only a friendly. At the end of the 1914-15 season, the Football League had been suspended and so had all payment to players. 'Professionalism' had been fiercely denounced in Parliament and the press: it was not right for men to earn money for 'playing' when others were dying for their country. Everton were, in fact, the title holders, having taken the First Division championship under the captaincy of Tim's close mate, the Scottish international Jimmy Galt. (Tim was long gone on his travels, gone but not forgotten.)

Real football had been forbidden for the duration on the home front, although it was different behind the lines. In other respects, the football scene was still thriving, and in the most British of ways: the papers remained full of football. Radio had not yet arrived in everyday life and football had not made it to the cinemas, so newspapers were the way the fans found out about the game when they weren't on those terraces. That January, as in the previous twenty years, Britons, and especially the English, were still buying 'football specials', those supplements to regular papers and others that were free-standing papers. Along with the sportier dailies, they took the game into the homes – and the imaginations – of millions.

For New Year, they were full of Tim. Feeding on rumours from the capital, the New Year's Day *Bradford Argus* had its obituary ready for press. 'Something of a humorist, he was always popular wherever he played,' it said. This is what everyone says about the fallen player. He was 'always popular' – everywhere he played, and he had played everywhere. These are the Coleman hallmarks: humour and a deep sense of popularity . . . and talent. Most obituaries say nice things about people, but his were different. The sheer volume of these vivid, instant memoirs brings back the lost image of a pre-war football hero. 'As far back as Bradford City's first season in the Second Division he came to Valley Parade with Woolwich Arsenal on that remarkable day when the great deluge caused play to be abandoned at halftime.'

By 1914, Bradford City had made it into the First Division and they were well placed when the war came, established in the Yorkshire heartlands of the game. There, the thought of Tim Coleman brought back already nostalgic memories of innocent days, when 'the great deluge' referred only to a rainy day.

The football strongholds of the North and Midlands were mourning the loss of this southern boy. The story hit people's feelings in Hull, Birmingham and Sheffield. One of the most moving reports came in the paper of the city that had been top of the football world at the turn of the century, when Sheffield United took both the League title and the FA Cup. Although they had fallen away since then, Sheffield remained football crazy. In what they called 'Football's Roll of Honour', they first highlighted 'among the latest names that of J.G. Coleman, always known as Tim'. Then the dignified clichés stop, and instead there is real sadness, touched strangely – and as it turns out fittingly – with wit: 'Alas, Poor Tim! There was nary a cheerier figure at football than poor "Tim" Coleman, who has fought the good fight and gone over.'

Another deep note came from the modern world's football city, which had a central place in Tim's story, though he never played for either of the clubs. The *Manchester Football Chronicle* launched its 'Roll of Honour' with a picture of Coleman, before giving their take on his story. They had heard he was still playing, right to the finish: 'He took part in a military match behind the firing line shortly after his arrival in France.' He had arrived at the front only in November, so it was a few weeks before. It was a strange idea, Coleman playing his last match within sound of the guns. The catch in the breath is audible: 'He played football for the love of it and forsook it for the love of his country.' They flicked back to the beginning of Coleman's career, when all the great northern clubs were competing for his signature: 'Before he was seventeen he had received many tempting offers.' From Nottingham came shock at 'the reported death of the ex-Evertonian Tim Coleman', a tremor echoed to the west in Bristol and the east in Norwich. This was a cult following in mourning.

But clearly there were also that New Year's Day some hints of confusion in London, where the *Football Star* reported that after Christmas: 'Mrs Coleman received a telegram from her husband.' He was not dead at all – despite all the obituaries! The real coup belonged to the *Athletic News*, the national sporting paper, based in Manchester, which had been making its own inquiries. Coming out that little bit later, on Monday 3 January, it devoted its front-page lead item to: 'The Welcome News in "Tim" Coleman's Home'. Next to the headline, it ran what was then an astonishing picture of Nelly, as Tim always called her, with their two sons, opening the telegram from her husband telling her that he was OK, as if for the first time. (She must have been performing it.) Young John Victor is proudly looking at his father's photograph in the frame: a miniature is inset into the picture. The older brother, Arthur, an awkward teenager, stands with an effort at dignified calm and offers his mother support. It would be a senti- mental scene except for the genuineness of the feelings they express. In the background, you can just see some of the domestic clutter of Christmas and New Year. The photo came out the day before the Tuesday on which Victor had his seventh birthday.

It had been all a false alarm – on a national scale. The truth that Tim had survived began to spread and, amid the confusion and the half-farce, the football community showed its strength. Tim became a national good news story in a difficult time. The London nationals were in the lead, notably the *Sporting Life*, which ran a story under the headline 'Tim Coleman Alive and Well'. It read: 'The many friends of Tim Coleman, the old Fulham and Arsenal footballer, will be much relieved to hear that the story that he had been killed in action is without foundation.'

One of the most widely read papers of them all, and in many ways the prototype for modern sports journalism, was D.C. Thomson's *Weekly News*. It was the pioneer of football personality journalism, and the place where Tim had found his own voice. Coming out of London, Manchester and Dundee, this was a real British football paper. 'Good News From Famous Players' ran its headline. They filled the story out: 'The tale that Tim Coleman and Bob Dalrymple, of the Footballers' Battalion, had been killed at the front was a very circumstantial one, and was circulated from three different sources, namely, London, Norwich and Northampton. Some time later all were gratified by the receipt of wires from Coleman and Dalrymple saying they were alive and well. It would be interesting to learn how the tale originated, but indignation has been forgotten in the relief felt by all that the players are alive and well.' The personality of Tim again took centre stage, 'for there is no greater favourite in the game than Tim Coleman, who is one of the recognised wits of the football world'. As the papers caught on to the story, the jokes grew: 'Tim . . . will be making a collection of all the splendid press notices.'

Dead and then alive, Coleman was a focus for heartfelt interest among the football media and its readers in 1916. It was one of several moments of real fame for Coleman, amid a steady flow of news and attention from the early years of the century until that ominous date in British history, looking as it does towards the horrors of the Somme and the unprecedented scale of the British loss of 60,000 soldiers on 1 July alone. Even so, a century or so later, he is not an obvious subject for a book. He was not an enduring superstar, as was Manchester United's Billy Meredith, the most long-lived celebrity of the period. So why Tim Coleman, and why now?

My interest began with the pre-war football world, the huge release of popular energy that drove the game to the forefront of British life and so prepared the way for its global domination in the decades after the First World War. James Walvin, in his classic account, *The People's Game*, reveals that in 1888-89, the first season of the Football League, a total attendance of 602,000 watched the games. By 1895, that figure had reached two million and in 1905 there were five million spectators of League games. It was an unprecedented explosion of public passion, centred on working-class men and yet including many women and also beginning to draw in people of other social classes. In the nineteenth century professionalism had arrived in football, beginning with expenses claims to cover being away from home. After initial resistance from the Football Association, by 1891 the Football League had 448 registered players, mainly professionals. Two decades on and, by 1914, there was a Players' Union, whose files recorded that there were 4,470 footballers, many part-timers and a hard core of full-time pros.

I wanted to tell a story that caught the human power of this development, one that goes beyond the impressive statistics and records the real atmosphere of the game and the grounds, what it felt like to be there, at the birth of the world's favourite sport. I read thousands of reports and articles from the time – the football press was already huge – and the subsequent histories. The story would need to have a character at its centre, someone who lived through the drama. I wanted someone who experienced a real football life, not merely the most famous or successful player.

Coleman attracted my attention first because of the warmth of the press reaction to him, and I began to find more and more references to him and his life, both on and off the field. His main fame as a player was won with the club that was then called Woolwich Arsenal and Bernard Joy's classic history, *Forwards Arsenal*, confirmed my feeling that here was someone special, someone with a story, someone at the heart of the football explosion. In John Harding's history of the players' union, *For The Good of The Game*, there is a picture of a side that called themselves The Outcasts, with Coleman in the front row, which reinforced this impression, even though the book itself does not otherwise mention him. Then I found Tim's own writing about his experiences and beliefs, which was featured in the *Weekly News* in 1909 and 1910. The paper, as Harding notes, had a readership of more than 300,000 and was one of the most influential voices on behalf of the players themselves.

A personality was emerging, as were the key episodes of a unique and exciting football life. I followed both Tim and his generation into the trenches. The glimpses were fewer, as one would expect of a private soldier in a mass slaughter. Yet he then came back into view, even as a player on one strange afternoon before the Somme when, on 1 April 1916, he played what was to prove the match of his life in several senses, a contest between two teams of front-line soldiers. This day will take us to the heart of the strange, lost world of what the men at the time knew as 'firing line football'. The image of football at the front has been restricted to the Christmas truce of 1914 when, as one officer reported: 'On Christmas Day a football match was played between us in front of the trench.' In fact, this one image of Anglo-German football has obscured the much larger picture of the game as a rare positive influence in the lives of the British soldiers. Tim's match in 1916 gives us a unique opportunity to do justice to the real role of football, and of its famous soldiers, amid the carnage.

His war even had its own climax, half-shrouded in smoke and yet all the more moving. Our fixed image of the Western Front has, naturally, been shaped by the prolonged experience of trench warfare, the often apparently static situations punctuated by the furious intervals of 'going over the top'. The war of 1918 has been overshadowed by the powerful pictures and memories of the earlier phase, the peculiarity of which sank deep into modern consciousness. But in August 1918, which we probably think of as the road to victory, British losses totalled 122,000. It was in this more mobile war that Tim was really drawn into the heart of the battle even beyond the experiences that he shared with others in the dark days of the Somme.

Through all his exploits, there was little sense of his private life, something that is all too apparent with the twenty-first century celebrity player. Coleman's family appeared only fleetingly in coverage of him, though still to touching effect. His was not a richly documented life, but I found myself more absorbed by him because of that, fascinated by the challenge of piecing together the essential drama of a life spent – in many senses – fighting for football. This was a life that reveals how the modern game was made, before and even during the First World War.

# Part One

# The Woolwich Arsenal Years

# Taking a Chance

September 1902, and the fourteenth season of the English Football League was beginning. The power of the game still lay firmly in the Midlands and the North. Sunderland were the reigning champions, Liverpool took the title before them and Aston Villa had won it in 1898 and '99. The only London club in the League was Woolwich Arsenal, who were struggling in the lower reaches of the second of the two divisions. It was here that Tim Coleman began his real football life.

The club was founded in 1886 and known briefly as Dial Square FC before taking up residence in Plumstead, south-east London, and changing its name to Woolwich Arsenal, which they were to retain until the move to Highbury, north London, in 1913. The Plumstead years are generally treated as a prelude to the formation of the Arsenal legend, meriting only a page or so in the official illustrated history of the club, and a short, though lively, account of 'Freaks from the Factory' in Jon Spurling's alternative chronicle, *Rebels for a Cause*. But those years were far more dramatic than that suggests and far more worthy of investigation.

Discovering that drama meant delving into the rich mass of football papers, from the local patriotism of the *Plumstead News* and the *Woolwich Flash* to the larger view of the London-based *Football Evening News*, the *Morning Leader*, the Manchester paper of national sport, the *Athletic News*, and dozens of other local and regional voices. There are also relevant details from more modern records of club and game. The most vivid overview of the club is still Bernard Joy's 1954 account, *Forward Arsenal*, Joy having been the last great amateur player at Highbury in the Thirties and Forties. This dignifiedly partisan book traces the origins of the Woolwich days among the workers at the armaments factory in south-east London, and the role of some former Nottingham Forest players, who brought their red shirts with them and so established the famous colours of the Arsenal club.

It is Joy's book that hints at the real power behind Arsenal's rise to become, as he said, 'the leading club in the south', beginning with their domination of London and southern cup competitions in the 1880s. There followed the momentous decision to join the second of the Football League's two divisions in 1893-94. No signs followed, though, of promotion to the top flight. On the contrary, they had a worsening struggle to survive, caused in part, according to Joy, by the Boer War. 'Soldiers were drafted abroad from the garrison and, worse still, the workers at Woolwich arsenal were kept behind on Saturday afternoons on munitions production,' he wrote. Crowds fell and money was tight. The club was saved by a local shopkeeper, G.H. Leavey, who gave £60 to pay outstanding wages.

Fortunately they were able to sign a sharp man as manager in the shape of Harry Bradshaw, and he combed the lower reaches of the game for cheap talent, including Tim himself, from Northampton, Jimmy Ashcroft, an amateur goalie from Sheppey, and Archie Cross, a Kent-born defender. To them he added the experienced Scot, Jimmy Jackson, as skipper. Jackson had played for Rangers and Newcastle and he came to London partly to set up a sports shop, so taking the pressure off his limited football wages. Still, the club depended on fund-raising through fêtes and raffles. This was how London was fighting for a place on football's national stage.

As a new recruit, Tim did not have long to wait for a game. He was picked for the first home match of that season, in League Division

Two, against the side then known as Burslem Port Vale. Woolwich Arsenal's home at that time was the Manor Ground, located just by the munitions factory that gave the club its name. Thousands of factory workers were packed in on the terraces to see their team begin another season. Many more were kept back by the demands of production. Those who did make it saw Tim come out in the red and white of the Woolwich Arsenal club, alongside his friend Everard Lawrence, who had been signed with him from Northampton Town. Together, they made up one flank of the forward line.

The team sheet, and newspaper announcements, might have listed him as John George Coleman, but already among his fellow players he was known by the name of Tim, which followed him from his previous clubs, Kettering Town and then Northampton. He was typically mocking about this nickname: 'Though I am known as Tim Coleman, my real name is John George Coleman. I don't know why I was called Tim but I suppose it was because I used to address lads whose Christian names I did not know as Tim, and by degrees they must have "done it on me".' There was a hint of aggression in the Coleman charm. It was fitting that his name should arise out of his irresistible urge to tease and entertain his fellow players, even when they did not like it. Certainly, though he had had a brief spell as 'Tiddy' at Kettering, he was firmly Tim from the moment he arrived at the Manor Ground.

The only variation on his nickname was the use of 'Tiny Tim', which, besides being the name of a character in Dickens's *A Christmas Carol*, was also appropriate: Coleman did not look like most pre-war footballers. There is some uncertainty about his exact height. In general, he seems to have claimed to be taller than he was. The Army found him out: his enlistment form testifies that he was no more than 5ft 5in, a mere couple of inches above the military minimum. At that time, a 5ft 10in centre-forward or centre-half was considered huge, but Tim was still a good few inches below the average for a footballer. It was not just his height. In an era of muscle-bound aggression, he was solid enough but delicately built. In team photographs, his boots seemed half the size of the clumping footwear worn by his colleagues, which were like modern climbing boots.

Despite his small stature, there was an aura about him, created in part by his boyish expression, sharp features and distinctive sideways grin. His hair was curly, and reddish-brown. Only in close-up could one see the lines that were there from early on, a sign of the hard childhood he endured. Being the middle of the seven children of George and Julia Coleman was a lively start in the world. His eldest brother, Arthur, had set him a sporting example, as a demon bowler in local cricket in the Kettering area. The trouble was that his father's dairyman's wage did not make keeping such a family easy.

As he came out to face Port Vale, Tim knew that a huge amount was at stake for him. The maximum wage for a footballer was four pounds a week, the same as that of a decent factor worker. Tim was on considerably less, three pounds a week at the most. Still that was a lot better than the income at the dairy where his father worked or on a farm, and he had spent part of his youth helping with the harvest. He had also done his time in the shoe factories around Kettering. If the streets were not paved with gold around Woolwich, they were a lot more welcoming than the muddy fields at dawn around Kettering, and a lot more promising than the trek to the dairy. He had worked hard to get this chance.

Tim wrote a little later, in his *Weekly News* column, how he always knew that 'the footballer's lot is not ideal'. Even after he had become a success, he remembered the early anxieties, which indeed never went away entirely: 'There is also the case of the injured player who may meet his death as a result of football injuries, and leave a widow and family,' he said. Professional football was a risky business in those hard times, when the world of medicine was still rough and ready, and anaesthetics and keyhole surgery were unheard of. A broken bone would end a man's season, and ten-month contracts gave the clubs the power to dispose of players seen as injury-prone more or less at will. Tim himself had several painful lay-offs. Still, he was also ready to look on the bright side, as he recognised in his own distinctive way: 'A characteristic of most footballers is that they are always confident of winning, and perhaps I'm usually inclined to be that way myself.' He was aware of the dangers and the difficulties, and yet he was confident of succeeding.

His football had begun as pure fun. At the age of fifteen, he was playing for the church team of Kettering St Phillips, and later on he remembered scoring five goals in one 9-1 victory. The team became virtually unbeatable in the Wellingborough and District League. His burgeoning reputation earned him a place with Kettering Town in 1899. The main competition they played in was the Midland League, and it brought them up against teams like Barnsley as well as local rivals like Wellingborough. In fact, his first game for 'The Ketts' had been against Wellingborough and, at the age of only seventeen, it took him about a minute to have his first long-range shot, which crashed into the side-netting to the amazement of the crowd. He was even smaller in those days, yet already the power of his right-foot shot took spectators and visiting teams alike by surprise. Soon he was hammering in 25-yard goals, and week after week the local journalist recorded admiringly that Coleman 'scored beautifully'.

With Tim in their ranks Kettering won the Midland League and they had a great FA Cup run in the first months of 1901, despite having one tie postponed because of the funeral of Queen Victoria. Most famously, they defeated Crewe Alexandria, northern experts from the real football country. Kettering also entered the newly reorganised Southern League, where they came up against bigger clubs like Southampton and West Ham, Woolwich Arsenal and Tottenham Hotspur. This was how Tim had first come to the notice of the Plumstead team. In between, there had been a season at Northampton in 1901-02, where his main highlight had been a Cup-tie against Sheffield United, who went on to win the FA Cup that year. Tim had gone close. It was another taste of the big time for him as United were led by the legendary 22st goalkeeper, Willie Foulke, a towering presence in the turn-of-the-century game.

Now here he was, inside-forward for Woolwich Arsenal, the most ambitious of the London clubs. He had had offers from the North, but had chosen not to go so far afield. This was alien enough to him. Looking across, he could see the centre-forward Billy Gooing, who had already introduced him to his main delight, billiards (Billy became a notable billiards player after he gave up the big ball game, winning tournaments). Behind them was the Scot, Jimmy Jackson, the captain, in the centre of defence. He was making a new start of a different kind, having been tempted to London with the promise from the club that it would help him to open a sports shop in Woolwich, a promise that was indeed honoured. This was how clubs managed to get round the issue of the maximum wage.

Tim always thought of these games between northern and southern clubs as the hardest matches. When he was preparing for the Merseyside derby between Liverpool and Everton in later years, he contrasted such a prospect with matches such as this one, between Woolwich and Port Vale. 'Though the play is always of the hardest, there seems to be an absence of that bitter antagonistic feeling that often prevails when teams many miles apart try conclusions,' he said. The North versus South rivalry was about far more than football. It was about two different Englands.

The whistle blew, and Tim's real football career was under way. There was a scrap for possession in the middle of the pitch, and then the home side went on the attack. Another whistle: the 1902-03 season began with a penalty. The obvious person to take it was Billy Gooing or maybe Tommy Briercliffe. Instead, to everyone's surprise, the new boy stepped up and insisted that this one was for him. It seemed that he was in a rush to get in on the act. He had that feeling of self-assurance that a great player needs; as he said, he knew what he could do: 'I consider that I am a pretty good judge of my form.' Without that, the touch of assertiveness and even of arrogance, there is no future at the top of football. But in that early moment of his Woolwich Arsenal career, he was not yet able to carry that confidence through into success. He hit the penalty reasonably hard, but the keeper guessed right, saved it, and the score remained 0-0.

The miss only made him fight harder. Arsenal came forward again and there was a sharp passage of inter-passing between Lawrence, Gooing and Coleman, another hint of things to come. Later, Tim highlighted the advantage it gave players when they were familiar with each other's game and had 'knowledge of each other's little ways'. That was one of the keys to success according to Tim, as he considered football to be all about anticipation and quick movement. In any case, that was the style he had brought with him from Northampton and it was looking as if it might fit with the Arsenal approach, in contrast to the more straightforward methods of some of the big northern clubs. The move criss-crossed the field and opened up the visitors' defence. It was only a question of who would finish it off. Tim was not shy of having a go that day and, with his nerves just beginning to settle after that penalty setback, 'with a glorious shot', he was on the Arsenal score sheet. Woolwich Arsenal ran out 3-0 winners, and both fans and press were happy with the summer purchase. 'Coleman, the new man from Northampton, played magnificently as inside-left, his passing and shooting being superb.'

Tim had begun well, enjoying a fine debut, but 'the new man from Northampton' had had a far from smooth transition to his new club. He told the tale about how he was woken in the middle of the night by Woolwich Arsenal officials, so eager were they for his signature. Despite his late-night capture, Tim had not come to London full of gratitude and nostalgia for his old town club. On the contrary, he had a wry, perhaps bitter, sense of how teams such as Northampton treated their promising players. They never paid these men properly, many believing that to do so would ruin such small clubs. Tim's response, uncompromising as ever and increasingly articulate, was: 'I hear that old rusty war cry that the weaker clubs would go to the wall, but how many of the so-called weaker clubs have put themselves on a sound financial footing by the sale of a player whom they have brought out?' As far as he was concerned, he owed Northampton nothing – if anything they owed him. Certainly this was logical. It was the club that had benefited financially, not the player. Beyond logic, there was also a streak of mischief and even menace. This attitude was all his own; it was more than half a century later that footballers started to become the heroes of a newly rebellious generation, when Rodney Marsh and Derek Dougan made themselves icons of the awkward squad in the 1970s. Marsh became a regular TV pundit after a career spent upsetting managers and creating numerous newspaper head-lines with his off-field behaviour, while Dougan's uncompromising stance and hard-nosed attitude eventually won him the chairmanship of the Professional Footballers' Association. These were men who were rebels in times when rebellion, though still a precarious business, also had its uses as a pathway to success. Tim is recognisably their type of footballer, but did not live in their type of world. It has much to recommend it, that defiant anger, but there was also a dangerous side as Tim did not always know when to stop. Sometimes that got him into trouble, when that bravery and defiance became destructive. Such characters are always going to be a mixed blessing for themselves and their team.

# London Upstarts

Tim's arrival coincided with a difficult period at Woolwich Arsenal. Continuing pressure of overtime at the vast local munitions factory, due to the demand caused by the Boer War, meant that attendances were lower and money ever tighter; the club was hanging on. Ironically it was this shortage of money that had forced them to recruit players from lowly Northampton and the South instead of taking more experienced professionals from northern clubs as they used to.

As the team had good and bad days, Tim was in and out of the side through the autumn and into the spring. He took the chances that came his way, bagging two goals against Lincoln as the December dark closed in on the action (there were no floodlights then, of course). He learnt from the experience and it helped to develop his sharp understanding of the anxiety of most players in that era, 'and particularly the player in straitened circumstances'. His defiance would always seem to some people like a chip on the shoulder, but better times were on the way and the dangerous side of Tim had to wait.

With the Boer War over, 1903-04 was to be one of the great seasons in Arsenal's history. Not only that, it would prove to be a turning point in the story of the English game. The Arsenal side was becoming more settled and Roddy McEachrane, the popular Irishman, arrived to strengthen the defence. The real boost, though, was a £1,200 windfall from an archery tournament that paid for signings and wages. Above all it brought in Tommy Shanks, from Wexford in Ireland, who gave the attack a new edge. The club was ready to mount a serious challenge for the first time.

Arsenal's push for promotion to the First Division struck deep at the established system of football in England. Players had received money since the 1860s, and the real professional game was established in the 1880s. The man who instigated the Football League, William McGregor, was still the director in charge at Aston Villa. The original Football League was based exclusively in the North and the Midlands. Most of the original sides were still there in 1903, although the addition of a Second Division had given clubs such as Liverpool and Manchester United a foothold in the game. Football had spread south, where leagues mushroomed in all areas, but the southern game remained defiantly separate, with a much more amateur atmosphere, though wages were paid to some players there too.

In 1901, Tottenham Hotspur became the first southern side to win the FA Cup since the foundation of the Football League. Regional rivalry was bitter and the FA Cup was the only national competition in which it could be fought out, that and the selection of the national team, which played an annual home nations tournament. The FA itself was based in London, unlike the League, which had its board meetings in the Midlands and further north. The FA's HQ in Russell Square, by the British Museum, was a highly gentlemanly place, still dominated by men who had made their reputations in the Victorian game, based around the public schools and the Royal Engineers. Lord Kinnaird, the leading figure at the FA, held the record for the number of FA Cup Final appearances, sported a grey beard and played in long flannel trousers. This did not stop him gaining a reputation for foul play. The northern world was ruled by the club directors, who were often leading industrialists. Yet the moment was promising, because something was already changing. As Tim observed, 'football has become a huge concern', the game was outgrowing its traditional roots. In that expansion, all kinds of new and strange things were becoming possible, even a London side in the top flight.

Tim's breakthrough really began when Arsenal went to Tottenham, already the needle match in London football, even though it was a decade before Arsenal moved from Woolwich to Highbury to become their North London neighbours. He had learnt about local rivalry on a smaller scale when he scored those goals for Kettering against Wellingborough, the Reds against the Blues of Northamptonshire football. He understood these occasions. 'In a local derby match,' he said, 'I have always the feeling that no stress can be laid on the forms displayed by the rival teams just prior to the game. However rocky one of them may be going, and even allowing that the other team is performing brilliantly, the tussle between local rivals is one regarding which it would be difficult to predict the result.'

At the start of September 1903, the game at White Hart Lane was already the be-all and end-all for the team from the arms factory. They no longer cared about the London League, which was the competition; this one game was all-important. At first nerves got the better of the little inside-forward. He slipped his markers, and found the ball at his feet, but the surge of energy took the shot miles over the bar. A few minutes later, he was through again, with only the goalkeeper to beat. As he took aim, the keeper panicked and rushed towards him, cap flying and arms waving. On any other day Tim would simply have accepted the invitation, and passed the ball into the now open net. On this particular day, however, he felt too edgy and tried to power it straight through the keeper, who saved without having a clue how he had done it.

It felt like the start of his first Arsenal season, when he missed that penalty. And just like that day, Tim bounced back, through the positive side of his self-will. The more things went wrong, the more he wanted to be the one to put them right. The moment came, and he answered his own – and other people's – doubts with what was becoming known as a Coleman special: a solo dribble and shot. 'Coleman was a treat. His goal was a gem,' said one report. Tim and his partner on the right flank, Tommy Briercliffe, were impressive and promised more to come. 'We are going to be well served by our present right wing, or I am greatly mistaken,' read another report. Would they live up to the hopes?

Soon, Woolwich Arsenal were fighting their way towards the top of that Second Division, where they were competing with Preston North End and Manchester United for the two promotion places. They thumped Blackpool 3-0 and Tim was fast becoming one of the heroes of this promotion charge from the southern upstarts. 'What a little gem Coleman is turning out at inside-right!' His goals started to stick in the mind of faithful Woolwich supporters. This was what the club meant, their hallmark: meanness in defence and then style on the break.

After that Blackpool match, they were all talking about the third goal, 'a masterpiece'. The goal was pure Tim. He got the ball from Tommy Briercliffe, and then cut inside. He set it up for one of his right-footed specials, but found the defenders blocking his path. Instead of just blasting his shot at them, or giving up and passing to someone else, he used a trick of his and 'changed feet', which is something you didn't see much at the time. On his less favoured side, he 'drove a left-footed beauty just inside the upright'. Even the keeper was caught out; he was waiting for the usual right-footed blast. It was a shock to the fans as well, even the Woolwich spectators. 'From where he was placed there surely could have been very little to shoot at but that little was quite enough for Tim.'

Some folk might have thought that there was something over-confident, even flashy, about the Tim Coleman, who was now becoming more widely known. He was not the type to fit in easily, that was true. He remained committed to his daring style of play and insisted that, whatever the inevitable mistakes, 'youth and energy make a full amends'. He knew this from his own career. There are few things in football more exciting than a young talent bursting on to the scene. Later on he acknowledged that there was something to be said for players who could draw on 'experience', and that they were the basis of the really strong teams. But nothing would ever quite equal the first shining impact of youth, like that change of feet he showed against Blackpool.

While Woolwich Arsenal were enjoying this League success, they remained committed to southern competitions, in which they were also flying. They demolished West Ham 4-1 and Tim ran rings round their defence, adding a touch of showmanship for good measure, until '[Aubrey] Fair [of West Ham] did not relish the way in which he was fooled by Coleman'. Tempers frayed: there is a fine line between entertaining the crowd and taking the mickey out of the opposition. A 'fracas' ended in Arsenal's Johnny Dick 'setting about' the irate Fair in defence of Coleman, until eventually 'the referee intervened'. The real character of Tim was emerging: his distinctive personality was stamped all over this London derby, his ruthlessness being combined with a touch of extravagance. Winning was good, but it was not enough – he wanted to do it with style, and he was always aware of the crowd, like an actor on stage, or a circus clown according to his detractors. Maybe he was too concerned with making an impression, but what would the game be without such characters?

Off the field, the talk around the club was about the Southern League and their disparaging remarks about the quality of the Second Division of the Football League. There were days, though, that proved even the harshest of Southern League's critics wrong and one of them was the first Saturday in October 1903, when Woolwich Arsenal welcomed Manchester United, their promotion rival, to the Manor Ground and, having lost to them the previous year, made sure there was no repetition.

United set off with a bang and it looked bad for the home side. Their defence, however, held firm and that allowed the attack to find their usual lethal rhythm. 'One-nil to the Arsenal', a chant that has become famous over the years, was not enough on that particular day. There was a point to be made. As Arsenal cleared their lines, 'the ball went out to Coleman, and the latter raced away for quite three-parts the length of the ground, and cleverly eluding opponent after opponent, he enticed Sutcliffe out of his goal' and it was 2-0 to the Arsenal. All the true Coleman hallmarks were there in that goal: the speed, the elusiveness, the trickery and the finish. It was the reporter's use of the word 'cleverly' that summed it up: he was as clever as any footballer you ever saw. That, indeed, was the impression that the whole Arsenal side were giving. Mr Bentley, the United chairman, acknowledged, sourly, that 'Woolwich undoubtedly possess a very clever side'.

Players create their own image, but it is one that comes from the public sense of the team they play for. Tim was the clever lad at the heart of a smart outfit. That was the image that came to define southern and London football: the clever types taking on the tough sides from the Midlands and the North, and some of the brawny West Country clubs too. The Arsenal team were just right for that moment. They were more than merely working men who were strong and tough, they represented new ideas of smartness, sharpness and cleverness. It was three years before the epoch-making General Election of 1906, which gave Herbert Asquith and the reforming Liberals 400 seats and the Labour Party its breakthrough intake of 30 MPs, a landslide that began the creation of the landscape of modern British politics, though universal suffrage was still more than two decades away. Something significant was going on here. It seemed that, as happened in future years, footballers were catching the mood of the moment. This was a modern football team – you could say it was the first twentieth-century team – and Coleman was becoming its talisman, though he had a way to go yet. Such cleverness, of course, was always on the verge of being 'too clever'.

Meanwhile, there was also something happening to the crowd. A League record attendance for the Manor Ground, 20,000 and more, turned out to see United, and it included groups of fans from other London clubs. There was 'a big batch of West Ham supporters'. True, when challenged, they claimed sheepishly that they had only come to see their former player Billy Grassam, who had moved to United, run rings round the Woolwich captain Jackson. There was also a band of Millwall supporters who were 'genuinely proud of the Reds'. When asked by the locals, they insisted that Arsenal were still second in London to the Blues of Millwall, which resulted in 'a very thick argument with a couple of dozen ardent Reds'. There were even some Tottenham fans there, though as the Arsenal lads pointed out they had had little enough to cheer about with Spurs so perhaps they just wanted a change. Altogether, the roar when the Arsenal put away their fourth and final goal was like nothing anyone had ever heard at a London ground before. The previous season, this had been just the Plumstead team, the munitions club; now they were the flagship of London in the national competition.

The image of Tim was also becoming lodged in football people's minds, first of all as a genuine favourite of Arsenal supporters but also as a national figure. This was how stardom worked, so when the national press came to Plumstead they responded to the local warmth towards their player and recognised the 'dapper little fellow, tripping about with his short legs, anticipating Briercliffe, darting forward to receive or hanging back to pick up, but always in the right place'. That was the perfect phrase for him, 'a dapper little fellow', with its suggestion of smartness in appearance as well as in style of play. His short stature was vital to this new image, because it made him so much the opposite of the average footballer. The final verdict summed up Tim: 'A class man, Coleman.'

In these early games for the Arsenal, Tim, selfishness and all, could charm the birds out of the trees, the fans down from the terraces and even the occasional referee. Arsenal took on Luton, who were near the top of the Southern League, in a very unfriendly friendly at the Manor Ground. Tim was already a marked man and at one point was surrounded by four defenders. Slipping past them, he set up an exchange of short passes and then went clear, offside, but clear. The referee, to the delight of the Arsenal supporters, let play go on while Tim dribbled another 30 yards of pure magic. It was clear to everyone that the official wanted to enjoy Tim's skill as much as the crowd did. Tim also knew he could be himself more freely this year, as the Arsenal had more steel in the centre of the team. It was Billy Gooing who 'bent double' to head the killer goal, after Tim's delightful touches had set the occasion alight.

Not surprisingly, the perpetrator of this selfish yet sometimes magical style of play was quick to understand that, as he said, players were 'the men who provide football entertainment' above anything else. Against all the stuffiness of Victorian values, the pompous phrases about sportsmanship and the importance of 'playing the game', Tim insisted that football was about entertaining huge crowds, and that only the really great players could do this. There was, of course, a touch of bitterness to his comments too, a slightly self-righteous resentment that other people were making the money, while the players were drawing the crowds. He would have felt grudging amusement to see this balance change in later years, after it was too late for him to benefit. Still, games such as the one against Luton were the signs of things to come in football.

As the autumn deepened, match by match, this Arsenal team prised London football out of its southern niche and made the capital part of the national scene. Then came the inevitable setback: they went down 2-1 to Barnsley, the ultimate northern side. It was the first defeat of the campaign, and allowed Preston to go top. Only by losing a game was it revealed just how important football had become in the life of the area. 'There is something the matter with the Borough of

Woolwich this week,' one report said. 'Something that is hard to define. Something that can be felt rather than seen. What is it, I wonder, that is causing all this unusual depression? Men who on Saturday morning walked to their work with a perky, cock o' the walk sort o' step with their noses tilted so high their eyes got a clear vision of the rain clouds that are always with us nowadays, were different beings in the same garments as they walked in yesterday. The perky step had deteriorated into a slouch, and the eyes that were lifted skyward are now cast down to the ground as though in search of something that has been dropped.' People's whole sense of themselves was caught up in the team. Supporting the club was part of a way of life, involving pride, passion, and dejection too. Woolwich Arsenal responded with plans for a new covered terrace to increase capacity at the ground, and also comfort. The whole status of football in London was changing.

Despite the occasional setbacks the League season was becoming a success story, especially at home. In November, Lincoln came to the Manor Ground and were thrashed 4-0, in front of a euphoric crowd of 15,000. Ashcroft, the goalkeeper, kept the visitors at bay to start with, and then Arsenal began to put together the attacking form that made them formidable on their own turf. Briercliffe and Coleman began a move with their neat interplay, drew the defenders and set big Billy Gooing free down the middle. He outran the central defenders and returned the ball to Briercliffe, who immediately put in a cross that was met by the Irish striker Tommy Shanks, who found the back of the net. This was the Woolwich style into which Tim fitted so seamlessly and this year it had, in Shanks, a man to finish the moves off with a killer touch. Tim, who was returning after a short injury absence, added a nice one of his own, through the keeper's legs!

Short on Christmas spirit, Arsenal celebrated on 25 December by beating Bradford 4-1 in front of nearly 20,000 spectators, which was becoming their regular size of crowd. It was 1-1 at half-time. Then came the most memorable moment of the game. The visiting goalie pushed out a shot instead of holding on to it. 'This is a dangerous mistake at any time,' said a report on the game, 'but with Coleman about it is absolutely suicidal, and on this occasion the little inside-right came up at full pelt and smashed the ball amongst the top rigging before Seymour could get anywhere near recovery.' Tim added a second and the match was all over as a contest. Tommy Shanks, as centre-forward, was bound to be the top scorer but Tim was confirmed now in people's minds as more than just an emerging talent; he was frustrating sometimes yet often deadly.

Keeping up the pressure on top spot into 1904, they headed off to Bradford to be greeted by the deluge that the *Argus* still remembered in 1916, when they associated it with reports of Tim's death. 'Referee Barker, of Hanley, acted wisely when he decided to abandon the Bradford City v. Woolwich Arsenal match at half-time. Rain poured down incessantly, and more pitiful objects than the players as they made their way through the mud it would be impossible to imagine.'

From October to March, football was largely a muddy occupation. There were no underground heating systems to keep pitches from freezing, no special drainage to avoid waterlogging. Add the leather ball, which soaked up water like a sponge, and you have a recipe for a war of attrition. To play with style and skill in those conditions took something that has passed from the game, some inner strength and passion. In those days, football was very much part of the natural world, whereas today it is played in a smoothly artificial world, with the only hint of nature often being the exaggerated greenness of the grass.

Through the mud of 1904, the Arsenal continued their relentless pursuit of the Second Division title. Down went Lincoln 2-0, Burnley 4-0 and Barnsley 3-0: it was the talk of the country, this southern machine. Stockport came south in early March and met the Arsenal in top gear. Three minutes on the clock and Tim, back from another short injury, met a high cross from the left-winger Bill Linward and hammered it home. His personality brought a tangle of comparisons and superlatives from the press: 'Coleman . . . was as sharp as a needle and as lively as a kitten with a ball of string'.

For Coleman, football was always a mind game, between attackers and defenders. 'We forwards will have something to do to outwit them,' he said. That afternoon, he had more than enough ways of outwitting the Stockport defenders and goalkeeper. In addition, Tim was also becoming a reliable part of a team pattern. The *Plumstead News* caught the rhythm of the front line as the season approached its climax: 'Shanks and Linward would often travel down the left with their long swings and 'through' passes, varied here and there by the in and out swerving attack of Coleman and Briercliffe, and the sudden dashes of Gooing.' Moves such as these stayed in the memory of the Woolwich faithful: 'A really lovely bit of work by the whole of the Reds' front line. The ball was slid on to Coleman, thence to Briercliffe, and Gooing was put in possession with a clever hook. Shanks was the next to take hold and a quick pass to Linward saw the outside return to the centre, where Coleman nipped up on the left, ran round Orr and shot hard and true just under the bar.'

Team man though he was now, Tim wanted to be on that score sheet too. He put another two in at home to Bristol City, the third-placed team at that stage. Preston, Manchester United and Woolwich Arsenal were chasing each other towards the finish line, but only two could be promoted. More than a century later, you can still sense the appeal of the league system taking hold on football's new mass public. 'The race for the Second League Championship is like an exciting cricket match in the last innings when the sides are so equally matched that nobody dares to predict the result,' was one observer's view. 'For this state of affairs in the league Preston, Arsenal and Manchester United are chiefly responsible.'

What the public loves about leagues is partly the way the pressure gets to the players themselves. Arsenal slipped away to Chesterfield and Manchester United were picking up steam. Down to the Manor

Ground came Bolton Wanderers, as fine a symbol of the old northern game as any club in the land, contesting the League since that first Saturday in September 1888. The crowd was up towards the 20,000 mark and the Arsenal contingent were delighted when Tim 'cleverly put his side one up'. He emerged from a maze of little passes – another new-fangled tactic – and manoeuvred round the last defender. He was 'sailing into goal' with the ease that belied his size and, as generations of strikers since have done, 'beat Davies with a shot that gave the goalkeeper no earthly chance of saving it'.

Then suddenly people were asking: were the wheels starting to come off Arsenal's promotion challenge? Burnley nicked a win on behalf of the Lancashire mill towns and then Preston were due at Plumstead for the return game. Meanwhile, while his club stuttered, Tim's own reputation flew higher and higher. He was the man of the moment: 'Some distance on the road to my ideal footballer,' wrote one admirer. 'He knows why and where he is kicking the ball.'

Fresh from victory at Leicester, Preston travelled the long journey to south-east London for what they would now call a 'six-pointer' – though it would have been four in those days. It was, they said, just like a Cup-tie – and the FA Cup was still the premier contest. The match had a crackle and a buzz about it that felt new. 'The air was charged with electricity. If Marconi had wanted to work his wireless telegraph there would have been no need to put down a dynamo plant to generate the motive power. He could have collected the electric fluid from the spectators.'

This atmosphere got to the teams. 'The players also had caught the infection, and caught it badly.' It was a goalless draw, but no one felt any sense of anti-climax: 'Most of the 28,000 spectators who congregated at the Manor Ground were caught in the spell of the League fiend, to whom "points" are more than mere prettinesses.' The League fiend that now produces billions of pounds for Premier League clubs began its work during that North-South struggle.

Arsenal swept aside Bradford to go back to the top of the division. It was looking good. At the end of April, Burslem Port Vale were back at the Manor for the final act of the League season. Manchester United had played at Bolton earlier that afternoon. If United won, then Arsenal had to get at least a draw, then they would be home and dry given 'the extraordinary goal average of the London club'. If their rivals lost, promotion was theirs whatever happened. During his career, many of Tim's best footballing mates were United players, and he often referred to 'all my friends of Manchester United'. Several times he was a transfer target for them. For that day, however, they were the real enemy, far more than poor Port Vale, who were in the middle of the battle.

The Plumstead kick-off was in the evening and as the fans were gathering for the crucial game a telegram brought news to the ground that United had managed only a draw. Despite this message, the rumour circulated that United had won and so the 20,000 and more supporters who crammed into the ground still believed that the Arsenal needed to draw to be promoted to the First Division.

They could have done with help from Mr Marconi that evening. That special atmosphere built up again: 'All the evening the air was charged with electricity and when the teams entered the field some gentlemen in a far away corner of the huge crowd told us on a cornet that 'England expects that every man this day would do his duty'.' Port Vale showed no sign of giving in, though, and Arsenal had their eye on that draw from the start, with their defence built around the rock-solid skipper, Jimmy Jackson. There were still flashes up front, mainly from 'Coleman, whose movements were always smart and clever' and who 'looked very dangerous'. He couldn't match the goals he got in his first game against the Potteries team the previous season, but it didn't matter that evening.

The Plumstead ground went mad as the final whistle blew. The Edwardian dignity of the occasion – and of the reports – was broken by an explosion of most un-English joy or, as they put it, 'a scene of extraordinary enthusiasm'. The local brass band was blaring out its patriotic best, and someone set off some rockets that startled some with their 'screaming' towards the evening sky. The fans invaded the pitch and would not stop chanting the names of the players. It was a demonstration of feeling that fits with American writer Barbara Ehrenreich's idea that football was keeping alive, or reviving, a sense of public carnival, amid the increasingly routine order of modern urban life.

Supporters climbed on to the roof of the home dressing-room and refused to come down until 'Jackson and his men' reappeared to take the cheers. 'It was a great day for the Arsenal' and also for 'the Londoner with any sense of loyalty for the game in the South', proclaimed the *Morning Leader*. There was something historic in that electric air: the Arsenal team 'will be remembered in the annals of League football as one of the most expert and dashing teams that ever went on the field'.

Tim loved these moments of adulation and excitement. He also knew what they meant. 'I am one of those who believe that a man should be paid according to his ability, and a good few, I reckon, are worth more than four quid a week,' he said. This was a lesson he learnt that day looking up at the roof of the dressing-room, and around the Manor Ground, where the gathered thousands were chanting the names of their heroes, including conspicuously his own. As the fireworks exploded over the London sky, he understood with lasting passion and resentment why these players were worth more than the so-called maximum wage. As he looked out over the celebrating masses, he was storing up both laughter and a bitter lesson for the future.

Joy's *Forward Arsenal*, written in the early Fifties by a star of the Thirties and Forties, still hums with the excitement of that first great Arsenal season. 'In that promotion season, they did not lose a match at home – and only drew the final two when the pressure rose. The home goal average was 67-5.' After a decade of struggle, Woolwich Arsenal had redrawn the football map for the new era, and the new century. Victorian football ended with those fireworks bombarding the South London calm that English spring evening, ten years before war swept many of those celebrating fans and players into the trenches – including the 'dapper little fellow' who had been so 'dangerous' right to the end.

# Unequal Battles

It had been a mould-breaking season for Woolwich Arsenal but soon after it ended, the club was brought crashing back down to earth. The biggest of the setbacks was the loss of the manager, Harry Bradshaw, who was poached by Fulham in their quest to bring about their own move from the London leagues to the national scene. In his place came Phil Kelso, a seasoned Scottish pro who had been coach of Hibernian. He did his best to strengthen the squad for the big time, bringing in Tommy Fitchie, a notable London amateur from Norwood, and Charlie Satterthwaite, formerly of Manchester United and West Ham. His half-backs were Johnny Dick, Percy Sands, a public school educated amateur who now turned pro, and Roddy McEachrane, an experienced Irishman. Everyone knew, though, that the going would be tough and this was hardly the kind of transfer dealing to frighten the likes of Newcastle or Aston Villa.

The summery early autumn of 1904 signalled Woolwich Arsenal's arrival in the top league. They had received an enormous amount of coverage and attention. They had broken all the rules of footballing etiquette; the Southern League was meant to be the place for London football teams. Football's top division belonged to the smoke-filled towns of the Midlands and the North. It was no place for southern gentlemen, a view which prevailed not only in the northern strongholds, but among the committee men of the South and the FA. There was something unnatural about the real League game going this far south.

On the pitch it was a hard battle. They began with a crushing 3-0 defeat away to Newcastle United. As everyone said at that time, it showed that the London team hardly belonged in such company. Their first home game had been a 0-0 draw against Preston, but that at least showed they could compete. It took until nearly the end of September for them even to score a goal, which coincided with the first Arsenal win in the top flight, the original London victory in football's First Division. It was at home to Wolves, and 20,000 increasingly frustrated fans were baying them on. A cartoon from the *Plumstead News* three days after the game showed a fan and his wife looking stunned: 'Lor' luv us 'Liza, our team's won, blow me if I don't tike you out to the gaff to-night,' he exclaimed in broad Cockney. Charlie Satterthwaite got the first – the season's big signing. It was Tim who got the second, the end product of a good old Tim and Tommy one-two down the right, when they showed 'remarkable cleverness . . . a knowledge of combination and the art of transferring that comes of a thorough mutual understanding'. The early-season nerves had got to the famous partnership but now there was a hint of the old style and freedom.

They hovered just above the relegation places. Come November, they managed their hallmark 0-0 result away to Derby County. They had achieved a kind of grudging acceptance among the commentators, pundits and rival fans but, as November came towards its end, the footballing jury was still out on the team's capability as a whole. The attack was particularly suspect. It was a hard time for Tim, after all the uproarious success of the great promotion season and because he had never had the patience to bear setbacks calmly.

Looking back on that period from 1909, when he was a more established star, he drew the battle lines as they had seemed to him at the time – players and directors, them and us, no sentimental working together for the good of the team, no good sportsmen and fellows. 'Some

Directors are largely to blame for this sort of thing,' he said, when talking about the insecurity of being a professional player. He then recalled from these earliest days in the First Division 'an individual who was elevated to the position of Club Director'. The contempt in that word 'individual' is still audible a century later, sharp or chippy depending on your point of view. The story is given a veneer of anonymity but it is all too obviously personal. 'Soon after his election, he requested that a certain player should be called upon to appear before the Board, to account for his poor display the previous Saturday.'

The dialogue was launched with a harsh inquiry: 'Why was it that you did not come up to expectations?' asked the new director. 'Now, come, tell me.' The rookie director was enjoying himself in his new role, on his new throne. Well, what right had the workers to fail to come up to the 'expectations' of the bosses? He had chosen the wrong man to pick his first fight with, even if Tim was off form just then. The reply he got was laced with sarcasm: 'Well, I consider that I was not fed well enough.'

It sounded good enough to Tim for him to recall the incident with relish. At the time, though, it was a dangerous move, with a family's livelihood at stake and a career not yet established. Even when recounting the event, Tim seems more satisfied with the immediate effect of his words than he was aware of the risk he was running. 'Fed well enough? How much does this man get a week, Mr . . .', the director said, addressing the secretary. The secretary of the club was Phil Kelso, the new team manager. You can feel the silence while he got the numbers right, checking his books. 'Three pounds a week,' Kelso replied. That was a pound below the maximum, as reimposed by the FA at the start of this 1904-05 season. Surely that was a good solid deal for a young man? In many ways it was a fair deal, by the standards of the time. Plenty of the readers of Tim's newspaper columns would have been glad of it. Was it worth putting all that at risk for the sake of scoring a point in an unequal contest? No true rebel would doubt it.

Tim recalled that 'the director seemed surprised' before respond-
ing: 'If he can't feed himself on that, how much does he want,
I wonder?' Then he looked round the room. The tension rose to a
pitch and one senses that even Tim was suddenly conscious of what he
was doing. He was not yet sure of a future in the game, yet here he
was taking on a director of his football club. Then the silence broke.
'The player, secretary, and Directors burst into a chorus of laughter
which had the effect of converting the boardroom into a veritable hall
of amusement.' Nowadays when a player insists he is worth even more
money than his already inflated salary his attitude can seem absurdly
grasping. The battle between player and club has become unequal in
reverse, as 90 per cent of many a club's turnover is consumed by
superstar wages. Yet if the player power of today has a beginning it is
in moments such as Tim's early gestures of defiance, knowing at the
time that it would get him nowhere, and half-guiltily aware of how
much he might be sacrificing for others as well as himself.

The maximum wage for a footballer had been fixed at £4 per week
only as recently as 1901-02, which reflected perhaps the beginnings of
pressure from men such as Tim. As James Walvin says, even with win
bonuses and unreliable payment in kind, top players were hard put
to get by. His overview gives the context for Tim's personal
experience: 'To the skilled player, the game offered a slight, though
invariably temporary, improvement in earnings and living standards
. . . the impermanence and insecurity of earnings from football can
be measured by the thousands of men who fell back from footballing
fame to the anonymity of their origins.'

One inevitable side-effect was that, though he could really feed
himself, a player such as Tim could not afford to bring a wife and young
child up to London with him, and they remained in Kettering, where he
and Nelly Moore had married in 1900. His first son, Arthur, was now
nearly four. Football was better in terms of money than the shoe factory,

but was still hardly an easy life. Tim's anger was more than just a result of his own quick temper. There was a bitter conflict brewing, in Walvin's terms: 'Football thus became another dimension of late nineteenth-century urban life, generating great commercial activity, but one in which the creators of the wealth, in this case the footballers, gained relatively little from their skills.' If there is a foolhardy side to Tim's bravado, it also had something serious behind it.

Meanwhile, battles on the pitch were also proving unequal. Even with such fireworks going on behind the scenes, it was generally a bleak season at the Manor Ground after all the cheer of the previous year. Yet there was still that extraordinary Woolwich atmosphere, and it was this that mattered in the long run, this and the success in avoiding relegation, always a struggle after promotion to the top tier. From the whole of the ground-breaking first season in the First Division, one afternoon stood out. It said everything about life at the Manor and what was being created there – and also provided the talking-point of the year. The match also had one of the most controversial outcomes in League history – and Tim was in the thick of it. In fact, it was a day that paid dividends later in his life.

The date was 26 November, 1904. Woolwich Arsenal v Everton, the two clubs meeting for the first time in the League. The Arsenal were toughening up; Kelso had brought in many players from northern clubs for this first raid on the top flight. At the centre of the defence, Jackson having moved on after securing promotion, was the Irishman Roddy McEachrane, with the Scot John Hunter alongside him on one side and the amateur Ashworth on the other. Tim and Tommy Briercliffe had one flank beginning to move, while Charlie Satterthwaite and Linward were joined by Billy Gooing in the centre. There had been many mutterings about the Arsenal attack in the national press: too many pointless passes, too little hard punch. It typified the supposed weakness of the southern character. Sooner or later, that had to be put right.

And if there was a Goliath for the southern David to take on that day, then surely it was Everton. They were one of only five teams to have occupied a permanent place in the First Division until that point. They were, as their fans proudly pointed out on every occasion, the senior partner on Merseyside, where Liverpool were still the newcomers. Goodison Park, Everton's ground, was one of the League's true, original homelands. This season, after some up-and-down years, Everton, the Toffees, were closing in on the title again. They had begun with an away win at Notts County, followed by a thumping 3-0 home victory over Sheffield United. They swept aside Wolves at home and Bury away. The week after, Everton had thrashed Forest 5-1. True, there had been some strange days as well. They had been 5-1 up at halftime away to Sheffield Wednesday but somehow managed a 5-5 draw in one of the most peculiar matches the League had yet seen. The previous week they had slipped to a surprising 1-0 defeat at home to Sunderland. All in all, Everton had a point to prove, as well as two points to win, that late November afternoon. It was a classic encounter: struggling newcomers against a top team eager to get back to winning ways. The stage was set.

Everton went for their best team, with Jack Sharp, the Lancashire cricket star, on the left wing and the Scotland international Sandy Young as the tall, target-man centre-forward. On the right wing was Harold Hardman, the amateur – and future FA official. The side was founded upon the platform given them by William Balmer and Jack Crelley, the League's most famous full-back partnership. They had had injury problems in goal, and the new man arrived only just in time. He was the distinctively named Leigh Richmond Roose, fresh from Aberystwyth by way, briefly, of Glasgow, where he played for Celtic. Roose was to play an important role in the life of Tim Coleman – starting that afternoon. It was the first meeting of two of the game's great personalities.

When the players reached the Manor Ground around midday, it

seemed unlikely that there was going to be any encounter at all, famous or otherwise. The pitch was frozen solid, ice hard with the first breath of winter. The clouds were low and getting lower. The referee, Fred Bye, had been out to have a look around. He pronounced the pitch playable, with luck. What followed was typical of the English weather: it warmed up enough to stop the game being frozen off, that was the good news. The bad news was that the cloud turned into thick, classic London fog, a genuine 'pea-souper'. By two o'clock, an hour before kick-off, the folk gathering on the terraces could hardly see the pitch. Floodlights were things of the future. Late November was always going to be murky by the final whistle. Today, it looked as if there was not even going to be a kick-off.

Mr Bye, however, was no routine official. A Sheffield solicitor, he had been the North's candidate for secretary of the FA a couple of years previously. He had been defeated, in the machinations of the committee room, by Fredrick Wall, the candidate for the amateur heartland of the South, a noted amateur half-back, rower and general sporting 'good fellow'. Now Mr Bye was going to show the soft southerners something about real football: of course the game was going ahead! It was a sport for men; what was a bit of fog to real professionals?

In the middle of that murky day, clusters of munitions workers still tramped down the freezing streets, through the London fog, and on to the terraces. It was something they were used to doing, going to the game straight from work, and it would take more than a bit of poor weather to stop them. As kick-off approached, there were 20,000 spectators in the ground, shrouded in cloud, hardly able to see each other let alone the goalposts, but they made up for the absentees with the noise they made, so the journalists present noticed.

The rules of the game, then as now, state that you must be able to see from one end of the pitch to the other for a match to take place. Mr Bye remained obstinate, however, and to everyone's amazement the teams came out to a huge, muffled cheer. Under that cloud, Percy

Sands, of Arsenal, tossed the coin with Jack Taylor, of Everton, and the local man called right. As he pointed to show which way they were going to kick, and the news spread as much by word of mouth as by actual witnesses, another enormous, almost ghostly cheer rang around the ground. Then the teams lined up for action.

The temperature seemed to be falling by the minute and the fog turning ever thicker. Then the whistle shrilled, which was, for many in the ground, the only evidence that the game had started. Tim was on the left of the Arsenal attack this particular afternoon, opposite McLaughlan and Hardman in the Everton attack. Somewhere in the distance were the big men who mattered for him that afternoon, Balmer and Crelley, the Goodison Park double act. Looking across, he could see Gooing at centre-forward, and Hunter was on his left, alongside him. Satterthwaite and Linward, on the far wing, were lost in the fog. In short, it was a perfect afternoon for Tim Coleman, romantic and ridiculous, a time for heroes.

Young kicked off for Everton and, as their breath merged with the freezing fog, Arsenal's original First Division players locked horns with mighty Everton. That afternoon, the 20,000 who were in the Manor Ground caught at best glimpses of the action. It was a shame for them, because the more difficult the conditions, the better they suited Tim Coleman. He was always at his best when things looked grim. It was the ordinary day that never suited 'Professor Timothy', as he was becoming known by the Arsenal faithful.

Breathing was not much fun in a London fog, even walking up the road could be difficult. To play football in it was a test of character that later generations could simply not appreciate. Tim had spent part of his youth rising before dawn to go to work; he had grown up with the cold and the dark. That experience was more help to him that day than any kind of training could have been, as the ball disappeared across the field and into the fog. Spectators along the touchline would have seen the glamorous Jack Sharp tearing down the Everton left, and those level with the Woolwich penalty area would have heard the bang as Roddy McEachrane, doing the job for which he had been brought south by Kelso, clattered into him. Suddenly, the ball popped up into Tim's view coming down the other side of the field. Then all he could see was Crelley booting it long and hard back the way it had come. Even for the players, let alone the fans, this was a match of snatches and glimpses, like a juddering silent film. Even the voices were muffled.

The Woolwich players started to find their rhythm and last season's confidence. The ball emerged from the fog, within range of the enemy goal, and Tim had the first shot of the game. It loomed up at Roose out of the murk and curled just over the bar. It was the first encounter between the celebrated double act, an appropriately crazy moment when the striker could hardly see the outcome of his attempt and the keeper had to guess at its beginning. Yet it all became strangely gripping, as players and fans strained to catch the next moment. This was truly the afternoon when First Division football arrived in London; everything else had been a rehearsal so far.

When the chips were down, the Arsenal came out fighting, underdogs though they were. Things became frantic in front of the Everton goal. Roose's clearance kick made it only halfway into his own half, and then came bounding back. Moments later Gooing had his first chance, the defenders having literally lost sight of the ball. It was all too much for him and he sent it, more like a rugby kick, high, wide and handsome. The next Arsenal attack came down the right through Linward, a snappy winger. Balmer knocked him flying as he closed in on goal, but the ball looped on ahead and Roose, seeing it late if at all, pushed it round the post for a corner. Every time they got the chance, the Everton defenders simply booted that increasingly weighty ball upfield, as far as they could.

Back came Everton down their left, but soon Balmer was pumping the ball away from his own goal again. Sharp, the Lancashire all-round superstar, hit back, left the Arsenal midfield for dead, including the amateur Ashworth who was meant to be marking him, and then scuffed his shot, when he was in the clear. You could see that Everton were the class team, if you could see anything at all. Their amateur cap, Hardman, left the Arsenal midfield standing and sent in a classic cross, which was bundled away by the Arsenal defenders.

Just when it looked as if the game had swung towards the favourites, the big-time side from Goodison, Arsenal came back again. Linward threaded the ball across from the right and Crelley was unable to stop it. By the time he turned, Tim had gone past him. His moment had come. Roose was left without a defence and Tim simply kept on dribbling. This was the manoeuvre for which he was most famous. Once he had the ball at his feet while in motion he was impossible to catch. As the crowd at that end were able to bring the action into focus, they saw the little man closing in on goal. Annoyed by his previous miss, Tim was taking no chances now. Poor Roose, making his First Division debut, did his best, spreading his arms and looking imposing but the shot, from short-range, was lethal. The net billowed and Tim was the Arsenal hero. The little inside-forward had put the ball past the only man with a doctorate in medical biochemistry to keep goal in the Football League. It was a classic Edwardian moment: the son of a dairyman, destined for a life scaring birds out of the Northamptonshire fields, or hammering shoe leather in a factory, outfoxing the public-school-educated, brilliant and eccentric scientific son of a Victorian clergyman. This was a few months before the first election in which all men aged twenty-one and over would have a vote, and also before Winston Churchill, the dangerously radical Chancellor of the Exchequer, launched the very beginnings of the welfare state for the Liberal Party. This was England in 1904-05, a society starting to unfreeze, where strange things were happening in the fog. Strangest of all was the path this was to open up for Coleman, one which led all the way back to Goodison, where he faced another challenge that really shaped his life, and the future of the game.

For the moment it was simply 1-0 to Woolwich Arsenal, and the battle remained unequal. Tim was not yet the kind of player who could win a whole game at this level, nor were Woolwich that strong a team. They had their moments but then the current flowed against them once more. Everton were back on the attack and it took only minutes for Sandy Young to cut right through the home defence and equalise. It was destined to be Sandy's afternoon from that point, a good day for one of Tim's close football friends in future seasons. The Everton crosses rained in after that. The whole occasion wound up to greater and greater intensity. It was different from the usual atmosphere in the ground. As one press report noted: 'The spectators evinced a demonstrative attitude.' The crowd impressed people, but they could also be a touch disturbing. What passion was being unleashed here? The fog made it all the more striking. This roar was the beginning not only of the modern, national Football League, but also of the modern relationship between the crowd and the game. It resulted in what a watching journalist described with total amazement as 'a running commentary of cheers'. The 'pea-souper' that day belongs to the pre-war world but those cheers bursting through it are the sound of the future, the sound not only of football but also of democracy.

Like most forwards, Tim saw football as really 'the battle' between 'the front lines'. Today, that meant the contest between the young southerner leading the Woolwich line and the Scottish international at the heart of the Everton attack. Tim knew the correct sporting language with which to dress up these attacking clashes when he talked about them: 'Of this I am sure, that the battle will be clean and vigorously fought, and that both teams will be out to win in the truest sense.' But his real feelings come through clearly: it is a fight, above anything else. On that day against Everton, in the fog, he was more than up for it, against the odds though it still was.

Some smart passing from Tim and the home side sent Satterthwaite through and the former Manchester United man let loose 'a hot shot' that produced a typical moment of drama in the Everton goal, where 'Roose cleared with a flying kick'. As the first of Merseyside's goal-keeping eccentrics, Roose would never do something simple if there were a more interesting alternative.

The whistle blew for half-time, ending the most intense forty-five minutes of football theatre in London history so far, the first of many. The Arsenal's early lead had been slow to crumble; only late in the half had the visitors gone 2-1 ahead with a goal by Hardman. It was the second half that made this match notorious, though for Tim the first forty-five minutes was where his promise was shown to a wider audience.

The half-time interval was spooky. As the spectators waited 'the density of the fog increased palpably' and by the time the teams returned the match was virtually invisible. Nevertheless, Mr Bye had his point to make: he was going to show the Londoners what real football men were all about. Amid the rising tempo of the uproar, Everton pounded in more and more shots. Then back the ball came down the Woolwich left, in an extraordinary zigzagging movement, a series of quickfire passes between the winger Hunter and Coleman, his inside-left. As Tim took control of the ball and the move, the match seemed to hang in the balance. This time, however, Balmer was too strong for him and the ball disappeared over the touchline for a throw. The disappointment ebbed noisily in the murk.

Arsenal did brilliantly to hold on and stay in the game. A quarter of an hour left and Everton had a corner. The man taking it could not see the goal towards which he was aiming, but he hardly needed to. Over the ball went, Young leapt, no one else caught sight of it quickly enough to counter – and it was 3-1 to Everton. It looked as if they would be back on top of the table, overtaking Sunderland.

But the afternoon had a final twist in store. As the Arsenal prepared to kick off, two goals behind and staring defeat in the face, neither goal was visible from the centre of the field. At last, Mr Bye summoned his linesmen for a conference and then took the teams off. 'The fog fiend' was the only winner, the result did not stand.

Coleman had begun the day as the young lad who was already a local hero. Even if he did not yet realise it, he ended it having made his first big impression on one of the really big clubs. That first twenty minutes, and perhaps the jinking and dazzling moment in the second half, meant that he finished as a man with a future, at least in the minds of those Everton directors present at the Manor Ground. Predictably, Everton went on to challenge for the title and they were riding high when they lost the rematch against Woolwich Arsenal just before Easter. In the end, they finished behind Newcastle United by exactly the margin of that cancelled victory in Plumstead. It remained a bitter talking-point among Everton supporters for decades. This was how Tim put it: 'In the words of the immortal Shakespeare – "We don't get much money, but we do see life".' He wasn't really smiling even then; you can feel the deadpan delivery.

What he had seen, through the fog, was that football was a world with wide horizons, an adventure full of irony and suspense, as good a source of stories for modern culture as the great drama of the past. He had also seen something else; that the players, like those who Shakespeare brought to visit Hamlet in Elsinore, were getting precious little for their pains. Referring to Shakespeare could be seen as overkill, of course, and Tim's reflections and his anecdotes sometimes have an overblown style but, as some of his words show, he was also able to put things plainly: 'We don't get much money.' He was consciously refusing to talk the simple language allotted to men such as him, and if he over-shot sometimes, that was only another part of his being out on his own. Pioneers are seldom moderates.

Another typical feature of Tim and his language is that word 'we', as in 'we don't get much money'. He always spoke on behalf of all the players, that was his style. Tim was never an official voice, like the union leaders of the coming years, Billy Meredith and Colin

Veitch. He was a pioneer of something much bigger than the Players' Union, though he was important to that too. He was searching, quite deliberately, for a voice for this new working-class profession, a forerunner of a new cultural order.

Meanwhile, the Arsenal's season continued to be one of the strangest imaginable. In December the club welcomed a France side to the Manor Ground – and annihilated them by twenty-six goals to one. Tim had a hat-trick by half-time and finished with five. Friendlies aside, complaints mounted among the Plumstead faithful. There was a run of injuries and 'there will have to be importations of players with the best credentials', said the *Plumstead News*, on behalf of the concerned fans. The sums involved were rather smaller than now, for a club that was promising to sink a massive £3,000 into ground improvements, and for whom the average takings from the 20,000-30,000 crowd was around £300. But the plea for new blood, then as now, rarely took these matters into consideration.

Tim's closing highlight of the season was his two goals to defeat the previous year's League champions, Sheffield Wednesday. Like the whole team, he seemed to do better when the pitches dried towards the end of the season. The fans complained that 'though able to hold their own on a dry, hard ground', they 'invariably go under when placed on a sodden turf'. This was seen by northern clubs and supporters as a sign of southern softness, and there was also a suspicion that it was due to their over-elaborate short passing game. Despite the criticism, they had held off the looming spectre of relegation that haunted the start of the season and established themselves as more than a one-season wonder. Division One was now definitely the national league, whatever Spurs and the southern snobs might say. For Tim, though, this had been a tough season, but one that had offered a few signs of better things to come. Life was far from smooth at the centre of the football boom.

# Drunkard?

Phil Kelso, the Arsenal club secretary and in practice the team manager as well, was beginning to shape his own squad, one that promised to do more than merely hang on in the top flight. As Jonathan Wilson shows in his history of football tactics, *Inverting the Pyramid*, Scottish players were often more used to the short-passing style of game favoured by the Arsenal, and so Kelso tended to sharpen this already distinctive aspect of the club. He added the pace of Bert Freeman up front and hopes were higher when the new season began. There was much tactical and strategic chat around the club and one theory that gained some credence was a suggestion that Tim should be given a trial at centre-forward. Could such a small man really be a centre-forward? It was a real attempt to overturn conventional wisdom; Kelso was always a bold thinker about the game.

Sure enough, Tim appeared in that role for the visit to Wolverhampton in October. It was literally a tall order, looking at the Wolves defenders. But Molineux, their famous ground, was in for a shock. After taking some time to settle into his new role, Tim was into his stride. At one point, one reporter wrote admiringly, 'Coleman reached the penalty line after a good spin.' Tim turning away from the big men and dribbling through a top-class defence – was a genuine First Division talent now being expressed? He shot from the edge of the area and found the net again. He got a second and that was the result, a much-needed win for the Arsenal. The *Plumstead News* was happy, though surprised that the experimental centre-forward had 'got both the goals of the match'. The potential was obvious but the question was, where did he best fit in to the team?

For the moment, he continued to enjoy individual success. A win over London rivals West Ham, always a happy event if not significant in footballing terms, featured a Tim special, 'a truly brainy effort' according to one report, and there was the rather more important matter of beating Sunderland in the League, where the reactions revealed a sense of surprise at Tim's success in his new position, with his 'nippy and tricky work'. This second season in the First Division, for all the struggles that the Arsenal experienced, there was a stronger sense of Tim's personality coming to the fore on the pitch. It hinted that he was ready to begin the next stage of his football development. That breakthrough, however, was delayed by a deepening crisis at Woolwich Arsenal.

This was an unrelenting period in his life. The following week he was absent from the Arsenal team and the press, ever alert to details of his personal life, revealed that 'Tim Coleman was attending the funeral of his brother'. The news was carried in many papers, another sure sign of the interest that surrounded his whole story, far beyond his adventures on the field. This glimpse is another poignant reminder of how little of the private life of such a man was visible in the press, in contrast to our routine expectations of disclosure in these gossip-hungry days. In fact, compared with his footballing peers, Tim was relatively forthcoming, limited though his personal remarks seem now. He spoke to the press often and always had something newsworthy to say. This particular week, knowing that he was going to miss the game, he let reporters know that he 'took up the centre-forward position at his own request' which they found 'gratifying to hear'. It was typical of Tim, making sure that everyone knew it was his decision, not someone else's, and letting the fans have that glimpse of the workings of the game, which almost no one else gave them.

The team lost in his absence but his return did not do the trick either. Though Tim retained his goal-scoring form, there followed five League defeats in a row. The criticism was getting louder: maybe the southern presence in the top flight was going to be a flash in the pan after all. There was more and more criticism of the Arsenal style, for which Tim and his fellow forwards were still the central symbol. Experts, a safe distance from the pitch, knew exactly how to put things right: 'The sooner the Reds' forwards lose their short-passing knowledge, and along with it their foolish desire to hold the ball and trick opponents', the sooner they would start to win games. It was the beginning of one of the major tactical debates of football, that between the passing game and the long ball, or as they put it back then 'a sharp swinging pass would be of more avail'. The advice did not change anything in terms of the Arsenal's performance and gave way, locally at least, to a doom-laden chorus of 'hopeless'.

On New Year's Eve they lost 3-0 at Liverpool. Worse still, they celebrated New Year's Day by losing 6-1 at Bolton. Who was going to be the scapegoat? Tim was in the eye of the storm, and he knew it. 'When a club is doing badly,' he said, 'have you ever thought of the abuse which the players are called upon to suffer from that great unseen army of anonymous critics?' That was the very beginning of modern football celebrity, or one of the downsides of it at least, put into words by one of the first men to understand how football was going to be affected by the media, what it would mean to live in the glare of publicity, even before TV or radio. 'Most people, I fancy, will not have given the subject much, if any, consideration, but let me assure them that the grievance to which I direct attention is by no means an imaginary one. I write from a knowledge of facts which have come under my notice from time to time.' It is a nice touch, 'facts that have come under my notice'. His tone is coolly mocking but, at the same time hints at real anger underneath. In Tim's recollections of this difficult period, there are also stronger signs of the troubled side of his personality. He was never slow to see himself as surrounded by enemies: 'The mud-throwing community, if I might so call it, is a very widely scattered one, and its members are past masters in the art which they practise.'

Mockingly, he sketched the bitter moment when the fans transform into a 'mud-throwing community'. It is still infused with all the humour that Tim also possessed – there were matches at the time where members of the crowd did pick up loose divots and hurl them at erring referees! But what Tim had his eye on was something more specific, and more apparently genteel: 'Some of them will retire to the privacy of their sanctums and write voluminous letters to the editors of local news sheets. What, I wonder, is their object?'

For Tim, he was facing not only personal enmity but also a kind of class conflict. He was surely right in part. Yet what was he going to do about it? How much would he be prepared to risk if pushed beyond his limits? This is where it all began, the love-hate passion between footballer and fan. This is the first sense of what it would mean to be a football star, from the player's point of view. But a man like Tim had none of the security of his privileged descendants. In his view, there was a particular edge to it, caught in that taunting turn of phrase about 'the privacy of their sanctums'. Many of these anonymous critics were middle-class gents, and the players they were abusing earned far less than they did. Typically, though, he did far more than just complain – and perhaps this saved him from over-reaching for now. He was also intrigued; he wanted to know what it was all about, this hostility, and this barrage of insults: 'If letter-writing is the safety valve to their feelings, then there is an acceptable excuse to offer on their behalf, but if the energy which they expend is directed with a view to the influencing of the players from any other course than that which they have been in the habit of following, then they labour in vain.' This is a strangely modern emotional analysis of fans and players, so much so that it is easy to miss its genius. There was nothing like this being said – no one talked about football as an emotional safety valve in Edwardian England. But if people thought that their abuse was going to change anything, then they had another think coming. As Tim said, who was going to play differently just because the fans told him to? Players had their ways, their habits, and they weren't going to learn new tricks from fans. Then there was the punch line: 'They only succeed in lacerating the players' feelings.'

The drama was personal too. It was not just about the failures of the team on the pitch. Tim knew that among those cheering fans there always lurked those who were, as he labelled them bitterly, the 'players' worst enemies'. These were the men he jeered back at as 'the anonymous critics' and he was their prime target. The magnetic personality is always going to be the one in the line of fire. They were going about it in the most poisonous way possible. The real way to destroy a player's career, said Tim, is to suggest that his bad form on the pitch is his own fault: 'But probably the footballers' worst enemies are those who, either by subterfuge or innuendo, convey to the minds of the directors that the reason for their falling off in form is due to misbehaviour. The anonymous letter is the medium which they most frequently adopt, and unfortunately there are some club directors whose ears are always open for bar-parlour chatter and communications of the kind.'

Tim called this period of his life 'The Story of Tim Coleman and the Anonymous Letter Writer'. The episode foreshadows many of football's subsequent rumours and scandals – he was accused of being a drunkard. That was, so the anonymous correspondent said, why his form had declined. For Tim even to tell the story afterwards, at a distance of four years, was a huge risk and a challenge to expectations. Having got away with that kind of scrape, the conventional thing would have been to keep quiet and be thankful. Tim went ahead and published the story of his own secret scandal, because he wanted to make a point more than he cared about the danger. Like all rebels he had the selfish streak that shrugs off consequences.

His version of the story appeared with the headline: 'A sample of what happens'. Tim then sought to put 'A case which proves how baseless, as a rule, are the accusations brought against players.' His story concerned 'a forward' who had been 'off form' – and the detail was totally personal and set precisely in this bad patch. Naturally the fans wondered what was wrong. 'No reason could be assigned for his lapse.' Then someone from that mud-throwing community kindly offered the directors some help in explaining why their striker was not scoring: '. . . until one bright morning a letter was handed into the office addressed to the secretary.'

More established in 1909, when he was recounting the incident, Tim could still picture that letter. And what he saw was not the document itself, but the sort of person the sender must have been – an outwardly genteel person, one of the gentlemen. 'The writing was that of an educated person, and the contents of the missive were to the effect that if the club official had any desire to ascertain for themselves the cause of the player going off form, they should make a call at a certain tavern in the town any evening between seven and eleven, where they would find him in a state of physical helplessness.' Welcome to football hell: the dock in the court of the rumour-mongers. The supposedly respectable classes have never been slow to take revenge on football's young upstarts.

Intriguingly, Tim admitted, in passing, that 'players are not angels'. How close was he to confessing some truth in the scandal? But then he furiously denied the slur: 'Now, what was the truth? The player in question was never known to have allowed intoxicating liquor of any kind to pass his lips, and on one of the particular dates which the writer specified it was proved that the player was in bed nursing a sore [an injury] which he had received the previous Saturday.' In this account, he made no attempt to keep up the anonymity. Was there a hint of desperation in the emphasis? It seems that this was not an isolated rumour: 'On the other occasion libelled it was proved that the player was in the company of the trainer during the whole of the evening.'

He managed to defend himself, for the moment, and then eventually they showed him the actual letter – and the spasm of revulsion that he felt was still sharp as he told the story four years on: 'You can have some idea of his feelings, I think, when the reasons for official investigation were made known to him.' This is a rebel under threat, the authorities closing in around him. Scandal – deserved or ill-founded – is one of the perils of rebellious notoriety. As Coleman came into his prime on the pitch, the darker side of life as a successful footballer was pressing in upon him. As a result of this pressure, there also emerged a darker side to his personality – a recklessness and rage that might someday ignore the limits and push him towards self-destruction.

There was also a huge talent, and for more than the playing side of the game. One really extraordinary thing is the voice that Tim used to fight back against the gentleman and his 'educated' writing. 'The more I think of such attempts to bring players into bad repute, the more vehement becomes my denunciation, because in the case of the anonymous writer the player always has to take the treatment meted out to him lying down. He simply can't do anything. Let me appeal, therefore, to that section of the public to whom these observations of mine have special reference, to give over their campaign of calumny.'

This was not how the Woolwich inside-left, the 'dapper little fellow', was meant to sound. It was perhaps hubris on his part to let such cleverness show in this situation. Retribution might be over the horizon. Better by far, as Tim also recognised, the old working-class abuse delivered in person from the terrace, destructive though that also was. 'Much rather would I prefer "the barracker" who, let me say, has been the ruin of many really promising players.' With raging courage, he stripped away the myths of Edwardian times, jolly sporting and polite, to reveal a much harsher world. 'When Woolwich Arsenal were going very badly, for instance, the players were inundated with anonymous letters, some of which, I can assure you, were of a very flattering nature,' he said sarcastically. 'Many epistles were also addressed to our manager, Phil Kelso, but very wisely he consigned them to the WPB [waste paper bin]. Some people were even courageous enough to adhibit their names to the charges which they preferred, but when the opportunity was afforded them of meeting those whom they accused they refused to accept it. Why? More than likely it was because they realised then that their libels were based upon some other body's statement, and which, had they inquired into the matter, would have been proved to have had no foundation in fact.'

It was Tim who first realised how far it would go, as he reflected on that close shave with the anonymous letter writer: 'To my mind you might as well stab a man in the dark as write anonymous letters about his behaviour to those who are in authority over him. Players are not angels, and are not expected to be such either, but still they like to be treated as human beings, and if they cannot get that from their own spectators, where are they to expect it?'

Of course it is some among a player's home fans who are most likely to turn nasty . . . as Tim also knew. He determinedly spoke up for the players who were supposed to just accept this treatment, as all men of their class did. 'On their behalf that I raise the voice of protest,' he once said. He was making himself into football's first member of the awkward squad, the first battler off as well as on the pitch, the first who understood what it meant to be a true football star. Here is Tim's motto for all footballers, right at the beginning: 'If players are treated fairly and with a little consideration better work will be got out of them than when they are subject to organised tirades of abuse by those from whom they have a right to expect better treatment.'

That was the point, 'they have a right'. But it was a radical idea in those days, that a footballer might have any rights – radical and risky, with a hint of the self-righteousness that belongs to the rare people who can fight a cause for a long time in unequal circumstances.

# Up for the Cup

After the toil and trouble, popularity and success was all the brighter when it came again. The same personality that provoked outrage and innuendo was bound to become a cult, given a chance. And just when Tim needed something to change, the FA Cup came to his rescue, the start of his climb to a new kind of popular acclaim. At last he was pushing on from the years of promise, towards a new maturity. Bernard Joy, himself a great Arsenal half-back, put at the centre of these Woolwich years the rise of 'John "Tim" Coleman, who was to blossom out as a great inside-forward'. He was never a goal machine but he was the most remarkable football talent to come out of London thus far.

The renaissance began in a cold corner. Woolwich Arsenal met Watford in the second round in early February. A howling wind welcomed the Southern Leaguers to Plumstead. Arsenal had never made it into the third round: the club had been rather more concerned with getting into the First Division. Now was the time to put that right. It was hardly the right climate for subtlety or skill: as the whistle went, there came swirls of bitter snow on that wind. Tim decided to follow the ball today, it was hardly the occasion for keeping in formation.

After ten minutes of jostling, big Tommy Fitchie, the former Norwood amateur and now the Arsenal centre-forward, managed to direct the game's first shot on goal. A Watford full-back got in the way – or perhaps he was just standing there. The ball cannoned off him and Tim saw his chance. Cutting inside, towards the penalty area, he was thinking as he ran that, in the high wind, there was no point in putting over a cross, or trying a spectacular looping shot. Instead, he thumped the ball back in along the ground. Everyone was taken by surprise and, amid the mayhem and the hacking, the ball simply kept on whizzing over the bumpy turf until it finished in the net. As one report said, it was 'one of those low shots which he seems to have made a speciality – and a very nice speciality too'. Tim was back on the victory trail.

One goal was hardly going to be enough in a game as tight as this. As the first half went on, the tempo got ever more frantic and the home team were reduced to ten men by a foul notable even in this battle. Tim decided again to introduce an element of order. He set up another of the much despised one-two passing moves and then 'when he secured his pass, as a result of that fine combined move', he charged in and 'beat Biggar with his pretty ground drive'. Those pretty passes and neat, sharp shots showed exactly what Tim said: you cannot change the way players play by insulting them from the terraces, in the papers or in letters to the directors. If that is their style, if it is in the blood, then that is how they have to play the game. It was always a matter of being true to your own talents . . . that was the message he was delivering in the Cup-tie, as he pushed them on to the next round.

As in later decades and as with so many clubs over the years, the Cup raised morale at Plumstead and they clambered painfully from the bottom of the table. Meanwhile they drew Sunderland at home again. The Wearsiders were genuine contenders for the Cup and the gate was another bonus: the tie produced record takings of more than £750. The match settled into a dour stalemate until the visitors, with their superior power, began to dominate. The hosts did manage a foray into the Sunderland penalty area, where Bert Freeman, who was trying the centre-forward role for the Arsenal, managed to miskick the best chance of a hitherto goalless game. It was not to be his season, although he and Tim were to have better times together in later years. As the ball screwed sideways, catching everyone out, Tim 'sprang up from nowhere', the nowhere that all really sharp forwards lurk in when nothing seems to be going on, 'and he transferred the sphere to the opposite side of the net'. It was, the national critics said, rather an odd 'low, slow shot', another of his specials. The floodgates opened as Sunderland were forced to chase the game. It was 3-0 by half-time and 5-0 at the finish. Arsenal had launched their first FA Cup challenge. 'Once in front the Arsenal were irresistible'; 'Hats off to the Arsenal!'. All those anonymous critics were having to eat their poisonous words! One of the most satisfying views on the game was that this victory 'told eloquently of the value of short, sharp, crisp, accurate shooting' and the Londoners' short passing style generally. All those demands that they give up and adopt the 'long swinging pass' of their northern adversaries now looked daft.

The luck of the draw could not last and they had to face Manchester United away for their unprecedented adventure into the quarter-final. Cartoons showed the Gunners gazing like Don Quixote towards the distant horizon, where the towers of Crystal Palace, the venue of the final, stood like a mirage. As everyone conceded: 'Now Southern quidnuncs [experts] perforce must count the Arsenal among the strong candidates for the blue riband of the football world.'

But Clayton, United's stronghold, was something different. The club had deep roots in this industrial heartland, having been born as Newton Heath, a railway team, in 1878 and moving to their Bank Street ground, still in the Clayton area, in 1902. This was where the name Manchester United was adopted, among the chimneys and the busy little shops, with the terraced streets all around and smoke everywhere. The London fans who made the long rail excursion mixed into a crowd of more than 30,000. The setting was forbidding to them, as the stadium seemed to be located at the very heart of a forest of chimneys, in what seemed like a clearing. 'Local colour! Black, all black, as black as pitch!' The soot of the industrial north: this was where the Cup belonged, after each season's annual invasion of the Crystal Palace. All around was 'a hissing vapour that threatened to envelop the whole place and a kind of feeling that you are at the other end of the world'.

Out came the teams, on to a field that seemed as black as the air. 'If I had seen a blade of grass on that alleged field I should have fallen down and worshipped it,' said the bemused correspondent for the *Plumstead News,* for whom this was evidently a foreign land. Amid the endless tinkering, Satterthwaite, Coleman and Freeman were now the front line, and it had been enough for the Arsenal to beat a path towards the sanctuary of the lower mid-table after the poor results of the autumn and New Year. The feeling of the fans was anxious. 'Any visiting team that can win at Clayton deserves gold medals,' said one. 'When I saw the "field" – save the mark! – I feared for the Arsenal,' admitted another. The question of style became disturbingly urgent. 'I never expected them to play the game they did or to conquer. The United ought to beat everything and anybody at Clayton.' It was hardly fair, there did not seem to be a level playing field. 'Rather should I say that the ground should beat any side that is not acquainted with its peculiarities . . . You cannot play the ordinary game at Clayton.' This was the ultimate home of the long ball game on which the North flourished. 'The ball is always in the air, and the United are up the field in three long passes.' Here, the short inter-passing method met its opposite. 'They rarely slip the ball from one to another and they do know their ground.' United were past masters of the aerial bombardment and they had prepared a field that suited their method. 'The occasions upon which the object went along the floor were few and far between.' It was a battle between the extremes of English football.

Inevitably perhaps, it was Manchester United that gave early encouragement to the roaring home crowd by taking the lead. But the

Arsenal were in no mood to give up. More to the point, they stuck to their guns, according to Tim's recipe for staying true to themselves. 'The Reds played real Cup-tie football on this occasion and they were cleverer than the United all the way through.' Arsenal came back strongly. The ball went out for a corner. Tim hovered on the fringe as he was not one of the players likely to win a header against the towering home defenders. Over it came and Tim watched as the keeper, Harry Moger, came out to punch clear. He saw how the goalie rushed into the milling crowd of players. It may have been obstruction, or just confusion, but no keeper reappeared, only the ball that he had punched despairingly over the top of the throng. As the roar deepened, Tim saw his moment and shifted just that vital touch to put himself in the perfect position. When the ball looped towards him, the temptation was to hit it hard, but there was a better way and, as the watching commentators noted, he 'pushed the ball into the net before Moger could regain' his position or his senses. That word 'pushed' is a Tim signature, an Arsenal theme tune: just placing it into the goal.

The Arsenal minority in the crowd went frantic with cheering and then got caught in 'alternate spasms of discomfiture and wild delight' as the fates hung in the balance. Twenty-five minutes into the second half and the scores remained level. Bert Freeman got the ball. 'He was just onside, though the referee was uncertain, for he made a move as though to blow his whistle. He did not do so, however, but the home defenders had anticipated him doing so, for they gave Freeman too much freedom, with the result that the centre forward rushed ahead and shot a capital goal, thus giving the victory to Woolwich.' It was a thoroughly modern Cup experience and it ended 3-2 to the Arsenal. The victory was one that would live long in the memory of 'those who braved the poisonous fumes of Clayton'. Tim got his share of the credit too. 'Coleman pleased everybody. He is a box of tricks' even though one report conceded that 'Clayton is not the place for jugglery'. The great thing for Tim, though, was that his panache and trickery were being balanced by the cutting edge of a more direct player like Freeman. It was a partnership with a future.

In retrospect, this was an historic match: Arsenal's first Cup win against Manchester United, the very beginning of one of the greatest football rivalries in the world game. Tim knew the importance of history, but he was really a man of the moment: 'I do not propose to go into ancient statistics of former meetings, for these, after all, have no bearing on the respective merits of the present day teams.' What concerned him was the next round – and those cheers from the terraces, at last.

The Cup had come south only once before, and that was to Spurs. Could this be the year when the Arsenal stopped their neighbours and greatest rivals from boasting at last? It had been the worst autumn of his career but Tim's fight back from the depths had been given more momentum from that Cup triumph. He was selected to be reserve forward in the next England international, even if it was with Walter Bull, of Spurs. That international fixture was where he met Charlie Thomson, the Scottish reserve and his future friend and skipper. No substitutes were allowed on in those days, once the game had started, so reserves had lots of time to chat and to invent their comedy routine of arguing in exaggerated English and Scottish accents.

Back on the Cup run, the semi-final was at Stoke City's Victoria Ground. They had been drawn against Newcastle United, League champions of the 1904-05 season and last year's beaten Cup finalists, one of the truly great sides in the history of the game. There was a tremendous atmosphere and the game was a focus of national interest. When the Woolwich team got into their railway carriage, a young steward held the door for them. 'How long will it take us to reach Stoke?' asked Phil Kelso of the boy. 'Not so long as it will take you to reach the Crystal Palace,' replied the youngster, as he slammed the door on the party.

The main threat in the Newcastle ranks was Colin Veitch, the young star of Tyneside, the most versatile and all-round talent in the game. As one newspaper said: 'Colin Veitch will be playing centre half-back next Saturday against Scotland. At Stoke he was a centre-forward – he is anything, as a matter of fact.' Veitch was to have a major impact on Tim's life, fighting together on and off the pitch. But that day he was a formidable opponent. Veitch was just coming into his prime, as was Tim. He was from the wrong side of the Newcastle tracks, in Byker, and he had dug himself out, first by winning a scholarship to grammar school and then by becoming a teenage sensation for United. He continued on both tracks, going to Durham University and playing football in the vacations. He was a multi-talented man, a theatre director who helped found the Newcastle People's Theatre, admired by George Bernard Shaw, a musician and composer, and a political activist in the rising Labour Party. Despite these many accomplishments, he was a quiet, modest character. 'A more unassuming player for a man of his abilities it is difficult to imagine. He does nothing apparently. He simply shoots the ball with singular accuracy at the opposing goal, or he passes or heads the ball to within a yard of a colleague, and then moves along to receive back the pass as though he was just doing it for fun. He simply does nothing but merely play football.'

When the players arrived at Stoke's Victoria Ground, conditions were ideal. The neutrality of the locals was more than compensated for by the passion of 500 Arsenal travellers and many more Geordies. The Londoners were in all ways underdogs and yet they sprang into action faster. After nine minutes, Bert Freeman 'sent in a rasping shot which Lawrence got hands to but could not stop, as the ball continued towards the line McCombie stepped into the breach and headed the ball out just as it was passing over the line.' Tim had a shot of his own too. There is rare photograph of him in action in this match and it shows a man fighting for all he is worth. The ball is coming towards Tim and he is holding Orr, of Newcastle, at bay with a well-placed elbow, while getting his balance for a shot. His gaze is fixed on that approaching ball. This is an instant showing a player poised even while under extreme pressure.

The north-easterners were more experienced: they were the League champions after all. A Woolwich journalist conceded that: 'Gradually the superior play of Newcastle asserted itself.' You could see what was coming. 'It was apparent that sooner or later their prowess would meet with due reward, Veitch in particular being a most dangerous shooting expert.' Veitch then gave his side the lead with an acrobatic shot, and they held on, adding another after the break to settle things down, despite one more good effort from Freeman.

The reports picked out Tim on the Arsenal side as 'their best forward' and 'the pick of the attackers'. He was more critical of his performance, though the day became another of his moments in the glare of the limelight. The game was to establish his lasting place in football folklore, at least until the First World War swept away most of those characters and stories like sandcastles from a beach. He gave his own version of what happened after that semi-final defeat, as part of his account of the ups-and-downs of football life. It was '. . . an incident which occurred at the close of the semi-final for the cup between Woolwich Arsenal and Newcastle United'. The Woolwich boys were trying to recover in their politely separate washing compartments: 'We had just retired to the dressing-rooms, when there came a knock at the door of the cubicle which I occupied.' A journalist had got into the Arsenal changing-room, which itself says something about the overbearing attitude of the press in that period.

' "Halloa!" ' I replied in answer to the application for admission.

' "Are you Percy Sands?" asked the visitor.' Sands was the Woolwich skipper, a strong defensive midfielder and an old boy of a public school.

Tim replied, in an appropriately modified accent, as was his habit: 'Yes.'

'To what do you attribute your defeat?' asked the reporter.

As a storyteller, Tim could lay claim to as much high-flown language as any Edwardian reporter could have used to write about him. As Tim said: 'I tumbled right away to the fact that the caller was a reporter, and that he was desirous of obtaining Percy's impressions of the game.

' "Oh, nothing in particular," I replied.

' "But surely there was something," he persisted.

' "Well, we were beaten by a better team, that is all."

' "And who do you think was the best player on your side?"

' "Tim Coleman undoubtedly."'

It probably wasn't really the humour that fascinated people even then. It was the notion of an uneducated lad, one of the pros, turning the tables on a writer. 'This closed the interview,' said Tim. 'Two hours afterwards I read in an evening paper that one of its representatives had had an interview with Percy Sands, who had very generously expressed the opinion that Tim Coleman was the best man on the Woolwich side. As a matter of fact he said Tim on that particular afternoon was just about the worst.' The third-person reference to 'Tim' is his way of playing around with the prevailing style of journalism at the time and also with his own public persona, as if it was someone else.

For years afterwards, the echoes of this episode followed Tim around, like a signature tune. People tended to introduce the tale as if it were a joke: 'Coleman is a bit of a practical joker. He once met an inexperienced reporter, who, unaware of the player's identity . . . rendered a glowing eulogy of Coleman's footballing abilities from Tim's own lips. Needless to say, they lost nothing in the telling.' The fact that he got his revenge for the reporter's intrusion into the dressing-room by mimicking his upper-class skipper adds another point, and that was the one Tim liked to dwell on himself, with his taste for seeking out class tensions and casting himself as the voice of the hard-done-by.

•

This was all part of Tim's emergence as a football character, on and off the pitch. They remembered, at Arsenal, along with the Stoke occasion, moments such as the club's end-of-season dinner. The drinks were flowing and the feast had been mainly consumed. As in later times, they had asked a showbiz guest, the music hall comedian and singer George Robey and he recognised a fellow wit and raconteur, according to those who were there: 'Tim Coleman is a born humorist, his powers of repartee being of a very high order. His wit is of the spontaneous variety, and on one occasion he convulsed the company at a club dinner by his bon mots. One of the most appreciative of his hearers was George Robey, who turned round to the gentleman next him and, with the inclination of his head towards Coleman, exclaimed: "Isn't he good?" When his playing days are over Tim might do worse than adopt a stage career.'

Humorist meant much more than joker, in the language of the time. It suggested someone who followed his own humour, who was mercurial and unconventional as much as funny. It was a word from a more polite age for acknowledging a man who went his own way, often bringing excitement and pleasure, and always with a hint of trouble.

# Chanting 'The Little Gunner'

The lights continued to shine and the cheers grew. In 1906-07 Tim turned twenty-three and was reaching the peak of his powers. Joy's classic account of the rise of the first great London club reaches its climax with this campaign, one that he hails as 'the peak season before the Chapman era'; that is, before the great days of the late Twenties and early Thirties when Arsenal were the greatest club in the land and even in the world. Joy picks out Tim and does so in terms that stand out amid the sober language of the era: 'Star of the team and also the humorist was Tim Coleman at inside-right. He was as nimble footed as he was quick-witted.' This was precisely the Coleman who was emerging at the end of the previous season, through his exploits, of all kinds, in the FA Cup. Like later 'humorists', or football originals, such as Marsh or Dougan, Tim never had the singleness of purpose to be a statistical great. But because of that, his moments of success shone all the brighter, for himself and for others.

The whole team was stronger and more settled in 1906-07. David Neave added width to the forward line and Satterthwaite looked threatening in front of goal. Tommy Hynds, an attacking midfielder, gave them added mobility and edge. The early highlight was when 30,000 spectators arrived for the visit of Newcastle to the Manor Ground. Increasingly, away supporters swelled the volume of the Plumstead roar – trains were improving and football excursions were getting cheaper. The local view was that Newcastle were mainly a strong-arm side: 'The Coalies are a heavier lot,' but there was a feeling that the home side might be a good match for them on 'the dry, hard turf' of September. Coleman and Satterthwaite shone, and Tim got on the score sheet as well – as he was to do with more frequency and confidence this season. Two-nil and £595 to swell the club coffers; not a bad day for the Arsenal.

The club was now very much a part of the big-time atmosphere surrounding the game. Football was enjoying a boom. A crowd of nearly 40,000 packed Villa Park to see the Reds' visit. Arsenal had their backs to the wall after their captain, Percy Sands, was taken ill on the morning of the game. The setting was tailor-made for Tim, whose spirits soared with the excitement and passion of the occasion. Villa went ahead after only ten minutes, but Arsenal got one back almost from the restart. And that's how it remained until half-time. Then, as so often happens in football, even to this day, the second half began with a goal, the home team going ahead again. But the Arsenal kept going; this season heads stayed high. Hope makes all the difference, in football as in life. There were three minutes of the ninety left, though, and surely only time for one last attack. Tim got the ball, a gap opened and he decided to let rip: 'Coleman put the shot in with the force of a heavy gun'. Two-all, and the journey to Birmingham suddenly seemed worth every penny as the 'Woolwich contingent' went 'wild with cheers'. It was one of those perfect football days, a draw that felt as good as any win. Tim remembered it as 'one of the finest games in which I have participated . . . a league match between the Arsenal and the Villa at Birmingham. It was so full of incident.' That was what he always needed: action, and a cheering crowd.

All the hate mail and rumours of drunkenness had been swept aside and instead he had become the hero of the hour, the wonder boy. His rise was also having other effects: recognition loomed. Tim was selected for the inter-league match between the English and Irish Leagues in Belfast. It was a kind of trial game, though something of a mismatch because the best Irish players, as nowadays, were already in the English League. Luck was running with him now, and Tim scored two goals against the Irish. The Arsenal man was felt to have 'distinguished himself'. It was the polar opposite of that time the previous year, when they were down in the dumps and the directors were starting to turn rough. A year on too from his brother's death.

When he came back from the game in Belfast, there was something special to greet him. The little man now had a unique rapport with the fans and, at the Arsenal's next game, at home to Notts County, there were scenes that amazed witnesses: 'Woolwich people were charmed when "Tim" Coleman was honoured by the English League last week and now they are chanting the little "Gunner". He is indeed the lion of the hour with the Plumstead patrons.' That chant from the terraces was the sound of something new – the birth of a cult figure.

The whole day was dramatic. Notts County put up a great fight at the Manor in a game that the home team were really expecting to win. Tim seemed to have put his side ahead with a neat shot and the referee was pointing to the centre circle when he noticed the linesman waving his flag. It was offside after all that. The scene that followed proved that modern players have not invented the art of hounding the referee: 'The referee was surrounded by players.' It was of no use, then as now! The minutes ticked away and the Arsenal forced a late corner. Over came the ball and the huge County goalkeeper Albert Iremonger punched it clear. It fell nicely for the lurking Roddy McEachrane, who centred first time towards Tim. 'As it dropped, Coleman shot on the run.' This was a real striker's instinct, the first-time volley, 'and the ball flew into the net'. The cheers rang around and the verdict was becoming familiar: 'Tim was the star of the field.' The highs did not cancel out the memory of the bitter lows, but they were sweet enough.

In the aftermath, the crowd flooded on to the pitch: 'There was then a scene of enthusiasm which beggars description, and Neave and Coleman in particular came in for quite an ovation . . . Coleman was the star artist of the front line.' And to complete the perfect day, victory meant that the Arsenal were top of the First Division, a point above Everton and with a game in hand. Though their squad was comparatively small, they hung on to their position as 1906 was coming to a close.

The whole atmosphere at the Manor Ground had increased a notch or two, but not everyone was happy with it: 'And one word to the Woolwich crowd. They are a loyal and well-meaning body of supporters, but they would do well to remember that the home team is not always the embodiment of all the virtues. The visiting players and referee have some good points. This continual cry of "Play the game, referee" and "Play the game, Bolton", or whoever the visiting team may be, is childish, to say the least.' This was a different side to London's football-going public, a new expression of the capital's identity. 'Play the game, referee' is mild by modern-day standards of referee criticism, but it was a novel and surprising sound then.

Tim was then selected to play for the South of England in the traditional trial match against the North, to be held at Stamford Bridge, the west London home of Chelsea. From that encounter the team would emerge to take on the other home countries in the spring. The North proved too strong, as usual, running out comfortable winners by four goals to one. Accounts of Tim's performance varied. Arsenal partisans insisted that he was let down by the winger outside him, who failed to understand his clever tactics. Others were less sure. But the rebel spirit was still bubbling inside him. Tim remembered something else from the day: 'I will never forget an incident at Chelsea when I was appearing in a North v South match. The gateman would not let me in. Perhaps he mistook me for a programme boy. Anyhow I was rescued by Mr Wall, the Secretary of the Football Association.' A light-hearted recollection, perhaps, but it was another story of pompous authority. Coleman always had an eye for the tale that would add to the image of Tim, the football personality. Long before footballers' agents and media advisers, he was a one-man story-making enterprise. Most of the stories, though, had an element of conflict and a sense of injustice was never far below the surface. Football fans, though, recognised someone they could identify with.

Meanwhile there was the FA Cup to enjoy, and it was becoming a Woolwich speciality. Could they go one round better this year? In front of more than 32,000 at the Manor Ground, they took on Bristol City. Coleman and his right wing Garbutt were 'worth going a long way to see'. There was partisan speculation around the ground that day about Tim in particular: 'It has been claimed for Coleman that he is the best inside-right in England.' The Arsenal opinion was that there was not 'another player' who 'could have shown such a brainy knowledge of the game and such adaptability of characteristics under unaccustomed conditions'.

An England call-up followed for the game in mid-February against Ireland. As the day approached, the editor of the popular London magazine *Football Chat* spoke for a community that stretched far beyond the Woolwich area when he extended 'my hearty congratulations to Tim Coleman, on his selection for England against Ireland.' It was the editor's widely shared view that 'Tim deserves his cap, and I hope he will play one of his best games.'

The match was scheduled to be played at Everton's Goodison Park ground, on 19 February. It was, in fact, something of a new-look England team. The forward line, in particular, was more promising than experienced. Alongside Tim, there was that young Newcastle United player Colin Veitch, who had ended the Arsenal's Cup run back in 1906. Together, he and Tim represented a new wave in more than just their football. A qualified teacher, theatre director, opera conductor and political activist, Veitch was an intellectual revolutionary to match Coleman the pirate. Their paths would converge more than once, in crises which would determine the very future of the game.

First, they shared top billing in 1907 as the young England strike-force, along with Joe Bache, another rising star from Villa. Anyone who followed the game at the time would have understood what was meant by the pairing of Veitch and Coleman, all the more so because one other name had disappeared from the selectors' list, that of Vivian John Woodward. If Veitch's life ran strangely parallel with Coleman's, in football and beyond, then Woodward represented an equally striking counterpoint. In the late winter of 1907, the London football scene moved between the poles of Tim Coleman and 'Jack' Woodward. They were the ultimate professional and the quintessential amateur, the pro and the sportsman, the clown prince and the gentleman prince. The team sheet for February's England game represented a temporary victory for the player over the gentleman on the London scene.

Jack, as he was known to friends and family, was the son of an architect and educated at Ascham's College in Clacton-on-Sea, Essex. By his late teens he was turning out for the local Clacton club side, and he soon moved on to play for his county. That was where he was spotted by Tottenham and he began to play for them just after the turn of the century. It was not long before he was in the England side, both the amateur and the 'full' one, alongside the professionals. He was soon top scorer for both. But, by the beginning of 1907 questions were being raised about the idol. Spurs had left the Southern League, where they had enjoyed much stylish success, for the rougher waters of Division Two of the Football League. There Woodward encountered the spirit of the professional players from the North, as Tim had before him. In Woodward's case the experience was even harder, because he was famous as the gentleman player, the pure amateur, who had resisted the rising tide of professionalism.

Matters came to a head in the game between Spurs and Hull, a dour goalless draw, and according to the indignant London commentator, 'Woodward was completely encircled.' A heated controversy arose, in London sporting circles, 'about the treatment of amateurs who take part in professional football'. Rumours that his career was finished began to circulate. It was almost civil war: South against North, gentlemen against professionals. Woodward's supporters in the capital felt that he was being deliberately driven from the game, to make space for a new breed. Tempers were frayed: 'Mr Woodward lost no time in sending forth a contradiction to the widely published statement, and I am informed by the Spurs that immediately he recovers (which, unfortunately, his doctor thinks will not be for another two or three weeks), he will again be out with his favourite club.'

Meanwhile, the rise of Coleman continued alongside the apparent fall of Woodward. More was at stake that mid-February at Goodison Park than a football victory. Conspiracy or not, skulduggery or merely chance, or possibly as a result of some 'decadence', some failure of character, Woodward was missing, and so the new boys got their opportunity. And in Tim's life, as ever, all roads led through Goodison Park.

That afternoon on Merseyside, however, was not one of Tim's treasured memories. He had only one chance, when he dribbled past the Irish defenders and had only the goalkeeper to beat. His moment of destiny arrived, he lined up a shot, one he would score from nine times out of ten, and hammered it wide. In front of a crowd of 25,000, England came away 1-0 winners, though they were felt to have been lucky. One report said: 'Hardman was the only forward in the England side to do himself credit.' So it was still an amateur, the man from Everton, who had the starring role! The London reporter lamented that 'I had great hopes of Coleman, of Woolwich Arsenal, who partnered the Newcastle forward Veitch on the right, but the Plumstead man must have been very excited, for he passed erratically and shot much less effectively than he did against Liverpool the previous week. He had a fine chance of a goal in the second half, but after steering promisingly past Connor and McCartney, he did not give the only remaining man, Scott, the opportunity of displaying his talent, for he put the ball out. Scott, naturally, permitted himself a breath after such an escape.' Surely, everyone thought, there would be more chances for Tim in an England shirt: it had not been such a bad beginning.

Not much could dent Tim's morale that year, in any case. He returned from England duty in even better form and the Arsenal knocked Bristol Rovers out of the Cup. It was his goal that did it. 'Tim Coleman was in his liveliest humour, and after he had found the measure of Cartlidge he gave him little peace. Three or four shots he gave the Rovers' custodian before the goal arrived after twenty-five minutes play.' Humour was now the trademark of the Tim cult, and not just his jokes. He had a few punch lines on the field too.

The start of March saw Arsenal falling back in the League, the general view being that the Cup was distracting them. Tim was still riding high and he was picked to play for the English League against the Scottish equivalent at Ibrox, the most intense stadium of them all. It was a creditable goalless draw and the verdict of the national commentators was more than positive: 'Coleman is a master on the ball. He holds it beautifully and dribbles well until his partner is in position. I like Coleman's play, inspired as it is by intelligence.' The only thing missing had been a goal. The London view was more sanguine: 'The licensed wit of the Arsenal team is worth another trial and we wish him success.'

The Cup was still the bright spot as far as his club was concerned. For nine shillings and sixpence an Arsenal fan could make the train excursion up to Yorkshire for the tie against Barnsley. It was a tempting offer and, as a result, the 'neat little bandbox', as the visitors patronisingly called it, was full to capacity at 14,000. The locals planned to mark Coleman out of the game: 'Perhaps his reputation as an international had something to do with the way he was watched . . . "Timmy" was very good-natured under the circumstances.' Shrugging his shoulders at the flailing defender, he set up the equaliser after the Tykes had the temerity to go one-up, and then he scored the winner too.

The Arsenal had not given up on the League either, as only a few points separated the London challengers from top place. In the end, they fell just short in both competitions. Sheffield Wednesday knocked them out of the FA Cup, inflicting more semi-final torment on Tim and his team-mates. In the League Arsenal finished on forty-four points, their best to date, one point behind the third-placed team, Everton. Newcastle were champions. Tim ended his season with a flurry of goals, as if he was trying to drag the club single-handedly to the summit of the game. Despite his goals, England did not recall him immediately. Instead, for the home game against the Scots that was the climax of the international season, the selectors returned to old favourites. Woodward was back in and so was Steve Bloomer, who was a top striker as far back as the 1890s. They had their nostalgic moments: 'Steve Bloomer got the ball past McBride, after good work by Vivian Woodward.' But 'Woodward again failed to do himself justice. He is obviously out of condition.' The saga of Tim and England, and the more personal story of Tim and 'Woody', had a long way to run. For now he was in his football element, taking the limelight with him wherever he went.

The summer brought one of the highlights of his whole career, an overseas tour. He told the tale in the *Weekly News*, which saw the whole thing as a comic episode judging by its headline: 'Amusing scene with Belgian customs officials'. As usual, Tim had something more to say, beneath the veneer of amusement. It all turned on an incident that certainly lent itself to a comic touch rather like *Three Men in a Boat*. 'I am presented with a "kissen"!' declared Tim's column. He did like the word 'kissen' – or cushion – it's true, but he noticed a lot more about Germany and Europe than that excerpt suggests. It was a scene from the halcyon days of his football life, and yet it had even then some darker portents.

Berlin, 1907. The whistle had blown for the end of a football match, in the summer sunshine. The German crowd spilled happily on to the pitch, wearing clothes that might seem to us today more suitable for a funeral or a city office: sober dark jackets and black hats. A young lad of, say, ten running on to that turf could still have been alive to watch West Germany – a country not born in 1907, now long gone – lose to England in the 1966 World Cup Final. If he had been present at Wembley fifty-nine years later, he may well have thought back to that day when he first saw English players beat a German team. What is striking now is not the wit in Tim's recollections of the occasion, but the foresight.

The crowd gathered in the centre of the pitch, eager to get close to the players. It is not the locals they want to greet, it is the red-shirted victors, the men of the Woolwich Arsenal FC, over for their continental tour as many of the leading English clubs did. There was little contact between leading English players and their foreign counterparts. The England team fielded amateurs in games against the likes of Germany and France; the full side turned out only against the other home countries for the annual tournament. The chance of a club competition between British and continental sides was even more remote than a proper international match. So the summer tour was one of the more pleasant parts of life for the leading players, a kind of paid holiday long before foreign tourism or package trips to the continent began.

British teams were especially popular in Germany. The fans in Berlin even brought a present for the visitors, an expensive embroidered cushion, and they gave it proudly to the Woolwich captain. The centre of the decoration was a golden German imperial eagle, symbol of the national pride and confidence. The English skipper gracefully received the gift. What really intrigued him, though, as he wrote about the experience afterwards, was the lack of any real understanding between the people of the two nations. A comic side to this was the way the German word for 'cushion' sounds like the English for 'kiss': 'I, as captain of the team, was presented with a "kissen".' He did relish the potential for confusion and mischief. There was in his account a sharp sense of just how little these two peoples knew about each other, even when they were standing on a football pitch together. He casts himself as a lost foreigner, and his hosts as aliens, equally at sea together with their mutual but baffled goodwill. He was at a loss to understand their present: 'What for? I don't know,' he said. What was he supposed to do with an ornamental 'kissen' in the middle of a football pitch? Why a cushion for that matter? It was a strange foreign custom, amusing rather than worrying, yet the gulf between Berlin and Woolwich carries overtones of something more dangerous. The next episode in his travels will reveal these dangers, for all the attempts at reassuring comedy.

First, though, the problem was how to thank the fans. There were no microphones, but the Woolwich skipper felt more than equal to the task of addressing this gathering. 'I accepted it, thanked them profusely – in my own language, of course – my remarks being cheered to the echo when I sat down, although not a single German understood one word I said. That probably mattered very little.' There were two sides of Tim in this passage. One was the chirpy comedian, who made the speech and won over the Germans with his charm. The other was more thoughtful, and more original. That was the man who, though not 'educated' like all those anonymous letter writers or FA officials, noticed the real extent of the gulf on that pitch, and was stunned by it. Yes, it was amusing in its way; but there was another point. If we did not understand one another when we were trying to be nice, what would happen when things got difficult?

The occasion had a happy ending. An interpreter was rushed into action and the speech proved as great a success in Berlin as Coleman's fluent humour usually was in London: 'When they were interpreted, however, the Germans cheered again, which proved pretty conclusively, I think, that as an English Ambassador I was not altogether a failure.'

The journey back to England, however, allowed Tim to explore his darker thoughts about Europe. Suddenly, the continent that had welcomed English footballers so enthusiastically seemed a more dangerous place. The train crossed Germany bound for the English Channel. 'All went well with me and my "kissen" until we reached the frontier station between Germany and Belgium, where two customs officials boarded the train, and after rummaging about for a time took me and the kissen on to the platform.' What followed was an absurd scene of mutual incomprehension, in which a bumbling, 'educated' Englishman failed to make good his boast of understanding other languages and people. As Tim recalled: 'I had made the acquaintance of an individual who reckoned that he was a doctor, and who professed that he was an excellent linguist. Very naturally I appealed to him to explain to the customs officers how I had come into possession of the kissen.' While this gentleman was struggling to communicate, Tim worked out what was going on for himself, and got right to the heart of a bigger problem: 'What they objected to, as far as I could understand, was the eagle which was sewn in the corner.' Six years after Tim wrote these words, the German eagle did indeed cross this border with 'gallant little Belgium'. Already, Tim's sharp eye could see the danger, while the gentleman bumbled on with ineffectual arrogance. Sensing the drama and conflict at the time, Tim felt an irresistible desire to stir the pot and see what happened next: 'My first intention was to pull it [the eagle] off and present it to them there and then.' The thought of giving the German eagle to the Belgian customs officers was born of an intense curiosity to see how far things would go. The story, told a year or so later, suggests that he had been thinking about it since, and had come to realise that the Germans, who had been so friendly on the pitch, might have given him a gift that was far from a benign kiss of peace, certainly on the Belgian border. Tim still rejoiced in the humiliating failure of his supposed interpreter: 'Would that my pen could convey a true portrait of the scene on the station platform. The doctor ignominiously failed to make the least impression on them; in fact, he could not even make himself intelligible.'

Exasperated, Tim sought to explain the situation himself, albeit in rather comic fashion. 'Then I tried my hand at it. I gave them some real Cockney. I gave them some "Lancasheer" and "Yorksheer"; I even tired them with "Hooch, ay, a wee bit Scotch," but it was all to no purpose. The officials, however, seemed to be convinced of my earnestness at any rate, for after our lengthy war of words, I was allowed to board the train and my "kissen" was duly handed over. But what a jabbering and jumping about there was.' He then added, ominously perhaps: 'Had these customs officers not succumbed to our eloquence, I am persuaded the treatment which the Woolwich boys intended to mete out to them would have precipitated a European war.' It was football bravado, of course, but reality was soon to make those words sound prescient nonetheless.

The menace of war was some way off yet. Back home, hope was high in Plumstead. After the previous season, it all looked good for another assault on the summit of the game – for Arsenal and for Tim. But it was then, with him right at the centre of the club and the sport, that there was to be another steep downturn in the Coleman rollercoaster ride. It would leave a bitter aftertaste and yet, ultimately, it propelled him to an even bigger role in football's front line.

# Goodbye to Woolwich

Tim started the 1907-08 season with a bang in the home game against Notts County. The star turn that afternoon had seemed likely to be the weather: 'Then the rain came down again. But what did the shouting, rejoicing crowd care about a few tons of water? Umbrellas went up by the hundred, until each bank was a huge, black mushroom bed. It threatened to be water polo every minute . . . with the increasing dampness the greensward was getting very treacherous, and slips and falls were many.' This was pure Edwardian football, the quagmire of a field surrounded by a forest of umbrellas. How did anyone see anything? It got worse too, for the light faded to almost nil, which was also the goal tally, since nobody seemed likely to be able to see the ball or stay on their feet for long enough to score that afternoon. But it took more than darkness and a flood to deter Tim. 'Garbutt and Coleman gained possession. In and out they passed and re-passed, that tricky, clever pair, and at the precise moment when a shot was wanted, Little Tim blazed away. Iremonger was simply not in the picture – but the ball was in the net.' That was it: neither side was going to add to the score. It was the perfect way to begin the new season and to indicate that the Arsenal were here to win. Tim was also back with a vengeance, looking for that England place again.

Then came the turning-point. It was to be a revolution in Tim's career and in his life. He was starting his fifth season for Arsenal, and was almost due a benefit match, what would become known as a testimonial. It was well known that the only way to make real money as a player was from benefit matches and a player became eligible for one after about three years' 'good service'. A good benefit game could net a player hundreds of pounds, enough for a house and a pot for old age: pensions were only just being introduced in a rudimentary way, and there was no health service in those days.

The club announced in early October that: 'The most popular and consistent men connected with Arsenal, Tim Coleman and Roddy McEachrane, take their benefit. The Directors have given them a good game – Liverpool . . . Players like Coleman deserve recognition.' True, but joint benefits were not that common, certainly not for the big players. The club was running into hard times and it looked awfully like a trick to save money – two for the price of one. The fact that the opposition was to be Liverpool did not make up for the shared deal. It was also known that clubs sometimes sold players just to prevent them having a benefit.

Yet on the day itself, 21 October 1907, the sun shone. 'The afternoon of the half-holiday proved gloriously fine and there must have been nearly twenty thousand people present.' So far, so good. Tim was ready to perform too: 'Kyle the Arsenal centre sent the ball to Coleman. Twas cleverly done . . . Well, twinkling Tim Coleman snapped up the fruits of Kyle's labour and before you could say "beneficiare", Hardy was pushing the ball away from close to the goal. But Tim Coleman remained harassing round, and promptly found the goal . . . To Plumstead the points, and the bills to Tim and Roddy.'

The proceeds amounted to £500 but here was the beginning of the trouble – and the end – for Tim at Woolwich. The money, his half-share of it at least, did not materialise. Instead there were the first drops in a shower of excuses that lasted for weeks, and that became a steady downpour towards Christmas. Arsenal had overstretched themselves in pursuit of success and now they had to cut back. They could not keep their promise to Tim or, more important in the wider picture, to their supporters.

The whole country was entering a more troubled phase in 1907. Strikes and industrial conflict were widespread, from the mines to the postal service, once the symbol of Victorian efficiency and order. There was a spreading fear of anarchist bomb plots in the capital. In this uneasy context, Woolwich Arsenal had specific problems of their own that made their accounts harder to balance. Bernard Joy explains the local difficulties: 'While Arsenal were winning, the financial position remained sound. As soon as the results fell away, however, the inherent weakness of the site at Plumstead became obvious. It was too far from London and local transport was not enough . . . It is true that the Manor Ground adjoined Plumstead station, but it was an uncomfortable journey in a crowded steam train from Cannon Street or London Bridge . . . Growing competition with the other London clubs made the position more critical.' When success slowed down, the crowds fell away more than at other big clubs.

There were still some epic moments, especially the inaugural First Division visit of the Reds to Chelsea at Stamford Bridge. It was one of the defining moments in the history of London football: 'The Stamford Bridge ground, awkward as it is to get to from Woolwich, is one of the great sights of the Metropolis when you get there. There is only one stand, and yet that is such a tremendous affair that it holds great masses of people in barred-off seats, as snugly as it is possible to be. But the masterpiece of it all is the half-crescent terrace, capable of holding I should imagine over 60,000 people of itself alone. There they stand, rows upon rows of men – and women – and on Saturday they were packed together so tightly that nothing but their heads were visible. Venturesome braves had swarmed up the advertisements, revenue which the Chelsea club must be finding considerable, until one wondered that the boards could sustain the weight. The total crowd is estimated at quite 70,000. It was a merry crowd, which did not need the spirited band to play it into good humour.' This was the modern game, taking away the breath of all the Edwardian witnesses.

That day, the 'Chelsea Buns', as the Woolwich fans called the west London team, were 'too tough' for the Reds. Only their ground was jolly; the team's style was stern, and they knocked the Arsenal out of their stride, making that lethal passing game impossible to sustain. 'Not a great game but decidedly a great occasion,' was the verdict of one Arsenal connoisseur when he had finished watching the home side win 2-1. It was really the crowd that fascinated the world that afternoon, rather than the players. Chelsea got the opener and the stadium sprang into life: 'The West End ladies who grace the rows in front of the Press stand stood up and waved programmes, gloves, handkerchiefs, anything to show their delight – while mere man shed his hat by the thousand and pointed to the sky. Woolwich spectators have the reputation of being able to shout. Bless you, their lungs are but tissue paper compared with the strength of those of the Chelsea brigade.'

Tim couldn't get his teeth into those Buns, and his one or two efforts were stopped by the big lad in the Chelsea goal, Bob Whiting, later a friend and team-mate in very different circumstances. Even on an off-day, with his spirits already sagging under the pressure of other anxieties off the pitch, Tim still rose to the stimulus of such an audience: 'The cleverest work in our forward line came from Coleman.' But he was stifled by a Chelsea midfield in no mood to allow entertainment.

The contest spilt over into music: 'The interval was an orgy of music. The Chelsea Borough Brass Band obliged again with melodies of the present and bygone times, an opposition cornet on the terrace put in solos which were not included in the band parts, and the Woolwich vocal contingent chanted anything which came handy and crackers cracked the whole time.' This was football becoming total entertainment; a carnival of music, drama and feeling. Despite losing, the Arsenal could also cheer at the end as they were still above the newly promoted Chelsea in the table.

While London was reaching new heights of football excitement, events at Woolwich were continuing to unravel. By the middle of January, Tim's form had gone, the mud was thick and Manchester City knocked the stuffing out of them by four goals to nil. The team was in another losing streak and even their home form was suffering. Then there came a fateful off-the-field event: 'On Wednesday week, the 29th inst., the half-yearly meeting of the shareholders of the Arsenal F.C. has been arranged to take place at the Woolwich Town Hall, Wellington Street. It is fairly safe to prophesy that the financial statement will be anything but a rosy one.'

Indeed it was anything but rosy. London football had its first full-scale financial crisis. The Plumstead papers were full of dark suggestions: something was wrong with the accounts. Too much money had been spent pursuing the grail of becoming League champions and when the crowds fell away, the figures slumped. They had got ahead of themselves. Shareholders were on the verge of revolt. They were prudent investors as well as football fans and they demanded savings. The first casualty was the manager, Phil Kelso, the key to their rise. He left in February and the golden era, such as it was, was over.

Respectable commentators appealed to fans to back the board, while new management stabilised the club: 'If only the local supporters will stick persistently loyal, the present directorate will pull through safely, and the season should be finished with the club well above half-way in the League table.' Those directors with whom Tim had had such a tough time were now in the line of fire themselves and they were looking to sell the only real assets the club had left – the players. Under the prevailing rules, they could dispose of them more or less as they wished, and almost the entire receipts would stay with the club. The players would receive only token acknowledgement of the cash that was changing hands.

The transfer system was deeply unpopular with players, because they had so little influence over it and felt that they were being traded to make money for others when they got almost nothing from it themselves. In 1908, a player got a maximum of £10 from a deal at a time when the highest fees were well into the hundreds and when £1,000 was the record takings for an Arsenal home match. A modest new house in London cost £200 and it was 6d to stand on the terrace at a match. Players also had no real say if they wanted to move clubs for whatever reason. There was not much they could do except wait and hope.

Tim was never an easy man to have around, from a director's point of view. He was quick to take offence and always ready for a confrontation, over comparatively minor troubles, and now he had something substantial to get his teeth into. He was particularly angry at what he termed a 'glaring instance' of oppression: 'the mandate which says that no player shall leave his club if offered the maximum wage unless he can prove that his circumstances justify the change.'

That was the sort of thing Tim could not bear. It was not as if the 'four quid' was a great deal, and yet if you got it, you forfeited all choice about where you lived, unless you could convince an obviously biased tribunal. Who else had to stick with such restrictions? He wrote that diatribe a year later, but the rage was still fresh, and indeed it was to drive him into reckless action.

The Woolwich club had made Coleman into the star player he was in 1907: they had taken a chance on a lad from a minor club, who had been struggling on the fringes of the game, and working in the shoe industry to supplement his football wages. They had given him time to develop his formidable and idiosyncratic talents, and they had taken him to their hearts. His position was no worse than that of his team-mates, and hugely better than that of most of the industrial workers who were even then discussing strike action across the country. He was quick to feel slighted, as with the delays in the benefit money, and he was never entirely able to keep such ups-and-downs from affecting his form. In all those ways, one can see that Coleman was a difficult man to deal with. Yet he was also right about the basic issues, even if he inevitably amplified the ills they caused.

As he analysed the trap he felt caught in after Kelso left Woolwich, Tim unleashed a battery of legal terms to describe a condition he saw as virtual slavery: 'In certain cases, such changes have been sanctioned, but how many players have had to stick to a certain district when they wished to go elsewhere?' By the early months of 1908, Tim was one of those who definitely 'wished to go elsewhere'. The club had not the money to put up a better show, and from his point of view as a free agent he had done what he could in Plumstead. 'Sometimes a player feels unhappy in a particular district, [despite] the fact of his getting £4 a week . . . And yet he has to stop. Verily the lot of the professional footballer is not all that it is cracked up to be by some individuals.' There is scathing irony behind that remark about the reward of £4 a week, as if it would make anyone blissfully happy. Yes, he over-did the arguments and he must have been a nightmare to negotiate with, but he was also – as other awkward spirits have been – a necessary voice on behalf of the game, as well as a rigid defender of his own interests as he saw them. He demanded to make his own decisions about who he played for and where he lived with what he called 'a modicum of independence'. Touchy and inflammable, perhaps ungrateful too, he was also quick to see the imbalance that had grown with the rapid expansion of football.

The crisis came to a climax in early March when Plumstead was rocked by transfer news: 'It came as a great surprise to hear that Tim Coleman had been transferred to Everton. The transfer fees, I understand, were rather heavy, though nothing has been disclosed.' With some regret, perhaps, the Arsenal club waved goodbye to their angry, wayward home-nurtured talent: 'We shall miss Tim's merry face, and the Arsenal team will miss one who, in the words of a member, "always kept the fun going".' The club hinted that he could have been more grateful for what he owed them: 'He came to Arsenal from Northampton in 1902-3 and during six seasons he has assisted the local team he has done much good work. He secured his cap in the English International against Ireland last season, and in October last year he divided with McEachrane a benefit of £500.'

That was all well and good, but from Tim's less rosy point of view, the money was still not his, not even as he prepared to pack his bags and head north. While others remembered the 'fun', Tim was in a much more sombre mood, ready for a fight rather than willing to make a graceful gesture of reconciliation. These experiences went deep. He talked about transfers as 'finding a crib for the outcast', a desperate business. He also learnt from this struggle that: 'It is all very well for some to say that the player could look after himself. Many of them find such a matter difficult.' It was, in modern terms, a 'radicalising' experience for him, partly because he refused to see any other side to it.

The *Athletic News* gave the perspective of the wider football world on this episode, as far as it was visible to the general public: 'Tis passing strange that Woolwich Arsenal, with the prospect of relegation staring them in the face, have allowed such a clever forward as Coleman to leave them . . . It is useless to hide the fact that Woolwich are labouring under the stress of financial trouble.'

The departure of Kelso was what finally ended the attempt to keep the team together and fight the relegation battle. (It was not, by any means, Tim's last encounter with a Scottish manager in the English League.) Soon, other Woolwich talent joined the flow of assets: Freeman went with Tim to Everton; Kyle, another forward, to Aston Villa; and Jimmy Sharp north to Glasgow Rangers.

It was Tim, though, whose move received most of the publicity. 'Coleman goes to Everton with a high reputation and we believe that his style of play will blend harmoniously with his new colleagues. He is a sinuous worker, speedy and a good shot. Coleman, in form, is a menace to the best defence. Always called "Tim" at Plumstead, he has the reputation of being something of a humorist.' Those were the two public sides to Tim: menace on the pitch and comic off it. The anecdote that always followed him was the one when Tim pretended to be Percy Sands to the reporter in the Arsenal dressing-room: 'At any rate he has a sense of humour, for when Arsenal played Newcastle United at Stoke in the semi-final of the Association Cup, he impersonated Percy Sands, the Arsenal Captain, and told a gullible reporter who desired Sands's opinion of the game, that he 'considered "Tim" Coleman the best inside-right in England or Scotland.'

The funny man of football had always carried a hint of a threat along with the affection, but the fighter was now emerging from behind the charm of the chirpy comic. They were two sides of the same character, but the balance between them was different now, and always would be from this point on.

The wandering years had begun. Goodison Park, the home of Everton, was a real football stronghold and, in a sense, the very opposite of Plumstead. The game had been played at the top level here for the twenty years of the Football League's existence, and supporting 'The Toffees' was a duty already being passed down the family line in many Merseyside households. The joint Everton and Liverpool programme greeted Tim with a hint of another layer of controversy in addition to his bitter departure from London. 'The Woolwich Arsenal inside-right has been secured by Everton, and the Blues are evidently determined not to let the opportunity pass of obtaining a good man. Rumour was wrong this time, for it was generally credited that he was coming to Liverpool.' There had been a bidding war, behind closed doors, in genteel secrecy. So while the Arsenal directors kept back Tim's benefit cash, they had been haggling to make the most from his departure.

Whatever the effect of the move and its circumstances, the welcome that followed must have soothed Tim's soul: 'He is a class player, and is the possessor of several international caps, and he appeared at inside-right last year at Goodison against Ireland. He was the most conspicuous forward on the field the other week against Liverpool, and his form is always reliable.' That remains the highest praise for a footballer, being known as 'a class player'. It is the seal of approval among football folk. Those 'several' caps included the appearances for the inter-league sides and as an international reserve. It was a long time before players could expect to have any kind of international 'career': there were too few games and the selectors treated an appearance as an honour. An international cap crowned a life in the game – though Tim was far from giving up hope of future caps too.

Everton fans were also given warning of the personality they were acquiring, that unique image had already come north before him: 'Coleman rejoices in the sobriquet of "Tim" and he comes from Northampton originally, and has always been a marked man by the authorities.' The Everton programme rightly recognised that this would add to his appeal with their fans. This was a different world, much more welcoming to a rebel. But it would not necessarily recommend Tim to the powers that be at Goodison. He was about to have a rough ride, even by his standards – he was to play hero and villain in the coming years.

The profile ended with a note that would still be true now: 'He is not available in the Cup-ties this season, having already represented Woolwich.' In fact, being in and out of the Cup team turned out to be a major part of Tim's life at Goodison, in the battles that he was now about to fight.

From now on he was always going to be playing away from home. The North had always felt to him like a foreign country, intriguing but also alien. He responded by getting stuck into the football. The first battle was the simplest: to avoid relegation. He began with a dire away game at Nottingham Forest, a debut that attracted plenty of national attention and some irony. 'Coleman assisted Everton at Nottingham Forest last Saturday' – and it made no difference: they lost by five goals to one. At least Tim knew what he had taken on. It was a tall order, even by the standards of the hard times he had had at Arsenal. But Tim was relishing being in a good old-fashioned football scrap and he was quite happy to take responsibility in what he saw as a pretty weak team, certainly up front: 'When first I came to Everton I played on average about two games a week, and seldom indeed did I have the same partner in two successive matches. The club at that time was in a rather uncomfortable position on the League table, and stood a chance of dropping into the Second Division. These were the days of stern and hard-fought fights for safety.' The understatement that they were in 'a rather uncomfortable position on the League table' is a characteristic Tim touch, but there is an edge of sarcasm to his enthusiasm. At ordinary clubs, he conceded, the odd complaint may get heard when the team does not win all their games. 'Fortunately in Everton we are immune from anything of the kind,' he said, pointedly. 'In the dark, drab days of defeat, as in the happy hours of triumph, nothing comes to our ears but tends to the promotion of harmony and good-feeling in our camp.' This was partly a dig at the Arsenal, where all did not tend to promote harmony – and then there is some irony to spare for Everton too. For the moment, it is a kind of benign black humour, or the football equivalent, relegation humour.

The end-of-season finishing positions were still a tight call. A disappointing narrow defeat away to Birmingham left Everton with work to do. Watching his team-mates struggling that day, Tim decided he had to manage the job on his own, and it showed. His play was coming back to life after the dark months of impasse at Arsenal: 'Coleman obtained the ball, and cleverly threaded his way through the whole Birmingham defence, finishing with a shot that left Dorrington helpless.' The cheers of his new fans were loud and long: 'This was the finest run of the afternoon and was deservedly applauded.' A Mersey star was born.

The knowledgeable locals were already deep in football conversation about the best way to use this new player's talent: 'The most effective branch of the Everton attack was furnished by the right wing, where Coleman and Sharp displayed fine combination. There is no doubt that the ex-Woolwich forward is an acquisition to the club and his bids fair to become the most suitable partner for Sharp that the outside right has ever experienced.' If Jack Sharp was let loose on the wing, then the following season could be a very different matter from the current year's struggle. Tim was the man to make the whole forward line move.

The season came to a climax with a visit to Plumstead in the April sunshine and this was where Coleman's Arsenal years really had their dramatic ending. The game was a dour tussle and then came the sudden twist: a foul in the home penalty area and it was a spot kick for the visitors. Everyone knew the situation. As the experts said: 'Normally Taylor takes them.' No chance today! With eyebrows raised, fans and journalists pondered how the little inside-right came to be taking the kick: 'I wonder if Tim asked for the privilege?' He had begun at Woolwich by taking a penalty against Port Vale – and he missed that one. Was he about to repeat the mistake? Plenty had happened in between, and Tim did not make those kinds of mistake any more. He wound himself up and went for broke: 'The ex-Gunner shot the ball hard and true over Ashcroft's head and into the net.' The local commentary recorded the mixed feelings of the crowd that had cheered Tim as their own attacking hero: 'The fact that funny little "Tim" scored the first goal against the Arsenal was another point of note.' Funny and little maybe, but not so easy to stop.

In the end, Arsenal did sneak a 2-1 win, the decisive goal coming right on the final whistle, but Everton finished above them on goal average, with both avoiding the drop. The other real action of the week concerned Tim's private campaign against his former directors. At the last gasp, perhaps spurred on by Tim's visit to Plumstead with Everton, they came up with his benefit money – and Roddy McEachrane also got his share. That was even better news than that penalty flashing into the top of the net. Now the Woolwich years were over, the accounts settled. He was moving on, taking with him a couple of hundred pounds, simmering anger, a growing understanding and a lot of great memories.

# *Part Two*

# Fighting for the Future

# Moment of Truth

The 1908-09 season was Tim's most successful in the Football League, in terms of the position of his team in the table. Everton pushed Newcastle United – his old nemesis – all the way. It was also the club's best performance to date. But that was only the prelude, really, to the real drama of the year, the events of which give it a strong claim to be one of the most important, certainly one of the most influential, in the history of the British game. Tim had his own unique part in these wider conflicts that ultimately dwarfed the battle between Goodison and St James' Park for the title. He also had his own angle on a struggle that, for once in football, really did have historic importance for the future of the game within and beyond these shores.

At the beginning of the season, the football prospects were much brighter for Tim. At Goodison, the end of the previous campaign had raised hopes of a better time to come: 'Everton's right wing – Sharp and Coleman – will be one of the finest and cleverest in the country this season, and will no doubt do the premier [part of scoring] for the Blues.' The Everton team was rich in promise, and beginning to shows signs of achievement too. They started, amid a rising tone of confidence around Merseyside, with a swaggering 4-0 win at Plumstead of all places. Tim was playing alongside his old Arsenal centre-forward, Bert Freeman. The locals in south-east London felt that both of them had been determined to take 'a very natural revenge'. From an Arsenal point of view, they 'were like dogs in the manger for last season, would not play themselves nor assist others to do it'. The bitterness on both sides persisted. Tim and Bert scored in each half of the game. The best goal of the match was Tim's first: 'Coleman's goal was the result of a splendid shot, one of the best bits of play seen in the match, and the keeper had no chance of stopping it.'

Everton picked up momentum as September advanced. A sign of what was to come was a hard-fought 3-2 win at Middlesbrough, followed by a staggering 6-3 home defeat of Manchester City. The crowds were rising: close on 20,000 were there for the start of the game against City, and by half-time there were 30,000 in the ground. The stars were Coleman and Sharp on the right in the first half, and then the same little man and Young. October began with a fanfare, victory at Liverpool by a single goal. Tim told the press how much he was enjoying the game and the life: 'I must say I like Liverpool very much. To my mind Lancashire is the finest sporting county in the country.' At last, he was at the heart of a real football world.

Tim was still growing as a player and was being seen increasingly as a goal-scorer, honing talents and skills he already possessed. 'Near goal he can shoot with deadly accuracy, and he thereby possesses all the attributes necessary to an inside-forward who desires to obtain the highest honours in the football world.' His claim for that next England cap was also growing louder. The locals held out the promise of good things to come: 'Coleman will, we trust, stay long at Everton. He has already received one benefit and if he qualifies for another at Goodison no one will begrudge him his reward.' And those Everton observers had already picked up on his other attributes. 'His reputation as a footballer is, perhaps, only equalled by his capabilities as a humorist,' one wrote.

By the end of October, Everton were leading the First Division. Before 40,000 people, Tim scored in their victory over Aston Villa. Sunderland then collapsed to a 4-0 thrashing. By mid-November Everton were two points clear of Newcastle at the top. Then, down in

London, Tim scored 'a brilliant equalising goal' in a wonderful 3-3 draw at Stamford Bridge. There were 50,000 people packed in to watch his 'cleverness' in 'drawing the keeper from his goal'. That November 'England's Best Side', as chosen by Billy Meredith, the revered Manchester City and Manchester United outside-right, gave a place to 'Coleman of Everton'.

The Merseysiders continued to lead the League and then, suddenly, it all changed. In a desperately hard-fought 3-2 home win over Manchester United, Tim was injured: 'Coleman was rendered useless by a severe kick early in the game.' He managed to make one goal for his wing partner Sharp, but then he was out of the game. It was his first real injury crisis. Deprived of their talisman, Everton lost their rhythm, and on Christmas Day went down to a home defeat against the relatively weak opposition of Notts County. More seriously, they lost to second-place Newcastle United on New Year's Day, also at Goodison. When Tim tried to come back, he had lost his touch and was forced to take another rest. At the end of January, they went down 4-0 to a resurgent Manchester City. By the time Tim found his form again, they were four points behind Newcastle. He led them to a fine win over Sheffield United: 'On the right wing Coleman was the chief performer, and he gave the best exhibition he has afforded for some weeks past.'

But they could not close the gap. It was clear that Tim's loss of fitness and form had made the difference to the club's entire season. Not that Tim was the top scorer, that honour belonged to Bert Freeman, but, as everyone said, it was Tim who made most of Freeman's goals, and when he was out Bert scored less. It was also clear that Goodison now adored 'Tim Coleman, who if he were not at Everton, would probably stand a good chance for his international cap.' They did finish second, seven points behind Newcastle and two ahead of Sunderland. Tim ended the season with two goals against Leicester, showing what was possible the following season. As long as he kept fit, the sky was the limit. An England place beckoned once more and there was no reason why Everton should not hang on to the top spot. In his review of the season, the Liverpool and England goalkeeper Sam Hardy gave these predictions as to who he thought was worthy of an England cap: 'Dick Bond . . . an injury to his knee prevented him from rising to the occasion. Bar anything of this kind happening Coleman of Everton, Whitson of Newcastle United and Albert Shepherd of Newcastle United are all likely men for the season 1909-10.' This was probably the peak of Coleman's playing career, though he had many other fine moments to come. He had become a national star, and yet he was never to make his way back on to the international stage. Nor was his time at Everton to bear the fruit of this rich beginning. Instead, he made one of those life-changing decisions and chose a different role in the longer history of the national game.

That season, 1908-09, was also the moment of the first serious attempt to create and sustain a union to represent professional footballers. There had been a founding meeting for an attempted players' union held as early as 1898 in Manchester, according to James Walvin in his story of *The People's Game*. As Walvin says, although this failed, the movement retained a hard core, mainly at Manchester United, well into the Edwardian era. In 1907, an earlier plan was revived by the Manchester United star Billy Meredith, whose far more sustained effort is recorded in John Harding's authorised history of the Professional Footballers' Association, *For the Good of the Game*. During December 1907, Meredith announced his plans to the press. An initial meeting on 2 December was attended by seven United players, including Charlie Roberts the skipper as well as some from others clubs such as Manchester City and Spurs. At first, they were even able to include FA officials and club chairmen. One plan was to have union representatives on FA committees. This time the whole enterprise seemed more practicable. George Robey, the comedian who enjoyed Tim Coleman's speech-making back at Woolwich Arsenal, was raising funds. At that moment, in 1907, the Variety Artistes' Federation was itself involved in a major industrial dispute, so there was a sense of common interest linking different types of entertainers.

Meanwhile, as Harding notes, the 1906 Trades' Disputes Act made it easier for all unions to become established and the new Workman's Compensation Act also strengthened their claims to represent players over specific grievances. Walvin puts these developments in perspective by adding that 'both the Union's militancy and the authority's resistance may well have been influenced by the wider militancy of the period'. In fact even the FA and the *Athletic News* were not entirely hostile to the idea of a players' union at first. The First Division clubs, for example, were themselves keen to breach the maximum wage limit. This was seen not so much as incipient socialism, more as free trade. After signs of getting tough, in March of 1908 the FA backed off temporarily from attempting to suppress the union and seemed to accept its existence. At the end of the season, however, the FA then reasserted the maximum wage limit, pushed to do so by the smaller clubs. There was also opposition towards the union after it began taking on compensation claims. In increasingly difficult financial circumstances, many club owners and directors, and their allies, were afraid for the financial future of the game.

Meanwhile, in August 1908, the union set up offices in Manchester, with Herbert Broomfield, formerly of Manchester United before joining Manchester City, as secretary. The *Weekly News*, with its 300,000 circulation on Thursdays, opened its columns to the players within and beyond the union, giving them a strong voice for the first time. This was how Tim came to write his highly personal pieces about his experiences and then about the dispute.

It was in 1909 that the confrontation between the Players' Union and the football authorities came to a head. The industrial atmosphere was fraught: postmen were on strike, and so were miners. There were incidents of police charging unemployed marchers and a more general climate of tension surrounding the rise of mass democracy as well as political rivalries with France and Germany. Amid all this, in December 1908, C.E. Sutcliffe, chairman of Burnley and a key figure among the owners, accused the new union of 'inward greed' and 'immoderate and unreasonable' demands. In response Meredith started referring to what might happen 'if the pros struck' in February 1909. By March the FA was trying to demand a loyalty pledge from players, promising that they would not join the union. Relations deteriorated further when Broomfield met officials of the General Federation of Trade Unions.

The FA and leading club chairmen decided to drive the union out of the game altogether, seeking a united front of non-recognition for the coming season. Through the leading paper, the *Athletic News*, FA officials denounced the union for its 'contemptible claptrap'. In reply Colin Veitch, of Newcastle, Tim's fellow international in 1907, declared that 'the players are joined in brotherhood through the agency of the Players' Union'. The mood darkened and the *Athletic News* carried the blunt headline: 'Who shall be the masters – players or clubs?'

The FA declared it was ready to fight. It was a question of establishing the right to manage the game. In response, the union's leadership began to talk about strike action. The chairman of Manchester United, J.J. Bentley, declared that the FA 'would stand no nonsense'. Gathering steam, the FA next demanded a loyalty pledge in every player's agreement to be signed at the start of the new season. The FA's management committee confidently declared that the players were bluffing when it came to the strike threat and it planned to make the situation clear using the new contracts. The union responded angrily to threats from above: 'We look upon the clubs as the enemies of the players.' The reaction was equally acidic: 'It will be necessary for players to withdraw from membership of the union if they desire to continue their connection with the FA.' The battle lines were drawn. The question was: whose nerve would fail first?

Writing in his favoured *Weekly News* in that heated and historic summer of 1909, Tim gave his own unique analysis of these events – a view full of emotion and yet also perceptive, to the point of prophecy, about the forces driving the game, and its future direction. Though a member, he was never part of any union leadership. He spoke for himself and that was how he wanted it. But he saw the union's battle as part of his own fight to make a proper living from the game, and he saw the FA bigwigs as his natural enemies. Being inclined to take a mocking view, he found them ridiculous rather than frightening. He was caustic about the pretentious way the FA tried to ignore the players as if they were beneath consideration: 'Now, where are we?' he said. 'Upon my word, I don't know. The FA have a rare faculty of keeping themselves to themselves.' Then he noticed wryly the difference it made when the union found some powerful allies: 'When they had the "mere players" to contend with they took precious good care not to consult them on the question at issue. Whenever that powerful body, the Federation of Trade Unions, took up the cudgels on our behalf there was a different complexion put on the matter.' He knew this was a fight for his own future and that of the whole game.

As the summer advanced, the real issue was how players at the big clubs would act: this was where the strike would have to bite, if it was going to succeed. Herbert Broomfield, the Players' Union chairman, decided to try to delay the start of the season and force the FA to negotiate. By now it was into July: brinkmanship was the name of the game. The FA dispatched a circular to every professional player, demanding that they resign from the union or face expulsion.

Stories of such disputes tend to be told, both at the time and in retrospect, through the eyes of the leaders, and in terms of demands and strategies from above on both sides. Tim told the story from a different perspective, that of a player on his own, trying to make decisions in the face of often surprising twists and turns, without the direct support of any organisation or colleagues. For him, this was about survival. The FA's demands reached Everton and were passed on to the players: 'I received through my club management a document emanating from the Football Association calling upon me to resign from the Players' Union.'

The issue was more than a matter of union rights, important though they were. It was all about who owned the game, whose game was football going to be. Was it their club or was it his? The 'club management', from Tim's uncompromising perspective, had betrayed their players and gone in with the FA: that was how Tim felt. He knew it was an unequal struggle but he was not about to give in: 'Of course, I refused to do so.'

This was a moment of emotional truth. When he opened that letter, he felt a surge of rage and it stayed with him. It was one of the defining feelings of his life: 'This brings me to a personal matter. When I was asked to hand in my resignation to the union the request came in a bare circular. The document stated no reason why I should resign, and, of course, I didn't.'

He was even angrier about another thing missing from that ultimatum: 'If the FA had explained to me in what way my refusal to resign from the union was to be derogatory to the best interests of the sport, then I should most certainly have resigned. But there was no explanation, and still being without any explanation from the FA, I hold that there is great scope for a union.'

By refusing to give any reasons of their own, the FA had reduced the players to children, as if they were incapable of thinking for themselves or making their own choices. Yet these were the same men who 'provided the football entertainment': what gave anyone else the right to dismiss them so arrogantly? They had a vote now, so why not a say in their own future? Tim was also furious at the timing of the FA's demand: 'Let me also pass a comment on the action of the FA in sending out their circulars in the close season. The majority of the players were on holiday, and distributed, as it were, all over the country.'

Together, the players would have been brave, as they were on the field every week. Alone, many were going to give in, looking at their families, at the cost of standing firm: 'I consider that such action was taking a mean advantage of the players as a union. There was no opportunity for combined effort on the part of the players, and in the confusion that ensued in certain quarters many players handed in their resignations who in other circumstances might not have done so.'

When he did get in touch with other players, and particularly his team-mates at Everton, Tim found that they had backed down, almost all of them. Even at the big northern clubs, further from the culture of the FA and London, the threat had been too strong. Veitch was a Newcastle star and yet even his presence could not keep his colleagues from leaving the union: 'It is scarcely necessary for me to detail any of the circumstances leading up to the present state of affairs, but I feel confident that the large majority of those who have handed in their resignations are still in sympathy with the objects of the union.' Tim had talked with the Goodison boys about the issues at stake and it was obvious that they were being intimidated from following their beliefs.

As the season approached, Tim knew that the fight was going to be lonely. Every other player at Everton had resigned from the union. The big northern clubs were the battleground and they seemed to be delivering victory to the FA. At Sunderland, as at Newcastle, the players had threatened to stick it out, but then they had almost all given way. Tim began to feel frustrated with his fellow pros: 'Had we all stuck together I do not think there would have been any cessation of summer wages or any drastic action taken, and I still entertain the feeling that the Players' Union will yet be a flourishing concern, and one that will be of great service to the players.'

Tim felt isolated, facing enemies and lacking friends, but he was not going to give an inch. Before the trial matches in August, players went back to their clubs to collect their summer pay, a reduced rate. Tim, whose family was still down south, went back to Merseyside. He always said he loved the city but this was no happy return. He had not submitted the reply demanded by the circular that had reached him while with his family. Now he came back to face the consequences. He went to the ground. He actually called at the office for his pay packet, knowing full well how the request would be handled. 'The other week, when I applied for my wages, they were not forthcoming,' he said.

This was the loneliest moment of all. Yet he could have spared himself, by simply staying away, knowing that he had effectively resigned from the club, at least for now, by not resigning instead from the union. Tim was not that sort of man. He went to Goodison to have the fight. From his point of view, he had saved Everton from relegation in his first season at the club and he had been the star of their brilliant autumn. Only a few weeks ago, the locals had been complaining at his omission from the England side. Yet now all those cheers counted for nothing: 'I do not know when next I shall draw my salary as a footballer,' he said. He saw the future and he had the language for it already. But the sense of loneliness began to get to Tim, however strongly he felt: 'I am, so far as my knowledge goes, the only player of the Everton team that has refused to resign from the Players' Union.' His head was full of the threats and rebukes of the other side, even of his own team-mates: 'And why?' He was challenged to defend his defiance. What was a mere player doing, thinking he could resist not only the directors but the game's ruling body?

As the struggle went on, he went public with his feelings and his arguments. The articles he wrote for Thomson's *Weekly News* had angry and uncompromising headlines: 'Is the FA tyrannical?'; 'T. Coleman thinks their laws too hard, and means to hold by the Union';

'Tim Coleman of Everton tells us why he sticks to Union and reviews present situation.' The only other voices raised against the ban belonged to official leaders of the union, especially Billy Meredith, of Manchester United, and Veitch. They had the support of the organisation. Tim was on his own.

His own bitter experiences were certainly involved when he talked about 'the player who needs to move clubs'. It was the transfer system that really revealed how the clubs saw their players – as bargaining counters and sources of cash: 'The union could step in there,' said Tim. 'They could present the facts of the case to the Football Association; they could plead on his behalf. They would be in communication with all the clubs . . . and be the best medium for finding a crib for the outcast.' The biggest need for a union arose, he thought, from the sheer scale of the game, as it expanded by the year: 'Unless there is a well organised union, players are bound to lose touch with each other.'

With all these feelings of solidarity, he could never quite get over his annoyance with his fellow players for being intimidated into submission: 'There is not a sincere footballer in the land but recognises that there is an urgent need for a union.' This was doubly barbed: the players who surrendered were divided by that remark into the insincere and those who lost their nerve. The criticism showed how Tim's feelings went so deep that he was almost as much at odds with his fellow professionals as with the authorities.

He was, in his way, being characteristically difficult. He brushed aside all the delicacies of diplomacy that a man such as Veitch was trying to apply to the situation. Ultimately it is such characters who are likely to take centre stage, but an outsider such as Coleman also has his value. In his sharp and perhaps over-bitter way, he got straight to the point of the dispute. He genuinely felt this battle was about the fate of football itself and not only the individual players involved. He was basically right: the issue was how much footballers counted. Did the game belong to the officials, or to the players and the fans who followed them? Was football to be just another factory, employing an anonymous workforce, or was it to be something different, the first great entertainment made for the people by men who came from their own world? 'We do not wish to be masters of the situation,' Tim said. 'We duly recognise the standing of the FA, but they are a stern body, and have overstepped the mark in laying down hard and fast rules which simply fasten the players down as a sort of vice.'

But life was bleak for Tim, back in the everyday world, as he wryly admitted: 'Speaking "pocketologically", I candidly confess that things are a bit dull.' He was well aware that other folk around him 'may know unfortunately what it means to go without wages for a couple of months'. It was part of a working life, but he was not recommending it: 'If they don't I should not advise them to try the experiment. Take it from me that the experience is not a joyful one.'

As the season approached, he felt cut off from the world to which he had belonged all his adult life: 'As matters now stand, I am a suspended player.' In the press, the Goodison management declared that their men were loyal only to the board, with just one exception. The vital moment was the return to training.

The FA felt it was winning. All of the big clubs returned for the new season, except one. The main players at Manchester United said that they were with the union. The club then suspended almost its entire squad. This included the great Meredith, the rising England star Sandy Turnbull and the skipper Charlie Roberts. Thrown out of the Manchester United training ground, the suspended players arranged to train at Fallowfield, which was basically a public park and was used by the Manchester athletic club for training. The drama caught people's attention and stirred their feelings. On one side, the players declared that they would not return until the union was recognised; on the other side, the club and the FA insisted on their right to rule.

What would happen for the first match of the season? Both club and players would have to put their money where their mouths were. The failure to field a side might result in the exclusion of United from the League.

At Everton, the other players were uncertain and divided. They appeared to be about to declare again for the union, but then they all reported for training, some with expressions of regret to the leadership, unable to hold out against the threats and promises of their club. They were all present, as the club programme reported with relief, for the start of the season and the trial matches. All, that is, except one. The sense of being isolated finally drove Tim to act. Instead of returning to Merseyside, he reported for training in Manchester, with United's union contingent. It was the act of the summer, the moment when an individual came into the limelight. The leaders on both sides had had plenty to say; now it was down to one person's conscience. On 11 August, Tim took the field at Fallowfield.

Meanwhile, at Everton, despite the official announcements, tensions were rising again. Would others follow Coleman? That was the question. The *Cricket and Football Field*, a northern-based sports paper, declared that outside Manchester United all the leading players were sticking with their clubs, 'apart from Coleman'. It needed no explanation, that remark. Everyone knew what Coleman had done, and not for the last time.

The Fallowfield players formed themselves into a team, which Charlie Roberts, another Edwardian with a nose for media attention, named The Outcasts FC. They posed for a team picture, in formal playing gear, exactly in the postures they would have adopted for the club portrait that was taken at the start of every season. At the centre of the front row, where the captain traditionally sat, was Roberts. At his feet, there was a wooden board on which was written 'The Outcasts FC' in white paint. On his right sat Sandy Turnbull, United's rising star, and beyond him George Wall, another England forward. On his left, there sat Tim Coleman, the outsider as the only non-Manchester United player in the line-up.

That fact was not the only way in which he stood out from the others. No one else in the photograph has that ghost of a smile. They look grim and frightened. Tim is smiling, a crooked and defiant grin. He looks straight at the camera and his expression, amid his Edwardian colleagues, is pure 1960s. This is the face of a modern footballer, a 'personality', a man who knows he is on display all the time. He was visibly making good the visiting journalists' prophecy that it would be his role to lift the spirits of the Outcasts.

This was Players against Gentlemen, the People's United – the force of the future – against Committee City. They were isolated partly because the union had missed several open goals in the negotiations, and mainly because it was simply too risky to go against the bosses. Four pounds a week, even with a few backhanders, did not allow anyone to accumulate much of an asset base for a rainy day. Everyone needed the new season. Famous athletes they might have been, cheered by tens of thousands, even hundreds of thousands for cup finals and internationals, yet they earned little more than factory workers. Even the factory worker could not be transferred to a rival company without his consent.

The programme of one of Tim's later clubs described this grin as 'his La Gioconda smile', the mystery smile of the Mona Lisa, someone who seems to have a secret; and so, in his way, did Coleman, as he sat next to Charlie Roberts and his Outcasts' board. His secret was that football would ultimately belong to the players, because they are the ones who make the game. It would remain secret for a long time yet, and Coleman paid a high price for knowing it too early.

The dispute was to get personal; his character and reputation were on trial. Those on the FA's side of the argument sneered that he was always just a joker, the game's comedian, and that he could not be taken seriously. That annoyed him more than anything. There was some vanity in his defence but it was also brave in the circumstances. He was refusing to shelter behind the cosier side of his reputation: 'Yes, the accusation has been made that I am the comedian of the football field, but the piece which is being enacted on the football stage at present does not present any comical side.' Yet even then he couldn't resist displaying his linguistic talents, with the same kind of energy that made him sometimes seem self-indulgent on the field too: 'A serious drama holds the boards, and it seems I am cast for the villain. There are a few in the same line as myself throughout the country, but I appear to be the only one in Liverpool.' But no one should think he of all people was acting lightly: 'At the present time I am debarred from the grounds of our own club.'

Tim needed the issue to be resolved, they all did. He just was not backing down. 'Many people are still under the impression – quite an erroneous one – that we are sticking out for more money. Indirectly we may have leanings that way – we are but ordinary mortals – but first and foremost we want to know why we should resign from the union. What wrong have we done? I don't know. Can anyone tell me? Surely we are entitled to a modicum of independence, and so long as we are not breaking any rule of the Association, I don't see what right they have to punish us.' His words carried the promise of a different future, even in the moment of approaching defeat. Tim began to acquire his own public voice and at the same time gain political credibility: 'In conclusion, may I say, in regard to the union, that we do not wish in any way to be hostile to the FA, but, in my opinion, we have been practically forced into our present position. My earnest wish is for an amicable settlement.'

Charlie Roberts gave an account of the atmosphere among the Outcasts at Fallowfield and in contrast to Tim's thoughts on the matter, Roberts told a picturesque story rather than an argument full of feeling and ideas. The headline read: 'Stick to it, boys, says Manchester.' Roberts then explained: 'You may occasionally hear some people suggest that the United players are making a stand out of sheer bravado. This is their view, but let me ask if you know any set of men for the mere sake of swanking a bit will toss away £4 a week, and let me say that we have now gone six weeks without our wages. Let me assure your readers that it is for principle that we are fighting and nothing else.

'. . . We are in a rather funny position as far as training is concerned. The majority of our players meet me outside my shop at Clayton each morning at 10.15. We then walk past our own ground in Bank Street, where we occasionally hear the ball being kicked by the few reserves that are left. While waiting for the car for Fallowfield we are frequently surrounded by the inevitable little crowd, and many a cheering message is conveyed to us. "Bravo, boys; stick to your union and we'll stick with you" and "United for ever!" are samples of their encouragement. The car moves off, and simultaneously there goes up a nice little cheer for the boys of Manchester United.'

As the season approached, Fallowfield became half-carnival and half-battlefield. The players trained in the glare of publicity. Ever keen to impress, they demonstrated the net-bursting power of their shots, a trick that Tim had always been good at. Coleman and Roberts between them also had a knack for the catchy phrase. Together, the players declared that they were 'training for a fight to the finish with the FA next week'.

Meanwhile, the Outcasts were having an effect. There were signs of players returning to the union, now that teams were together again, as Tim had foreseen. He underlined this changing mood in case the authorities had missed it: 'FA's obstinacy will spell ruin' said the head-line. 'Already we have abundant proof of this in reports just to hand that the players of Newcastle United, Sunderland, and Middlesbrough are all to stand by the union. The fact of a trio of such powerful northern clubs taking up this bold attitude is calculated to make the FA consider the situation as a trifle more critical than they at first imagined it to be.'

The players were going on the attack as the season approached, led by union chairman Herbert Broomfield: 'Mr Broomfield's successful tour in the North will, I have no doubt, induce him to make many more visitations, and developments are almost bound to ensue, day by day.' The resolution was approaching, for Tim and for the game as a whole. The Everton practice matches went ahead without, as the programme noted markedly, Coleman. His very livelihood was at risk. His second child was a year old. It was all or nothing. The Manchester United players had the strength of numbers on their side. Faced with their combined refusal, the club had to cancel the opening fixture of the season. At Everton, as everywhere else, the normal fixtures were going ahead. Tim was very aware of the difference in their situation: 'As the governing body they stand in a curious position. If they punish the players they must also punish the clubs, who are innocent of the whole affair. Of course, do not for one moment imagine that I am referring to Everton. One man in a case of this kind has no material bearing, but in the case of Manchester United, for instance, where nearly the whole of the first team is holding out, you will agree that the club's loss at this stage – if suspension be continued – would be tremendous. It would simply mean ruin during the coming season.' Tim realised all too clearly that it was only his future that was genuinely at risk, as they booted the ball into the bulging net to impress the journalists. In the end, United would have to reach a deal with Meredith and Turnbull, Wall and Roberts: after all, those players *were* the club. The United chairman, J.J. Bentley, prudently expressed his admiration for their honesty, even if he thought them misguided. No one at Everton was expressing any admiration for Tim Coleman. He was on his own.

On the last Monday in August, Everton were in action, except for the one black sheep. There were plenty of men to take his place. The Outcasts made a point of turning up on that Monday for training, which, as the papers said, was normally a day off for football players.

Meanwhile, the dispute had to find its resolution. The balance was changing; the threat of the strike spreading was real. The Fallowfield Outcasts had forced the authorities to negotiate after all, try as they might to disguise it. It was Tim who had turned the Manchester United issue into a national incident: he had made the Outcasts into something more than the Clayton side in exile.

The FA held a meeting in Birmingham to which the players were invited. There was initially an attempt to exclude the union men, then everyone recognised there would be no point in the meeting if that happened. The players were back in the frame, indeed at the centre of the stage. Eventually, guided by the negotiating skills of Colin Veitch, whose power to engage the other side's perspective reached far beyond Coleman's bitter insight, a deal began to emerge. It took weeks to finalise, but essentially the union secured basic recognition, although they could make no impact on the maximum wage. They were also forced to pull out of the Federation of Trade Unions that had supported their action. But the transfer system was going to change, to give players a better deal. At least they would get a more realistic percentage of the money that was, after all, being created by their accomplishments. The players had made their stand count.

Walvin puts this outcome in perspective, describing it as a founding moment in the development of the structure of the modern game, 'the compromise of the 1909-10 . . . in which a non-TUC players' union was accepted'. Harding picks out a contemporary cartoon to capture the flavour of the day. For the meeting in Birmingham on 31 August, the *Daily Despatch* ran a picture with the heading: 'Truce declared in football war'. In other words, unequal though the odds had been, the players had staked their claim, and would never be pushed aside again. The Manchester United players went back to work. They took the field for their first match wearing union armbands, which were soon to be banned. That was the point: they were in it together. The crowd cheered them, and it felt as if they were on the winning side in the dispute. They had at least forced the club to accept them on something like their own terms. True, Charlie Roberts lost at least £500 in a promised benefit match, but at the very least they had gained an honourable draw – and against tough odds.

Tim was no part of the official union leadership, he was too much of a maverick for that. It was his individual act of commitment, however, along with his passionate and distinct argument, that meant that Tim had such a central role in the crisis. His eccentric courage caught the mood of the Outcast drama and projected it as a more national gesture. The fruits of their efforts were considerable, as well. Although it would take half a century more to overthrow the maximum wage, players would get a better deal out of transfers that, as Tim said, were laying the financial foundation of many clubs. It was more than that, though. The players could never be reduced to silence again, seen and not heard. This threat lingered in the memory: the FA had got away with it, but it could not be so sure the next time. The professionals had begun the march from deferential hired workers to the stars of the most popular game in the world.

Being by nature a rebel and an individualist, rather than a politician or an organiser, Coleman has been largely ignored in accounts of those historic days for football. Awkward to handle on and off the pitch at the time, Tim has been too awkward to include in football's history. Without such figures, however, football, like other fields, has only a colourless past.

# Fighting On Alone

Tim may have been a marginal figure when it came to the deal being struck, but he had nevertheless been the most articulate and personal voice in the game at that critical moment. Now, after the resolution, there was the reckoning. He went back to Goodison Park, which was no longer welcoming. In mid-August the Liverpool *Football Echo*, a paper that had sung his praises throughout the previous season, published its 'Motto for Tim': 'Delays are dangerous'. It was referring to his refusal to return to training. It turned out that the warning was right: that delay proved very dangerous, in fact fatal, to Tim's stay at Everton. So far in his career, he had got away with challenging directors and other authorities in the game. Now the cost was coming home.

His return to his club was greeted with a renewed warning: 'With one exception – Coleman – the Everton players have turned in to their training in the ordinary way.' When he came back, they left him out of the side, saying that he had done only 'Fallowfield training', which had left him unfit. Then the team struggled to get going and he was soon playing. As Tim regained his old touch, the side picked up steam. They defeated Notts County by two goals to nil and 'Coleman was the only real live Everton forward'. They even defeated Newcastle, who had done them out of the title the previous season.

That victory at St. James' Park was the Saturday before the home game against Liverpool. Tim wrote a lively article about the derby match, in an attempt to restore his image as a football enthusiast and humorist. For the first time he had to try to heal the damage. He began with a deftly picturesque touch that often went down well in those openly sentimental times. Remarking that 'many were surprised at us defeating Newcastle on their own ground on Saturday', he declared firmly: 'I wasn't!' He then revealed the 'circumstance that prompted me to the belief that we would carry off the points. Just listen!' He was trying to re-create the more acceptable side of Coleman, the eccentric, funny commentator with a sharp football brain, rather than the dangerous rebel. First, he stuck to the humour: 'We had a visit from our mascot this week. I suppose I surprise a lot of my readers, but we do have a mascot. It is not of the ordinary brand, and it is not always with us. It pays us "flying" visits. It is a seagull and it honoured us last week.' Tim was in full flow but the image of the seagull's flying visits had unfortunate connotations as far as Tim was concerned. That's exactly what his career at Everton was threatening to be.

As ever, though, Tim let the public into the private world of the football club, as no one else did: 'Whenever I saw it I remarked to some of my colleagues that when it put in an appearance we never lost. And its record has yet to be soiled.' How did he know it was the same seagull? The question is, of course, absurd! Then he came to the real issue, that week's game: 'I'm wondering, too, if it will give us a look this week. We have something important on. It is nothing less than our first encounter with Liverpool in the League.' The Merseyside derby hooked Tim. In this week, of all weeks, he recovered that sense of 'we', the feeling of belonging. The previous year, Everton had won both home and away. 'In this week's match, therefore, our Anfield friends have a little score to wipe out.' Everything was ready for a great afternoon's drama: 'That is how I feel in regard to this week's meeting.'

Having been on the outside of the game and on his own, Tim wanted to get back inside the theatre and experience the enter-tainment and the passion of a simple match day. He was not above turning the knife about the previous season: 'They did not have the best of luck, and latterly, you will recollect, they were struggling to retain their place in the First Division. Everton, on the other hand, were going strong, and in the running for the League championship.' He was also trying to remind everybody of the good times that previous season, perhaps trying to bring them back. He sounds entirely modern: 'Our own victory at Newcastle should inspire us with some confidence.' He wants to make one thing clear, though: 'But, whatever happens, we shall strive our hardest.' Normally, that might be just a platitude. For Tim, returning from a kind of voluntary exile and still not yet accepted, it was a kind of pledge. He needed to get back to the centre of the club if he was to survive.

In the style of a pundit half a century later, he built up the atmosphere: 'Interest in the forthcoming game is keen, and I shall not be surprised though the gate and the crowd shall establish new records.' He runs through the teams, comparing the different elements. The goalkeepers are equal. There is nothing to choose between Liverpool's Sam Hardy and Everton's Billy Scott: 'Between the sticks at either end will be found a goalkeeper that has nothing to learn in the art of custodianship.' The Everton defenders 'are considered by several of the critics to be superior to those of Liverpool'. The midfields are about equal: 'I consider that the present half-back line of our opponents is as strong as ever, and I have a great admiration for them.' Then he gets down to detail: 'Where Liverpool lacked early last season was in their inside-forwards, but they seem to have found the right men.' Overall, he just tips the balance in Everton's favour: 'Summing the teams up, I should say there is nothing to pick and choose between the goalkeepers. By reason of experience and knowledge of each other's little ways, our backs and half-backs may have the pull over Liverpool's, some of whom are yet winning their spurs.' Beneath the wit and wordplay, there was a razor-sharp analyst. He was trying to show that it was this intelligence, what they called his 'cleverness', that he could still offer to the Goodison Park club.

The whistle blew, with 45,000 people in the ground. Only a minute had gone when Tim headed a loose ball towards Bert Freeman and Hardy was forced to tip the shot away for a corner. From that corner kick, Young hit the bar 'and Coleman headed the rebound into the net'. Everything he had been trying to say about himself was contained in that moment, as the Everton official account of the game admitted: 'This was all head work and a bit of brain goes a long way.' That, if anything, should have been the motto for Tim.

It turned into an exciting contest, as the little man had predicted. He settled into his old style: 'There had been some pretty passing between Bert Freeman and Coleman.' At half-time it was one-all, Hardy narrowly saving a late shot from Tim. In the end, Liverpool ran out 3-2 winners but the Goodison crowd recognised that they had witnessed the return of last season's star: 'Some of Coleman's deft touches have never been surpassed – and we have seen some clever footballers.' His point was made, though two points were lost. Goodison needed him, at least as much as he did them.

Sam Hardy gave the Liverpool angle on the game: 'The players faced each other with the avowed intention of giving of their best amid the great crowd that witnessed this match would go away with the feeling that they had seen as finely contested a game as ever it had been their lot to witness between us. And despite the great rivalry, round after round of applause went up from the vast crowd in its entirety at the respective efforts in a magnificent struggle for supremacy. To be quite honest, Everton, on paper, had a better team than ourselves, and, of course, took the field hot favourites. They played up to their reputations . . . We won because on the day's play we were a shade – only a little – better than Everton.'

A real Merseyside epic, it should have been enough to bring anyone in from the cold. But those were hard times and the wounds of the summer were not so easy to heal. The Everton management were still angry and afraid, and Tim was in the line of fire: 'We go further and say that the majority of the men at Goodison Park and Anfield are satisfied with their present position, and we trust that if the question of their allegiance to their club or to their union, as at present constituted, should arise, they will not be led astray by outside influences.' So the Everton and Liverpool programme declared at the start of October. There is no doubt about who was the strongest of those 'outside influences'.

When the Arsenal managed a 1-0 victory, the sarcastic local comment was that 'Tim Coleman has had no luck this season. Is he anxious about many things?' The remark was sinister. In the national press, Tim was still receiving favourable reviews. As the *Athletic News* said: 'No man in the Everton forward line did better than the good-humoured Tim Coleman.' It seemed that the local view of Tim had changed. His magnetism and individuality was now working against him.

The price of his rebel gesture still had to be paid. Soon he was in and out of the Everton team. For Tim, the decisive moment was an FA Cup tie away to Middlesbrough in January 1910. He previewed the game with his deft touch: 'I think it will be a good game and we are quietly confident that we shall at least draw if not win. We quite understand that it will be no walkover, and that we shall have to go all the way, but I fancy we shall just about win.' They drew the away game and managed narrowly to defeat Middlesbrough at home. But Tim was not involved. The official comment was barbed: 'The supercession of Coleman was one of the unexpected happenings. But doubtless the directors have their right and proper reasons.'

Not surprisingly, Tim saw things differently and was quick to recognise that he was being hard done by. 'I was willing and always ready to do for Everton when I got the chance.' Looking back in anger from the end of that poisoned season, he saw himself as having been systematically and pointedly 'excluded from Cup-ties'. He was outraged and now there was plenty to bear out his suspicions of ill treatment, even of victimisation. He expressed that anger with a force that foreshadowed the confidence of future players' protests about managers or clubs: 'Mark the last phrase, "when I got the chance". And my word, the opportunities were not very numerous last season. This is what I cannot explain. I consider that I was playing quite at the top of my form just prior to the Cup-tie at Middlesbrough, and when we journeyed there I was fully expecting to participate in that game. Yet at practically the last moment there was a change in the team, and said change was the exclusion of yours truly.'

Tim's situation was critical. A hostile club could destroy a player, by refusing to play him or by letting him go. Yet he was at the peak of his ability, poised for more caps and on the verge of League success. Being Tim, instead of toning down his comments, he took the fight to the enemy, armed only with his reputation on the pitch and his eloquent advocacy off it. He felt betrayed and perhaps relished the feeling more than was helpful to him: 'Whatever others may say, I am convinced of this, that on that date I ceased to be a recognised, regular first-eleven player for Everton. Certainly I have appeared in several League games, and, though I felt I was playing as well as ever, I was excluded from participating in Cup-ties.' He went on to describe the hurt he felt. 'Now a footballer has feelings, just the same as any other person, and if he imagines that his play was worthy of ranking with the first he feels sore if he has to play second fiddle. I don't mind at all saying this to the open.' Other players may have had the same feelings, but he was the one who spoke them out loud.

As the season went on his anger evidently boiled into rage: 'I sincerely don't think I was below my best at the time in question. I was not even asked to travel as reserve in the ties.' No one said things like this, no footballer talked so openly about his lot, but then no one had done things like Tim did the previous summer either. After the brief attempt at appearing more conciliatory, he was breaking a kind of unspoken agreement about how football was discussed. Instead of sporting clichés, these were real feelings and human drama, rights and wrongs, ambitions and resentment. His view of the game was as distinctive as his way of playing. Nor was he afraid to address the fundamental issues behind the situation. 'At one stage I had it in my mind that the original root of the business was to be found in the attitude that I took up at the beginning of the season in regard to the Players' Union. Indeed, I have faint suspicions yet that had something to do with my lack of opportunities this season. I may say, however, that I questioned one of the officials on the matter, and he assured me that the Players' Union question had nothing to do with it.' Tim was fighting for himself, and for what he understood to be the right future of the game. But was he doing so at the cost of survival in the present?

**Everton FC team photograph** Back row from left: W. C. Cuff (Secretary), V. Harris, R. Balmer, W. Scott, J. Maconachie, H. Makepeace (Vice Captain), J. Elliott (Trainer). Front row from left: J. Sharp (Captain), J.G. Coleman, W. White, B.C. Freeman, A. Young, R.F. Turner. Getty Images

## Cigarette cards from Coleman's era

V. J. Woodward: Chelsea, 1910.

Charlie Buchan: Sunderland, 1911.

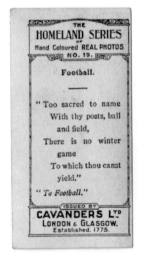

The Homeland Series, No.19: 'Football', 1924.

A typical crowd scene from the pre-war period from the terraces. This was the fiercely partisan world where even journalists yelled unsportingly "Play up, referee!" when faced with unfavourable decisions. Getty Images

Joe Mercer was a mate of Tim's in his season at Forest, and it was his enlistment that helped make him decide to become Private Coleman in February 1915. Joe was an articulate letter writer from the front, often giving glimpses of Tim. Colorsport

Tim found a place for what he termed wryly 'another shift' at Nottingham Forest in the summer of 1914, after his time at Fulham. He was welcomed as 'Forest's popular' new signing and an international man, and had a goal-scoring Indian summer in 1914-15. Colorsport

Corporal Joe Bailey served in the Footballer's Battalion between 1915-16 and is pictured here after he rose to captain of the Suffolk Regiment, 1918. Imperial War Museum: cat ref 3501 box no74/127/1

Frank Buckley, who rose to be second in command of the First Footballers' Battalion and achieved the rank of major, the highest rank accorded to any football pro. He played mainly for Derby County, gaining one cap, and was later an important manager of Wolves and Leeds. Colorsport

**The Second Footballers' Battalion** Set up in 1915 once the First Footballers, Coleman's outfit, was filled, using professional players, amateur enthusiasts and fans, with officers from elsewhere in the army. Sandy Turnbull, of the Outcasts FC, was an early recruit. Colorsport

Tim's wife Nellie and his sons, Arthur, the older, and John Victor, opening his telegram revealing that he has survived the first round of the trenches, despite rumours, on the front page of the *Athletic News* for January 3rd 1916. © The British Library Board

Football final of the 48th Divisional (Fanshawe) Cup between the 1/7 Battalion, Worcestershire Regiment and 1/7 Battalion, Warwickshire Regiment, played at Trissino, Italy in 1918. Imperial War Museum: Q 26357.

# The Wanderer

Footballers are known today for their big egos. Tim was one of the first to show this tendency because he had no fear of the authorities, he relished taking them on, and because he brought to life a sense of being embattled and wronged that made the consequences seem natural to him. In this time of feeling betrayed by Everton, he was galvanised to tell a player's story as no one else had done. He was effectively writing the death notice on his career at the very top of the game, and yet he was also bringing the experience of a footballer into view for people for the first time. For us now, a century on, this is a unique personal testimony to a life at the centre of the football explosion.

'Why have I left Everton?' was the headline on his next column in the *Weekly News*. 'Tim Coleman gives his reasons and considers that he has not been well treated.' He put it in a nutshell: 'I had no alternative! These four words briefly, but none the less eloquently, summarise my position in regard to my departure for Sunderland.'

He felt he was entitled to make choices for himself, to have an alternative in fact: that was what he had demanded when he got fed up with Arsenal and it was more so now, after the conflict of the previous summer. A year on, he was taking his personal campaign to the fans, and the issue was the same: why are the men who make the game what it is treated as second-class citizens? He answered back to the management and the directors. He spoke for himself.

Dismissing the club, he stayed loyal to the people, within the team and in the city: 'Don't imagine for a moment that I am going North unwillingly. After what has happened during the season just closed I have no regrets in saying goodbye to the Everton Football Club. My only sorrow is that I shall leave quite a host of good friends behind me in Liverpool. I thought I had settled comfortably in the Mersey city and that with Everton I would continue to serve, hoping, of course, when the allotted time elapsed, that I would earn what foot-ballers nowadays are prone to look forward to, i.e. a substantial benefit. But it is not to be, and in the respect alluded to almost three seasons of my football life have been thrown away.'

He had done the job for the management, so he felt, and they had let him down. Instead of that vital benefit – not too much to ask for keeping them up and then nearly winning the League – he had been simply left to rot. It was like being banned from the ground, this time permanently: 'This is but one rift in the lute, but it is a pretty hefty one. You ask why I went to Sunderland. I have given you the answer. Everton did not ask me to re-sign for them. Where was I? What could I do?' This was exactly the rotten transfer system that the players had campaigned to change the previous year, and Tim refused to accept its bias against him, against all of them. His anger breaking through, he said bluntly: 'Everton had the fixing of the transfer fee, and I just had to go to whoever would find the wherewithal. I don't know the amount of the transfer fee. To me it matters not what the sum was. My share of the spoils that may be going is £10. The system of bonus on transfers is come too late for me. But never mind. I won't cry over that.' The Players' Union might have won an improvement, but for Tim it was too little and too late. He let the full bitterness that had been driving him on for years come to the fore: 'Now I am getting my reward for past services in being treated like – well, I won't say hard things. They never asked me to sign on. That was enough, I think.'

So, he was on his way to Sunderland, who had been, for that matter, League champions in 1901-02, their fourth title success:

'Though I hail from the South, I am happy to go North, and I'm glad I'm going to Sunderland. I know a lot of the boys there, and they are all good sorts. I shall do my very best for them.' Instantly the other side of Coleman comes into play, the rover, the adventurer, off to seek his fortune, that 'joyful existence and companionship' which he had wanted from football since the early days.

Another Tim column was headlined: 'Do my best for Sunderland'. In it he said: 'I might mention that Jack Mordue and I were club mates during my stay at Woolwich, which club, by the way, I served for five years. I have played alongside Arthur Bridgett in an Inter-League game, and also made the personal acquaintance of Charlie Thomson when he was reserve for Scotland, Walter Bull and I acting in a similar capacity for England.' This was Tim the team man, but he was not backing down, as he warned the world and indeed his new bosses: 'And, by the way, the officials and rabid supporters of the union will perhaps be interested in view of current events to learn of a strange dream I had as lately as last week. A man came up to me and without any introduction or preliminaries, he observed, "Look here, Tim, are you prepared to do what you did at the beginning of last season?" I didn't know what he was talking about, and naturally my response was "Do what?" "Stick out for and stand by the union," he said. I could see the fellow looking at me as if he was anticipating trouble. "I'll consider it," said I, and then all was oblivion. In the morning I had to pinch myself to be sure it was a dream. I wonder if there is anything in it?' Meredith had announced the coming of the strike with a prophetic 'dream'; now Tim made a story out of the same idea, to show that the players had not surrendered. Even now, he was ready for trouble. It was grand, and it was a touch suicidal too.

Charlie Thomson, the Sunderland skipper, welcomed him with genuine and above all public enthusiasm. Having declared that 'this season we ought to reach the high-water mark in Sunderland football', Thomson paid particular tribute to one of the club's new arrivals.

'Roker Park has ever been rich in comedians. As soon as one humorist leaves our ranks another comes to take his place, so that the dressing-rooms always ring with laughter. Our chief laughter-maker this season will undoubtedly be Tim Coleman, who has already been elevated to the chair of mirth.'

Thomson was making a point as well as greeting his fellow player: Everton might not want him, but Sunderland knew what they had got! Tim's popularity continued to thrive and spread, though he was maybe no longer the cheerful soul it suggested. Thomson gave a clue about how Tim's comic act worked: 'Tim is full of fun, and his jokes are all the more ticklish because the ex-Evertonian has acquired the art of refraining from laughing at his own humour. No matter how funny a tale he is relating Tim's face is always solemn.'

Thomson was also the next in a line of Scottish friends and mock-foes that Tim had encountered, a list that already included Sandy Young and Walter White at Everton. It sounds as if Tim was mellowing by the time he arrived at Roker Park, at least for a while: 'How amusing it is to hear him struggling with the Scottish language, and the boys enjoy nothing better than to listen to Tim and I debating some fine point.'

At the start of the season, the Liverpool *Football Echo*, once so keen on Tim, noted: 'Among the forwards there is one notable, but not unexpected, departure viz, Tim Coleman to Sunderland.' The official programme added its view: 'Tim Coleman is a clever player, but last season he seemed to be under a cloud.'

The verdict on Coleman at Sunderland, on the other hand, was a rousing hurrah: 'Tim Coleman, a noted centre-forward from Everton, is a great acquisition. He is not great so far as inches are concerned, but he is a thing of life all over, and better than the awkward big ones.'

# Mellow At Last?

On a fine September day in 1910, Tim Coleman began his season for Sunderland Football Club. It was an away game. There were 25,000 people in the crowd at Bramall Lane to watch Sheffield United, the great team of the decade before, face the Black Cats, the rising side of late Edwardian times. The crowd included a fair number of away fans, eager to see the club regain its place at the top of the game, and replace Newcastle United, ever their great rivals, as the dominant side of the north-east.

Coleman was a sign of this ambition. His arrival showed that the club would not settle for second best: it was the League championship they wanted to win once more, and nothing short of it. This was the kind of flair player a club should be spending its money on when they wanted to get to the top and stay there.

Out through the shadow of the stand came Sunderland in their red and white stripes. With a roar, the new season was under way, the twenty-second in Football League history. A few minutes in, and Mordue sent a long pass out to Tim on the wing. It looked as if his arrival might pay immediate dividends. He was through the home defence and bearing down on goal. He looked up, took aim and then sent his first shot of the new campaign whistling just wide, like his first shot back at Kettering. There were groans from the Sunderland side, cheers from the home supporters. The Yorkshiremen were safe only for a moment. This was a Sunderland team looking to win, to show what they could do, setting out their stall to intimidate their rivals for the championship, and the Sheffield United keeper had a busy first half. Before the interval, Tim cut through again, hammering a shot on target which the keeper saved. The teams went in for the break at 0-0.

The pace was unrelenting when the teams reappeared for the second half. Sheffield United, the home side but who would have seemed to any unsuspecting visitor to be the away team such was their lack of dominance, continued to defend until the heat wore them down. Down the wing again came Sunderland, and the ball was tucked inside where Coleman was waiting for the pass. He swivelled, as he had been doing for a decade, left the defenders for dead, and gave poor Lievesley in the United goal no chance. Sunderland were on their way.

That was how the game finished, 1-0, maybe neither side had the energy to add to the score in the summery sunshine. The result was a victory for the little man playing at inside-left for Sunderland, the southerner who had come north to be at the real heart of the game. In the press that season there was an even stronger sense of Tim being football's national folk hero: 'Coleman played superbly at Bramall Lane. It would have been more appropriate to call him "Coolman".' 'Tim Coleman was "mustard" at Bramall Lane last Saturday. He scored Sunderland's winning goal. Play was so "hot" and "keen" that even the stand caught fire.' Humour and danger mixed: that was the recipe.

Into the Sunderland side came another figure from Tim's past: Leigh Richmond Roose, the Welsh goalkeeper against whom he had scored that goal in the fog against Everton six seasons before, the goal that had led him to England, Everton and now Wearside. Roose and Coleman were a perfect double act, even as opponents; as team-mates, they were heaven-sent, for the papers and also for the crowd. Two such larger-than-life personalities on the pitch together! Sunderland were becoming not only the top footballing side, but also the celebrity outfit, the media favourite.

Like all great double acts, Roose and Coleman were twinned opposites. One thing they did share, however, was the gift of the gab, a love of words. While most players were seen and not heard, like the children of the Victorian generations, ideas and phrases flowed from the pair of them. In Tim's case, the eloquence was as natural as the leaves growing on a tree. He had not been brought up as an actor or a comedian, it was simply his nature. Roose, on the other hand, was the son of a preacher, offspring of Welsh oratory. He was also, it seems clear in retrospect and seemed so to his contemporaries, a true genius: thinker, writer, goalkeeper. No category could hold him and he was the best at everything he touched – apart, that is, from leading a balanced life. Whereas Tim had the anchor of Nelly and the children, even though they were usually far away down south, Roose was a loner, endlessly quarrelling, always restless. His life was a series of brilliant, starry beginnings. He was an author, contributing some of the finest articles about football tactics yet written. He was also a scientist, with a doctorate in medical biochemistry. And he was a total, 100 per cent clown, cap pulled at a rakish angle and all. Yet he was amazingly athletic, though slightly stout: unbeatable, irrepressible and crazy. He had already passed through Aberystwyth Town, Celtic, Stoke, Everton and several other clubs. He was a fixture for the Wales international team, but no club could live with him for long. In the end the streak of craziness turned out to contain real madness, and tragedy was waiting.

Sunderland were unbeaten in September. In the account of their victory over Everton, there was just a hint of a new factor concerning Tim: 'Sunderland have a very fine line of forwards, and if Tim Coleman is approaching the veteran stage, he is still one of the "finest inside-lefts in the world".' There was the first hint of the passing of time. If Tim was going to get back to the pinnacle of the game, this was his moment. If he could not seize it, then it would be gone for good.

Through September and October, Sunderland's success became a national story and it was underpinned by those two heroes: Roose in goal and Coleman in attack. After a stunning win at Blackburn, 'Roose is credited with having accomplished wonderful things in the way of saving, being both effective and entertaining'. Roose may have been an amateur but he was one after Coleman's own heart. On the same day, 'The right wing made most headway. Mordue and Coleman were a merry pair, as the home defenders were made aware.'

In mid-October Sunderland took on Nottingham Forest at Roker Park. Manchester United were one point above them and Forest just below. Coleman 'evinced much keenness and all his old cleverness and calculation'. On 22 October Sunderland managed a creditable away draw at Manchester City. Tim got an uncharacteristic goal in an untidy scramble. The Wearside press was triumphant: 'Sunderland are still unbeaten, and have been showing very fine form.' The finest of them all was Tim: 'The best forward on the field was Coleman. His footwork was delightful and his passing, which is his strong point, was as good as anything that has been seen up Hyde Park for a very long time.' It was not only his passing, though, that caught the eye that day; he scored again too: 'Coleman putting the ball into the net in characteristic fashion following the flag kick.' Powered by Roose and Coleman, Sunderland were having a terrific season.

The end of October brought a different announcement: 'Sunderland players will figure prominently in the match to be decided at the Manchester City ground on 5 December for the benefit of the Players' Union funds. The game is between the Players' Union team and the joint strength of Manchester United and Manchester City, and a powerful side the Manchester clubs will put into the field.' The Sunderland *Football Echo* added that: 'Tim Coleman is always a safe card to play in a representative game. There are some men who are representative match players, and I should assume Coleman to be one of them. Others of the same order are Colin Veitch of Newcastle United.'

Meanwhile, Sunderland kept top spot, pushing Manchester United into second as November began. They thumped Everton by four goals to nil. This was on the same day that the union team was announced – a happy coincidence for Tim. They hammered Spurs 4-0 and kept their unbeaten record, with Tim scoring the fourth of the goals. The praise of Roose was glowing: 'Roose is the best custodian living.'

Then came a fateful day. It was another of the great local derbies in which Tim took part, with Newcastle hosting Sunderland at St James' Park. In his write-up of the prospects for the match and the likely teams, Veitch asked hopefully: 'Will Sunderland's record be broken by Newcastle United this week?' He was generous about the Black Cats, even though they were deadly and local rivals on the pitch: 'Since achieving victory over our forces on September 1, the Wearsiders have gone on their way rejoicing, and added several victories to their total.' He acclaimed their record: 'The Roker Park eleven stands out as the only unbeaten League team in Great Britain. That is a record of which they can be pardonably proud. Beyond that, however, their position is the outcome of no fluke, but one attained as the result of sheer merit on the field of play.' He went on to pick out their strengths: 'Roose everyone knows, and his abilities need no reference from them. In Troughear the Wearsiders can claim to have unearthed another right back of the highest calibre . . . The halves are a strong trio. "Charlie" Thomson works as hard as anyone playing football today . . . on the right, Mordue and "Tim" Coleman are revealing form reminiscent of their former days when they were the pride of Woolwich Arsenal's supporter team.'

Sunderland's record survived, just! The upshot was that Newcastle held them to a draw at St James' Park. Coleman scored the equaliser in front of 50,000 spectators. Some estimates put the crowd as high as 59,000, a record for the ground. All of which was overshadowed by one incident. Roose collided with a Newcastle forward and broke his left arm above the wrist. It was the end of the keeper's season, and more than that.

The next week, the unbeaten record finally fell – against Middlesbrough of all people. Yet Tim was still flying, top scorer on eleven, all the more impressive considering that he was 'not a centre-forward and one is inclined to think that his eleven successes are even more meritorious than others.' These were fast becoming the days of real recognition for Tim: 'The footwork of Coleman was in advance of anything else in the match, his perfect passing on the run being unequalled by any other player. He was undoubtedly the finest forward on the field.' And 'Coleman was as cool and clever as ever.' Every great football career has such a moment of perfection, but it was not Tim's nature, nor the logic of his life, to stay at the peak – or anywhere else – for long. Drawing against Preston, Sunderland dropped to second, just behind Aston Villa.

One more comic scene was recorded years later by a young lad watching that day from the sidelines, Charlie Buchan. He had just signed for Sunderland and was waiting for his chance in the forward line. Decades later, having had a famous career of his own at Herbert Chapman's Arsenal and then founded the long running *Charlie Buchan's Football Monthly*, he recalled that day at Preston: 'One of the games that first season was against Preston North End at Deepdale. Tim Coleman, inside-left that day, put on a thick, black moustache and played throughout the first half with it stuck on his upper lip.' The amazement of the young man was still evident in the Fifties. How it felt at the time is hard to imagine. There was more to come: 'During the interval he removed it and took the field with an innocent expression. The referee at once noticed the difference and spoke to Coleman about it. He thought we had put on a substitute.' No subs were allowed in those days. The gesture also says something about Tim and hinted at an increasing distance from the Roker Park set-up, a growing disaffection, and a hint of self-destruction. Why else would he even think of playing a practical joke in the middle of a serious game?

Yet the locals remained loyal: 'It is still a mystery why Everton parted with Coleman.' They were sure that international recognition was still due: 'Mordue and Coleman had never been absent, and between them they have shot seventeen out of the thirty-nine goals credited to the club. The operations have been so fine that they certainly ought to be considered as a pair in view of the international matches.' The national critics joined in: 'Any football enthusiast seeing Tim Coleman and Mordue playing will be quite satisfied of England's winning in April.' The press even revealed another Coleman talent: 'Tim Coleman, of Sunderland, is an expert bowler, and has won numerous trophies with the woods.'

By February, Tim was still banging in the goals, his tally was up to fifteen, and Sunderland were hanging on in third place. The commentators were still full of admiration for Tim: 'Few men can pass the ball as well as he, and in addition he is a great goal-getter.' Unfortunately, that same week, the Black Cats could only draw at home to Blackburn and fell back into third place, four points behind the leaders. The peak was passed, the circuit was broken. Despite continuing to score frequently, and make even more goals, Tim eventually lost his place in the team at the close of the season. In came young Charlie Buchan, a different voice of the future.

Tim was to meet Charlie Buchan for one last showdown, later. For the moment, he was on his way again. Yet he had nineteen goals that season and was Sunderland's top scorer. He was still a hot property. The press was already asking: 'What team will Tim Coleman play for next season? He's evidently tired of the Roker Park.' *The Weekly*, where Billy Meredith gave his views, asked the question: 'Does Tim Coleman want to go to Manchester United? Meredith and Coleman would make a great wing.' The seagull was restless again: 'It is widely rumoured that Tim Coleman is bent on leaving Sunderland at the end of this season.' Coleman and Meredith: that would have been the final fusion of all the aspects of Tim's football life. Perhaps sadly, his life never managed to achieve that kind of balance. It was a different drama, as is always the case with the game's truly awkward customers. They have an instinct for avoiding the best places.

Instead of Manchester United, Tim found a home at Fulham, back in the capital after a long journey. At last, he was able to settle down domestically. The family home was now in Lower Richmond Road, near to the ground, after years of keeping the home at Kettering while he roamed the country. Life was more stable, after all the travels, and it seemed as if the adventures of the game's rebel were drawing to a comfortable close. He was still the club's top scorer in the Second Division, and he seemed to put almost as much creative energy into his performance off the pitch. His comic act became a little more mellow, and more theatrical, though it still had an edge.

The 1911-12 season began at Fulham with Tim being interviewed about his new club's prospects. 'I agree with my college friends, Mr James Augustus Leonard Sharp, Mr Walter William Wilson White, and Mr Arthur Harold Hugh Collins, that we should do very well this season. I am glad to say that all my men have come back from their vacation sound and well.' He loved talking about football in the stolen tones of posh students. It was still an unmatched act. No one else would dream of saying this: 'I venture to think that the Cup and promotion is not outside our grasp this year. It's a beastly elusive goblet – at college, we frequently said goblet instead of cup, for the latter is a common word – but I think you will see us at the Palace next year.'

The rebel had mellowed, but not sold out completely: he was still out to mock the snobs who had been his enemy since he 'was not fed well enough'. He also had a nice line in barbed comment on the management of Fulham, where his friend Phil Kelso, who had been his manager at Woolwich Arsenal, was running the team and others controlled the budget: 'We have not thought it necessary to encroach upon the thousands of pounds we have in the bank to the purchase of new players, for the very good and sufficient reason that we are perfectly satisfied with the skilled talent at our disposal.' In fact, as Tim knew, the owner, Mr Norris, was using his cash for other purposes – in particular, taking over at the Arsenal and shifting them to Highbury in north London. Fulham would have to get along with no new money and no star recruits. For now, though, Tim let the humour slip into self-mockery: 'And before saying goodbye for the nonce, let me add that this is going to be Fulham's greatest season. I am not given to straining after effect, or excessive adulation – I seldom talk! – but I am full of optimism and confidence on this threshold of what promises to be a great and glorious season. Good-bye!'

Though the bitterness was still there, Tim made more and more of a music hall act out of his football. These seemed to be the last warm days of the Edwardian cult: 'Tim Coleman has only one complaint. It is against his friend "Wattie" White. He does not like Wattie's foreign accent, as he calls it. Wattie you know was born in Hurlford, where they use the broadest of broad Scotch.' Tim and White, his pal from their Goodison days, had a comic routine in which Walter was the straight man: 'The other day Wattie had reason to express his opinion on a full flush served on him. It was a real piece of the best Hurlford – too much for Tim Coleman. Timothy: "I say, young fellah! I wish you would take a little more soda with it. What did you say?" '

The rebellious streak was never far below the surface though: 'Tim is irresponsible at times. Recently one of the "heads" blew in to see the manager. Mr K was out but Timothy requested the messenger to say "that Mr Coleman was here, and could be seen in his office in a few minutes".' Tim was becoming the carnival king, always ready to turn things on their head. The old days were obviously on his mind, and he told a few Coleman specials about them too: 'Lawrence was an outside-left that, I believe, was an old partner of Tim Coleman. Lawrence had only one fault, the fatal gift of fat. His spirit was willing, but his flesh was overpowering. They said he had lost his form, but the bare fact was that his form was "not lost, but gone before".'

He also worked that college student act into everyday life in the Second Division. One report regarding his former Woolwich team-mate Tommy Fitchie was a case in point: 'There was not much the matter with Tommy Fitchie's display against Clapton Orient, in fact I thought it was quite good, particularly as Tommy had not kicked a ball this season before Monday's match. Tommy, in a voice loud enough for the irrepressible Tim Coleman to hear, told me so in the dressing-room just before the start of the game. Said Timothy in his best college tones: "*Nil desperandum*, Tommy." And the beauty of Tim's effort was that he knew what he said – I put it to him.'

Nostalgia began to creep into Tim's performance off the pitch, softening the edges. He still kept his edge on the pitch, though: 'I hope that the Orient like their second emphatic defeat by Fulham this season ... Our goals were nicely got, and I liked Tim Coleman's as well as any. Tim, I understand, is a little hurt by some gentle press criticism bestowed upon him in this game. However, Tim is too good a foot-baller to think much about it.'

Backed by his goals, Tim's vocal style started to be heard in the local coverage, especially when he had a good day: 'What Ho! Timothy' said one headline. 'Tim Coleman's hat-trick against Wolverhampton Wanderers was a very pretty event. Do you know the one and only Tim shares with Herbert Jon Pearce the distinction of being the leading goal-scorer in the League team just now? Each up to this morning has scored nine of the best. But Timothy's feat against the Wanderers is our first hat-trick of the season.'

Meanwhile, those Coleman stories kept on flowing, just like the Thames: 'I also like Tim as a humorist. He is always bubbling over with it. This is one of his latest: I blew into the dressing-room just before the start of a recent match. Tim was on the "slab", and was being oiled all over – a preparation against cold. Said I (innocently),

"What are you putting all that oil on for, Tim?" Tim: "Oh! Just to slip through the opposing defence, Aubrey." ' It was pure music hall repartee, made-up names and all. He was going to finish his career on his own terms, in his own words.

He always made sure to score against Arsenal and kept his best speeches for those days, such as the one in mid-November 1913, when he actually ended his appreciation of his own goal with the music hall comedian's catch-phrase: 'Thank you, thank you!' The more seasons he played, the better the goals got, at least the more people enjoyed them, like this one in 1914: 'Tim's first against Glossop was one of the best goals I have ever seen him score – a dribble round two men, and then, swish, when going at full speed. I wonder if Tim is going to finish up as our leading scorer.'

4 April 1914: Boat Race day – and what would prove to be the last of the era. This was exactly the world of college chums and goblets that Tim now made into his comic speciality. Somehow, nostalgia seemed to be in the air, even at the time, let alone in retrospect. Tim went for a stroll along the Thames towpath, just by Fulham's Craven Cottage ground, with Kelso. There can't have been anyone sharper in the vicinity that day, however many colleges had come to London for the race. Tim had been having a lull in scoring and, in reply to Kelso's inquiry as to his form, he declared that 'my old school Cambridge' were going to win the race, while he would score a goal to celebrate, the goal of the season – and both predictions came true.

At the end of the 1913-14 season, Tim had to look about him again. His stay by the river was over, goals and all. The club was even harder up than back in 1912, and he was too expensive. It was a situation he had foreseen and tried to fight against: 'Take, for instance, the case of a player on whose head there is a transfer of, say, £250. The man is past the stage of being reckoned a first-class exponent, and no first-class team (who after all are the clubs best able to pay such a fee) is anxious for his services. While this player is perhaps not worth £4 per week, he might prove a useful man to a club of lesser standing who are perfectly willing to pay him 30s or £2 a week – are willing, indeed, to pay the man a living wage. But they are barred by this heavy transfer fee. It does not necessarily require to be £250. Even £100 or £50 might be too heavy a drain on the finances of the club wishing to sign the man on, but all the same they are willing and able to pay him a living wage. And yet the poor fellow has to wander about doing nothing.' Fulham were sufficiently broke to stick it out until they got as much cash for Coleman as they could. Whether he would get anything for himself out of the deal was another question.

The *Weekly News* wondered about 'The Destination of Tim Coleman': 'Conjecture has been rife in Fulham as to the destination of Tim Coleman. Next season will find the genial one located in the Midlands. Tim is such a clever footballer that he can hardly fail to do as well in the Black Country, more especially as he will be backed up by players of a vigorous order who are likely to profit from the openings made by such an astute forward as Coleman is.'

So it was going to be Wolves, against whom he had scored many times down the seasons. That was the picture in May. But Fulham were too demanding: 'Early in the term Wolverhampton Wanderers made a bid for Tim's services, but negotiations, which looked hopeful at one stage, fell through.' There was some Scottish interest, perhaps based on Kelso's contacts: 'Later Partick Thistle appeared on the scene, and it seemed a certainty that Tim would migrate to Clydeside, but [once] again a hitch occurred.'

As he had recognised years back, a player could be entirely destroyed by a club that put its interests ruthlessly before his. It went down to the wire and then in late July there came a rescuer: 'At last Tim Coleman has, in football parlance, "got a shop" for on Saturday he was fixed up by Notts Forest. That third time is lucky has once more come true, and in this case both Notts Forest and Coleman may be considered gainers, for the red-shirted foresters of Nottingham sadly lacked last season a player of the ability and generality of Coleman.'

The ups and downs of 'Timothy's transfer' made another kind of Coleman story, to which he gave a defiant punchline by declaring that he was just 'glad of a chance of another shift'. While Fulham were remarking that 'Professor Tim Coleman is now with Nottingham Forest', Tim had moved on. He saw himself as being back on the factory floor, no more 'Aubrey' or 'goblet' jokes for this crisis of his family and career. He received this chance of a new 'shift' in late July 1914. Then on 4 August the world changed.

*Part Three*

A Footballer's War

# Rebel and Recruit

Nottingham Forest had had an indifferent season in the Second Division the previous year. The commentators were agreed that 'in signing Fiske, Neave and Coleman they have gone a long way in consolidating the side'. There were grounds for optimism at the Forest for the approaching campaign of 1914-15. Except, of course, that on 4 August 1914 the Great War broke out about a week before the first trial and practice matches were due to be played.

On Monday 10 August the *Athletic News* was still announcing 'The Advent of League Football'. The practice matches went ahead, though any gate money was to be donated to appropriate charitable funds under the sponsorship of the Prince of Wales, patron of the FA. This did not stem the tide of complaints and criticism heading football's way, and from sources that would always have been calculated to antagonise a man such as Coleman: 'The difficulty, of course, is that professional football is not a sport at all. It is a business just as much as the running of a picture palace or a public house.' That denunciation by *The Times* was close to condemning the whole idea of 'professional football', exactly as had been commonplace in Victorian times.

The FA was a natural ally of the recruiters and it was not long before posters and advertisements were flowing from 42 Russell Square: 'An Appeal to Good Sportsmen. Show that they are good sportsmen and enlist now and help other good sportsmen who are so bravely fighting

Britain's battle against the world's enemy.' This was signed by Frederick Wall, the FA secretary. That kind of call to 'sportsmen' would have pushed all the buttons that made Tim object to the FA committee men. He was firmly on the side of the professionals and suspicious of all such notions as 'good sportsmen'. In fact, the FA announced that it would consider cancelling the season if asked: 'I am also instructed to say that the FA is prepared to request all its members to stop the playing of matches if the War Office is of the opinion that such a course would assist them in their duties,' said Wall.

Meanwhile, under the sunshine of that warm summer of 1914, Tim Coleman was moving into new lodgings on Tierney Street in the Trent Bridge area of Nottingham. They were bachelor digs, since he did not have time to move the family and it was only another short-term deal. Nelly and the boys remained in their home in London as they had in Kettering before. At the age of thirty-one, the rover was on the move again, about to start his twelfth season as a professional player in the Football League, and his fourteenth in all, with his latest club. It had been a relief that he did not have to go so far as Clydeside. The family were not so far away, which was important at such a time. The local welcome was as enthusiastic as ever. The *Football Post*, a Nottingham-based paper, hailed the arrival of 'Forest's popular new forward'. The players were noticeably friendly, indeed he knew many of them already from tussles in previous seasons with Forest. Some of the older men, notably Tommy Gibson and Joe Mercer, were just his kind of footballers and they soon became a close-knit group.

So another season began, on 5 September 1914. By now the British Expeditionary Force was in retreat from Mons. The first casualty figures had been announced: more than 2,000 British soldiers lost already. Many of the match-day programmes carried Lord Kitchener's first famous appeal for recruits to the flag. The *Football Post* restricted itself to the half joke that 'it is the duty of every footballer to learn to shoot'. One compromise was for players to sign up for military training, while carrying on playing for the moment. Aston Villa volunteered for such instruction, under the pressure of their chairman. At Forest the atmosphere was more relaxed, at least to start with: the directors were arguing in the press that to cancel the season would ruin the clubs and the gentlemen who had loaned them money.

To Tim's contrary spirit, this was a provocative stance. His form improved with every successive denunciation. By early October he was clattering past the Preston North End defence, one of the strongest in that division: 'Hayes was out to clear but Coleman was much too quick for him and he sent it into the net'. In November, Forest travelled to London to play Fulham, and so gave Tim a welcome chance to see his family. The Fulham people reported that 'Tim Coleman arrived all smiles but this was nothing to his smile when he scored against us'.

In his trips down memory lane, he went on to play against Arsenal, who visited Forest in late November. As everyone expected, Coleman scored for Forest and only a penalty gave Arsenal a draw. The *Arsenal Magazine* praised the form of 'Tim Coleman, once the favourite of Woolwich'. None of the old bitterness remained on either side. There was something richly nostalgic about Coleman now. It was as if he reminded people of better and simpler times. Still, in the face of all the hostility to football, he had eleven goals, only one behind the leading scorer in the division. Meanwhile, the press revealed that Tim and the Forest players had remembered poor Tommy Fiske, the Forest goalie who, being an ex-soldier, had gone to the front already: 'They have sent him a knitted string vest which, as Mrs Fiske says, will be found very useful.'

Yet, before the next spring arrived, Tim and his merry Nottingham men were headed towards the war themselves. It was the call of football itself that made the difference, that and the appeal of friendship. The sudden transformation of happy-go-lucky Tim into Private Coleman was really the outcome of events just before Christmas 1914.

The War Office had started to issue statements attacking football, and blaming the game for the slowness of recruiting. In response, the FA offered to found a Footballers' Battalion, under the patronage of sympathetic MPs and the Duke of Cambridge's Middlesex Regiment, of which it would be the 17th Battalion, recruited if possible from professionals, supplemented by amateurs and supporters. This outfit would raise the flag of the game, and answer all the insults.

Several notable football figures came to be associated with the battalion. Among them was Frank Buckley, whose life as player, soldier and manager has been told by Patrick A. Quirke in *The Major*, and Buckley's fellow officer Vivian Woodward, as recorded in Norman Jacobs' biography. The most famous of footballing soldiers was undoubtedly Walter Tull, one of the earliest black professional players and the first non-white officer to have a regular commission in the British Army. Tull, who served mainly with the 23rd Middlesex, the 2nd Footballers' Battalion after a short period with the 17th, has been carefully researched by Phil Vasili as part of his history of black players, *Colouring Over the White Line*. He has also been celebrated by a Remembrance Day programme on television and an accompanying dramatisation. There is also a recent study focusing especially on the military campaigns of the battalion by Andrew Riddoch and John Kemp.

The core sources for their experiences are the war diaries of the Battalion, an official record that was required of every battalion that focuses on day-to-day military operations. Then there are a few personal diaries and letters, and the interest taken in them and in the whole story by the contemporary press, especially the *Athletic News* and other football papers. In addition, there are many surviving individual service records. Eyewitness accounts also illuminate some key events.

Going over the original material from the specific perspective of Tim Coleman brings to light a number of otherwise neglected sources.

Naturally he comes in and out of the picture, both in the recruitment phase and even more at the front line. His story is patchy, but it is also uniquely revealing about the whole strange saga of football and the war, of which the only widely known event is the Christmas truce in 1914, when the game played a role in bringing together some British and German soldiers across the lines. That was moving, and important, but there is far more to football at the front and Tim's story reveals much of this extraordinary subject.

The first recruitment meeting for footballers was held in London, at Fulham Town Hall on Tuesday 15 December. Tim was still playing football a month later when Forest, recovering after a slump in form, won away against Huddersfield Town, one of the strongest sides in the division. In that game, Tim fastened on to the ball and 'deposited it in the net after 17 minutes' play'. That set the adrenalin flowing and he played one of his best matches: 'Coleman after dribbling through was only inches out with a low shot just outside the post.' He was forming the last, as it turned out, of his successful attacking partnerships, with young John Derrick, completing the series that had begun with Lawrence at Northampton Town, and at Woolwich Arsenal with men such as Tommy Briercliffe, Tommy Shanks and Bert Freeman.

By the start of February, 'Coleman was playing a grand game'. He was right at the top of the Second Division list of scorers. Some of his old jest had returned, making him more like the Coleman of his successful days at Woolwich or when Everton were chasing the title. But his best times were always during the most insecure moments. Forest were having their best season in years, then the FA's recruitment campaign for the Footballers' Battalion reached Nottingham. The authorities hired the Queen's Hotel, and the County Football Association held a meeting. The message went out that 'efforts are to be made to stimulate recruiting in Nottingham for the Footballers' Battalion'. A special committee was appointed, on the model of London. The head of the County Association made a speech, pointing out that more than 1,000 local amateur players had already joined other battalions. A special poster was produced and fifty copies of it were sent to Nottingham by Frederick Wall.

The first to step up was Tim's mate Tommy Gibson, who had been a soldier before taking up football. In London it was soon reported that he was 'one of the most zealous among the Footballers' Battalion'. In the *Football Post*, when they revealed that Gibson had enlisted, they also announced: 'Footballers' Battalion – spaces to let.' The question was: who was going to be next?

There was a sense of urgency in the air. By 1915, according to Max Arthur and the Imperial War Museum collection of *Lost Voices*, France had lost ten per cent of her territory and a third of her industry, indicating that the Germans had managed to occupy the most prosperous and powerful parts of the country, in the north and around the capital. On the Western Front, 110 Allied divisions faced 100 German divisions in what was increasingly a stalemate punctuated by bloody incursions. All the time, as the sense of crisis was deepening, the pressure on recruitment was stepped up. Conscription was still ruled out but everything short of it was now legitimate.

The FA next sent out a letter to individual players in mid-February: 'Every League player in the country received a circular from the FA last week appealing to them on behalf of the Footballers' Battalion.' It was a strange parallel with the circular calling on the men to desert their union in the summer of 1909. Tim had a different reaction in 1915. When Nottingham Forest were due to go away to Blackpool later in February, he announced that he was 'unable to play owing to a swollen ankle'. It was probably true: he acquired that injury quite readily. He also had other things on his mind. He needed to think seriously by himself, in those lodgings in Tierney Street, Trent Bridge. The effect of his thoughts appeared on the Monday morning, after that lonely weekend without a cheering crowd: he went down to the Trent Bridge recruiting office, where he enlisted for the Footballers' Battalion. What

Tommy Gibson and Joe Mercer, mere midfielders, could do, Tim had to equal for the honour of the forwards. That was his argument anyway, when challenged. He had sufficient reasons to excuse him. At that stage, family men were still not under as much pressure to enlist as their single friends. But Tim was always going to be on the side of the game, his mates and the honour of football – it was, for him, the same kind of decision as joining the union. The form that he filled in shows that there was a lively argument with the recruiting officer. In the space at the top, his name is listed as 'John George Coleman', while the signature reads 'Timothy Coleman'. (In general the bureaucracy was unfriendly towards nicknames.) He signed his name as he wanted it, determined to be himself.

# Parting Shots

The Footballers' Battalion recruits had their own deal. During the working week, the men were Army novices, based at White City in west London. On Saturdays, the Army paid the train fares to enable them to complete the League fixtures for the season. That deal had been done to avoid breaking their one-year contracts. At the end of the season there would be no more professional football for the duration of the war. Meanwhile, with increasing numbers of military ranks in the programmes, the leagues would continue.

It took two weeks to process a completed 'attestation' paper. The following Saturday, his last as a civilian player, Tim was back in the first team to face local rivals Leicester. He was notably in high spirits and free of ankle trouble too: 'Coleman went very close with a beautiful cross shot', and again 'during a hot engagement Coleman was all but through'. His energies always rose in the face of danger. It was boredom he could not stand; with risk he was in his element.

One week later, on 27 February 1915, the news about Tim Coleman enlisting became public. The *Football Post* gave him front-page treatment: 'Tim Coleman, the Nottingham Forest international inside-right, has enlisted in the Footballers' Battalion.' It then pointed proudly to the list including Gibson, Mercer and Iremonger. Forest were becoming the team with the most recruits, rivalled by Clapton Orient. The national press took up the theme, with the *Athletic News* declaring that Coleman was the right man to keep up the spirits of the players in the trenches, as on the football field.

When he arrived in London, he found himself among familiar faces. Charlie Satterthwaite, another member of Woolwich Arsenal's original First Division outfit, was also a football soldier now. Bob Whiting, once the Chelsea goalie keeping Tim at bay in front of 70,000 fans, had come from his latest club, Brighton, to join the Footballers' Battalion. They had made him a corporal already. Alf West, who had been on Merseyside with Liverpool when Tim went there with Everton, had also made the trip from Nottingham, where he was with Notts County. From Tim's Fulham days there was the hard-tackling full-back, Ernest Coquet.

And then there were the men running the show. Colonel Grantham, of course, was a professional soldier, not a popular man among the players and fans who served under him at White City. He disliked football and resented the fact that there were not more football recruits yet. Other officers were more familiar with the game. From the London football scene where Tim began there was the tall gentleman footballer, Vivian Woodward, who had shaved off his dashing moustache when becoming a lieutenant. He was the man left out when Tim got his international cap. He had stood for the amateur way as strongly as Tim had represented professionalism. Now V.J. was in charge of the pros in a new game. He was worried about men who had shown 'an extraordinary temperament', and 'have been very queer people to manage', when on the football field. Tim was certainly one of the latter group. Looking around him, Woodward declared that: 'I had my doubts about them submitting to military rule.'

Woodward, with his senior football officer, Frank Buckley, of Birmingham City and Derby County, now Lieutenant and soon-to-be Captain Buckley, had the job of 'putting in order the new lads'. This was done every afternoon, with a couple of hours marching around the huge parade ground. That was Tim's introduction to military life, being drilled by an ex-Derby County centre-half and the game's great amateur centre-forward.

Buckley was really in charge. He was a natural leader, as the rest of his life was to prove. He had served in the Boer War at the age of sixteen and was from a military background. He had been spotted when playing football in the Army, gone to Aston Villa for a trial and, though he had not made that highest grade, he settled into a solid professional career. He was a big man, 5ft 11in, and by the end of his playing days weighed well over 13st. The way he played had made many spectators smile: 'Buckley employed his weight to considerable advantage', 'none of the half-backs compared with Buckley, who seems to be getting heavier, though his energy is not impaired, and his worrying tactics quite disconcerted Chapman at times.' He may have looked quite different, but Frank Buckley was exactly the same age as Tim. Along with his brother Chris, by now a director of Aston Villa, he had bought a livestock farm in the West Midlands. He was a man who had, as they said, done well out of the game but he was also in his way a fighter and a man who thought things out for himself.

The Footballers' Battalion spent most of its days marching around London: 'Sometimes the men march from the White City to the West End, halting perhaps at the Marble Arch end of Hyde Park for quarter of an hour's rest prior to setting off on the return journey.' Then, on precious Saturdays, Coleman was allowed to be his old self. When they beat Glossop, he 'put the Forest ahead with a neat header', anticipating just right a nice cross from his partner Derrick. At the end of the match 'Coleman put in a shot that rebounded from one of the defenders'. He could not bear to let any more chances go. It was as if he had to score every possible goal while there was still time.

There were other bright moments in the military boredom and gloom. One was recorded much later in the war, 'an evening spent in a quiet London restaurant'. Present were 'J.G. Coleman, in the garb of a private soldier, three international players, and other lesser lights'.

Alongside them were some stars of the music hall, including Harry Weldon, who had created a stand-up comedy character known as 'Stiffy the Goalkeeper'. Weldon was a good friend of Tim's and they regarded each other as rival football comedians. The group were well into the evening of banter when 'into the room walked Templeton', who had played with Coleman at Woolwich Arsenal. He had caught the train to this reunion from far away Kilmarnock, where he was now playing. Bobby Templeton insisted that it was the players who had 'provided more fun for the British public than you ever did', challenging Weldon the comic. They recalled how Templeton used to race 'at top speed, bamboozling the opponents as he showed them his heels'. Then he would stand still, 'calmly rest a foot on the ball, smile at the back and say "how do you do?".' He was another of Tim's kindred spirits. Tim remembered the evening becoming 'a regular battle of wits among that little circle!' The contest raged between Weldon and Templeton on one side of the table, and Tim Coleman with his old Everton and Fulham mate Walter White on the other. The old rage seemed to be subsiding. The days were drawing in for Tim's football generation and their world already felt nostalgic.

The season ended for Tim with the most surprising result of the year. Forest visited the Arsenal, as they were now called, having dropped the Woolwich name. They were now at their new ground in Highbury and the home side won 7-0! The result was beyond football logic, as if there was something strange in the air. That was, in fact, Tim's last game in the Football League. He had completed his 186 League goals and his 404 appearances.

With the half-and-half season over, the Battalion moved camp to Holmbury, near Dorking, in the Surrey countryside. This was the estate of William Joynson-Hicks MP, their patron. The press announced that they were 1,500 strong, though there were disputes about how many players had joined. In fact, Colonel Grantham – to the outrage of football folk – complained that there were too few professionals present. The FA, at last galvanised to defend its players, replied that many had joined other battalions, which was true. Still it was clear that the FA would not manage to raise a 1,500-strong battalion entirely of footballers, unless you counted the enthusiasts who were attracted by the name and the company. Meanwhile, there was, as the press announced: 'Serious work for the Footballers' Battalion.' They were now 'under the able guidance of Captain W.W. Scotland'. Here in the countryside the aim was to learn the techniques of front-line survival: 'Trench digging and route marching are important items in their training.' In general, the announcements coming out of the Battalion were of 'splendid progress'.

Tim had his own point of view, which still appealed to the press: 'Private Tim Coleman, the wit of the Battalion, declares they will put up a record digging themselves in when they get to the front.' That wasn't exactly the stereotypically cheery spirit that Tim was supposed to embody. The comment betrayed a blunt side to his tongue: 'To see us,' said Tim, 'you would gamble we had never done anything else but navvy work all our lives.'

He saw the coming struggle in dramatic terms: 'With German bullets spurring us on we will sink into the ground about as quick as the Demon King disappears through the stage at pantomime time.' The grim reality of the First World War may seem obvious, in retrospect, with all the reports and poems to bring home the truth. At the time, Tim's was still a striking and discordant voice. Before he got to the trenches, Tim knew there would be nothing glorious about it: those would be real bullets, even if the rest felt like a military pantomime. This was not a man under the spell of glorious war.

The autumn approached, which would ordinarily have brought the excitement of a new season. Instead of all the normal speculation about signings and prospects of promotion, the football press was impatient for other action: 'When will the Footballers' Battalion go out to the front?' asked one headline. That was what the journalists wanted to know this year. The *Athletic News* published profiles of each club, but this time they presented which regiment each player had joined, rather than the position they were going to play. In fact, these were all former players, since no contracts remained in force.

Although the Football League was suspended, for the 'football soldiers' the game went on while they waited to go 'out to the front'. There was some excitement too. The Saturday deal continued, even though the real business was ended. Players got a match wherever they could: 'Chelsea have a hot side out against the Orient at Stamford Bridge and the latter too will carry some weight with them, seeing that they have such stars as Barber [Aston Villa], Sheldon [Liverpool] and Coleman [Notts Forest] in the ranks.' For the moment Tim was taking on a Chelsea side starring Charlie Buchan, Tim's successor at Sunderland. It was Buchan's great chance to upstage the old master he had already replaced at Roker Park before joining up with the Scots Guards. There were 12,000 in the crowd at Stamford Bridge, not quite like the old days but good enough for now. Buchan hit three to give the home side victory and Tommy Barber went close for Clapton Orient.

As September ended, the Footballers' Battalion itself started to put out official teams. Kitted out in all white, they had no home ground as such. They played against the professional, and a few semi-pro, clubs within half a day or so of travelling of their base camp on Salisbury Plain. They had an early victory against Birmingham City and managed to beat Cardiff at Ninian Park in a more difficult game on a wretchedly rainy Saturday. The crowds were normally around 5,000, not bad when all the travel difficulties were taken into account. The Battalion band paraded and at half-time there were speeches addressing the young men on the terraces, some delivered in football kit and greatcoat by Captain Buckley and Lieutenant Woodward. On one occasion, some lads on the terraces at Birmingham's St Andrew's ground were so enthusiastic in celebrating a Battalion goal that they enlisted on the spot.

The team was selected by Captain Buckley, who also captained the side from midfield. He later became a manager with a talent for spotting players and picking sides. For now, Buckley tended to pick his men on the basis of suitability from a military and recruiting or propaganda perspective. Amateurs and officers, commissioned and non-commissioned, were his main selections. Tommy Gibson, of Forest, had been a soldier before he became a footballer and he was already a sergeant, before quickly rising to higher NCO ranks. He was a definite Buckley choice. Young Joe Bailey was a corporal and he also had the recommendation of having two England amateur caps. The list stretched down to the Grimsby skipper Sid Wheelhouse, a pro if ever there was one, but he had the advantage of being another corporal. Tim got an occasional stand-in role – he was a crowd-puller still, but he was not a first-choice man in such a time.

Tim made one final appearance before he set off for war. On Saturday, 22 October 1915, he played for Queens Park Rangers against Chelsea. That was a bad weekend in London. German bombs hit the city only four days earlier. The match still went ahead. Now football symbolised not treachery but defiance of the enemy. For Tim, this was a last chance to get his own back on Chelsea, and Charlie Buchan. He had spent several earlier occasions on the losing side against the Stamford Bridge team, and young Buchan had stepped into his place at Roker Park. Half-time came with the score 0-0. Nobody had really got going yet. That was a success for the home team, little QPR from the Southern League.

The atmosphere improved after half-time. Everyone got into the game and forgot about the war for a while. The crowd perked up: there wasn't much to smile about, and they appreciated this attempt at 'football entertainment', as Tim called it. The referee blew the whistle and Tim began his last forty-five minutes before leaving for the trenches. The game was faster this half. Taylor took the ball on for Rangers and was knocked flying by a Chelsea midfielder. He had to go off for treatment but was soon on again. No one wanted to miss this. Tim had come back into midfield, looking to get involved as ever. He found the ball at his feet, one more time. It was a sight that a generation of football fans across the country would have recognised. The curly light brown hair, the speed, the cunning, the slight figure and the ball under total control. It was like an action replay of the pre-war world. The Zeppelins were over London, British soldiers were falling at Loos and at Gallipoli, and here was Tim Coleman, the football field comedian, star artist of the front line. The programme listed him as 'Private Coleman' – there would be no promotion even to corporal for Tim.

He was near the halfway line when this final run started. He was never going to pass! Starting to dribble, he put on a burst of acceleration and it took him through a floundering defence one last time. Shaking off the Chelsea full-back, he closed in on goal. Denoon, Chelsea's wartime goalie, was on the line. He was a good player but Tim called on all his years of experience to make one final footballing decision. Looking up, with that extra few seconds that great players seem to have, he decided against blasting his shot past Denoon and instead placed a subtle shot beyond the keeper. Tim Coleman had ended on a high. It was the only goal of the game – not even Charlie Buchan could equalise. So Tim had the last word.

# To the Front

The autumn of 1915 on the Western Front was dominated by the Battle of Loos, fought from 25 September to 10 October, just as the Footballers' Battalion prepared to travel. Martin Gilbert describes it as beginning with an initial Allied bombardment along a six-and-a-half-mile front. This was the occasion for the first British use of poison gas, with 150 tons of chlorine being dispersed, although much of it caught in the wind and some blew back over the advancing Allied soldiers. At the same time, Loos was also the end of an older idea of war, almost of glorious chivalry, stretching back to Agincourt. One eyewitness report refers to 'many squadrons of cavalry' deployed in the same Allied attack as the gas. The age of chivalry, though, was well and truly over. This was modern, mass war: 'We very soon found ourselves picking our way over the bodies of men who had fallen in the earlier attack and wounded men who were trying to crawl into shell-holes.' That was where the Footballers' Battalion was headed and even with censorship preventing the full horror of events from reaching the public, the picture was clear. The press were becoming more insistent: 'What we want to know is: when are the Footballers' going to France?'

By the end of that dark October on the Western Front the offensive at Loos had well and truly failed in the mud. Now the Allies desperately needed the arrival of Lord Kitchener's 'New Army' to hold the line. The trench landscape had evolved across the coalfields and the canals of the Loos-La Bassée region, waiting to claim more men.

It was mid-November when the Footballers' Battalion finally received their call to embark. Colonel Grantham had been replaced by the much more supportive Colonel Fenwick, veteran of the Boer War. Even he made a grandiose speech, which he recorded in the Battalion Diary, declaring that they were departing: 'On active service to France to take part in the greatest war in the annals of history.' In the week they set off, Captain Buckley, through his wife Madge, announced to the public that signed photographs of himself and Lieutenant Woodward in uniform would be on sale – in aid of the Battalion charity. They were still football stars, albeit of a strange, ambiguous kind.

Colonel Fenwick took charge of B Company, which included Tim and most of the professionals he knew among the recruits. They set off from Salisbury Plain by train, one belonging to Southeastern railways, with upholstered seats and heavy wooden doors. They left early in the afternoon on a Thursday to cross the damp autumn countryside to Folkestone. It was dark by the time they boarded the boat that was to take them to the giant camp at Boulogne. The voyage was tense, talking forbidden, because only the day before a hospital ship had been sunk in the Channel with the loss of many lives. They landed in pouring rain and had to wait until the next afternoon for their train towards the front. It was very different from Southeastern railways and its comparatively luxurious carriages. When this train drew in it was merely a long line of wooden wagons, hitched to a huge engine. The Footballers' Battalion climbed aboard the cattle trucks: inside there was just straw and once the huge doors were closed there was no light. When the train slowed, the men would lever these doors open and station names would go past: Calais, St Omer, Hazebrouck.

When they got off the train they had to march for several miles through the night before snatching three hours' sleep. The next morning, at about eight o'clock, they heard the sound of the enemy guns. Then it was a twenty-mile route march to camp. For the moment, the countryside around them was more or less intact: the trees still had their branches. In the distance was the continuous booming sound of the front. Other reports made clear just how bad conditions had become along the front line left by the failed offensive: 'It being the later part of November, it was pretty filthy weather. The Germans were only about fifty yards away and they had highly specialised snipers, which made life pretty unbearable.' The pressure was intense and at the same time everything was being bogged down by the hardening winter.

The officers went to receive their introduction to the trenches, Buckley and Woodward among them. Meanwhile, those in the ranks were left with a skeleton staff in charge to acclimatise. By now, they were at Guarbecque, inching closer to the trenches. A steady hour of driving from Boulogne today would bring you to this little town, set amid the flat fields. It is all much nearer the Channel coast than you might think: no wonder the sound of the guns could sometimes be heard on the south coast of England.

After a few days in camp, a lad called Harry Remnings arrived to see Corporal Joe Bailey of the 17th Middlesex, alias W.G. Bailey, who played on the wing for Reading. Remnings was from the Northamptonshire Regiment and he had come to bring a challenge to his friend. Were the Footballers' Battalion up for a game? Two days later, a Battalion side, though not an official one this time, was back in action – football action that is. In the early days, according to Bailey's Letts Pocket Diary, they had trouble finding the bags with the proper kit and, more important in this mud, the boots. They had been moved around too many times, everything was jumbled. Enough kit turned up to let the game go ahead. The 17th had had no time to choose a flat patch and improvise a ground, as more settled battalions had across the front. It would be an away fixture, just like in England. Scraping together their gear, the Footballers' also scraped together a team.

The match itself is visible only in glimpses through a fog thicker than the one that had enshrouded Plumstead a decade earlier. Bailey recorded the bare facts in his field diary, where a huge asterisk testified to their happiness at playing again, after the turmoil and the tedium of the journey and before the terrors of the trenches. Scraps in the Northamptonshire papers a few weeks later also reveal that Tim himself had had a game, as Buckley had not been around to fix the team selection and ensure that only officers and NCOs represented his beloved battalion. This was a spontaneous line-up and there was naturally a place for Private Coleman in the football front line.

There had been matches of every kind behind the trenches since the start of the war in 1914 when, according to a Glossop winger (they were a League side then) football had 'broken out'. Most famously, British soldiers had tried to have a game with the Germans during the so-called 'Christmas Truce'. They had managed a little more under-standing, perhaps, than the mutual incomprehension Tim had so vividly recorded back in Berlin with Woolwich Arsenal. Then there were some officially authorised British Army games – even whole tournaments. On other occasions, men laid down jackets for goalposts and played their hearts out, as a few frames of juddering film reveal.

The Footballers' Battalion versus the Northants was a match somewhere in between the formal and the entirely improvised. There were teams, a pitch, a referee and officials and goalposts. Bailey's brief note suggests that the game lasted the right length of time, and that it was as proper a contest as they could manage. Eyewitness accounts of similar games reported that there was likely to be a discrepancy between expectation and reality. Lieutenant Mason was amazed when, a little later, he joined the Footballers' and went eagerly to see their side play. The names on the sheet were well-known: it would have been a strong line-up in the League. Yet as the ball splashed to a stop in the mud, he found the play almost farcical. Perhaps he was too cynical: other days certainly brought more excitement and many men were at least able to connect what they witnessed more happily with their memories of games back home.

The score certainly suggests that the Footballers' were able to get the ball moving this particular day. By the final whistle they had won by seven goals to nil. Alas, no one, not even Joe, recorded who scored. It wasn't that kind of experience: everyone was just overwhelmed to be playing at all. Nobody cared who got the goals. It probably wasn't easy to tell anyway. Goals tended to be close range in the mud, the ball being forced over the line more like a rolling scrum in rugby. Winning did still count, as the corporal's diary testifies: poignant little pencil-written pages in the Imperial War Museum.

Yet all this was happening not far from the battlefields where the most horrific military innovation so far had just been tested: the gas barrage. In John Singer Sargent's famous picture from the front entitled *Gassed* from 1918, games like this one were both acknowledged and put into a kind of double perspective. Martin Gilbert describes the classic canvas: 'More than twenty men are lying in a field in the foreground, their eyes bandaged . . . In the far distance, on the horizon, dwarfed by the men who have been gassed, a football match is in progress.' Football was absurd, in such a setting, yet at the same time the game had never been a more moving assertion of life in the face of widespread death.

The real business of war approached quickly. Captain Buckley was back from his inspection of the trenches and it was time to initiate the football soldiers. Another Saturday, 11 December, and the Footballers' were in a different kind of action. Again, the distances in our world are incredibly small and the consequences at the time so immense. A half hour of gentle driving would take you from Guarbecque to Cambrin, where they first went into the trenches. It was past Béthune, the most welcoming town in the area, and near to La Bassée, which gave its name to the whole sector of the front.

Buckley led B Company to their places in the lines, at around one o'clock. It was a quiet interlude, with not much going on. Then darkness fell and there was a change of sentries. One of the new boys was Private James MacDonald, a lad who had joined to be with the players. Around eight o'clock in the evening, he took his position. Perhaps he moved, or it could have been just bad luck, but within a minute or so of taking guard, Private J. McDonald was B Company's first fatal casualty on active service, killed instantly.

From this began the confusion that led to the story of the death of Tim and his friends that Christmas. There was another MacDonald in B Company, a Norwich full-back. He, in fact, was back in London with an old football injury, undergoing an operation. But the names were enough to give rise to a misunderstanding that gathered pace in the intense atmosphere of the time. Before long reports of Tim's demise were featuring vividly in the English press.

It was only a brief first visit to the trenches. It was long enough, though, to show that some men appeared to have no nerves. The Clapton Orient goalie Jimmy Hugall, for instance, watched stunned as his friend Bob Dalrymple rescued a wounded man under fire. It was the start of another whole set of football stories. Perhaps that incident also contributed to the rumoured deaths.

That winter had none of the strangely nostalgic festiveness of the first front-line Christmas. On 19 December 1915, Douglas Haig replaced Sir John French as Commander in Chief. In retrospect at least, this change marks the moment that the First World War on the Western Front became a new kind of conflict. As Gilbert puts it: 'As 1915 came to an end, it was clear that the war that was to have ended by Christmas 1914 was certainly not going to be over by Christmas 1915.'

At least they pulled back a bit for the festive interval. By 30 December 1915, B Company were on parade in camp at Busnes. This is now a mere five minutes in the car from Cambrin; then it was the distance from the front line to some kind of half-respite. A hundred or so kilometres away was Lille and then the Belgian border. It is now only just over an hour to Mons, where the first great Allied defeat had started this whole catastrophe in motion. They were hardly out of the woods and not surprisingly the atmosphere was tense.

It had been a mixed Christmas. On Christmas Eve, they had managed an entertainment, if you could call it that, mainly Highland songs performed by Major MacLean. Then during the night there had been a gas alert, which they were getting used to. The routine of putting on gas masks was still tricky and frightening. It turned out to be a false alarm. Suspicions were rife that High Command had contrived this alert to make sure there was no risk of fraternising with the enemy for a second Christmas.

Although there was no football between the lines, the game went on behind them. On Christmas Day, Tim watched as some of his friends beat the local Royal Engineers by nineteen goals to one. Christmas morning had been a traditional football morning before the war – there were games going on at home. The star behind the lines that day was Tim's friend Bob Dalrymple. There was also a good deal of football gossip. Back in England, unofficial local leagues were still in progress. Much discussion followed about who would win the London and the Midlands competitions. Forest were top of their league, as Tommy Gibson recorded with delight.

But then they had moved on to a new camp, and the Colonel made his usual fuss that the place was 'in a wretched condition, being dirty, wet and practically uninhabitable'. As a result they spent the days after Christmas frantically cleaning the site. Now, they were on parade, with Sergeant Gibson in the row near to Tim. The usual routine was interrupted by the arrival of a wire from the British press. It was the inquiry about the possible death of Private Coleman, in action on the front line. Gibson was near enough to watch for Tim's reaction when the question was put to him. It seems likely that the senior officer doing the asking was Frank Buckley, since he was in charge of B Company. The press wanted to know, then, whether there was any truth in the rumour that Tim Coleman was dead. As Tommy read out this latest story from the papers, Tim stood upright on the mud and announced in the polished tones he used for his theatrical performances: 'I am pleased to say, gentlemen, there's absolutely no truth in the report at all.' He was meant to stick to 'Sir' of course: 'Gentlemen' was a word, as he knew full well, an officer might use to his peers. He also understood perfectly what it meant for a mere private soldier to adopt the Duke of Wellington's famous saying about rumours of his death being much exaggerated.

Tommy Gibson found it made him smile as they stood in line, a welcome diversion from the terrors to come, with another spell in the trenches moving ever closer. The darker side to the story was still plain to everyone. Most rumours of death were justified, and who knew how long it would be before this became true in its turn?

The officers promised to send return telegrams announcing that the men were safe. Sergeant Dalrymple sent one to his wife at home in Catford, south London: 'Alive and well.' Tim's read: 'Alive and well. Wire mother.' That was the telegram that Nelly Coleman was opening, or pretending to open, on the front page of the first *Athletic News* of 1916. The new year's papers contained more straightforward heroic news from Captain Buckley: 'Under fire,' said the headline. 'As members of the Football Battalion, both Captain Frank Buckley and Lieutenant Harold Walden have recently been under fire in France.' Buckley had instinctively provided what the FA had wanted: a morale-boosting cameo of football at war and playing its part. Coleman's 'death' and his wry response gave people back home a different angle. Even at the front, each of these strong football personalities remained himself.

A letter home written by Tommy Gibson told how, in the next few days, the Battalion received many of the obituaries written for Tim, along with some for the Sergeant. They provided a poignant experience for the two men and the *Sporting Life* put it best: 'A doubtful pleasure,' ran the headline on their piece. 'It is not given to every man to read his own biography. Sergeant Dalrymple and Private Tim

Coleman have had an opportunity to indulge in that doubtful delight.' Early in 1916, it took the papers less than a week to get out to the Western Front, when all went well. So Tim received all those front pages, including that picture of his sons and wife, within a few days of that parade. He must have had them by the time his son celebrated his seventh birthday back home in the first week of January. Tommy Gibson's note carries a hint of the state of Tim's mind that New Year week. What a man needed, above all, was to keep the idea of death out of his mind. This was the secret of mental survival. Tim was having to face the thought of his own disappearance and how that would look and feel to others. It must have made life feel paper thin.

The papers did at least enable Tim to put together the story of what had gone on back at home. There was the awful realisation that his wife had received her 'widow's telegram', announcing his death, and confirmed by the newspapers, before Christmas, while he was tramping back to camp from the front line. According to the press, it was his younger son, John Victor, who refused to believe it. He then learnt how Nelly had gone to Phil Kelso, at Fulham, for help. Kelso let her know that he had just received a letter from Ernest Coquet, the Fulham defender and fellow member of the Footballers' Battalion. Coquet would certainly have mentioned the death of Tim, had any such event occurred. On the contrary, he said that everyone from the club was well, and that would have included Tim.

The papers also told Tim how Kelso had arrived on Boxing Day for a game between Clapton Orient and Fulham and there 'was told the news with a wealth of detail, and on the authority of those who should have known the information was not confirmed'. Tim's old manager even received a telephone call from the manager of Nottingham Forest 'who suggested that a collection should be made on the ground for the benefit of Mrs Coleman, and intimated that they intended doing so at Nottingham'. Kelso's reply reveals why he and Tim were friends: 'It is a kindly suggestion and does you credit, but we had better wait and see if Tim has been killed. I have my doubts about it.' Kelso and Nelly went to the War Office and found no confirmation of the report. Then on Boxing Day one of Tim's letters arrived, saying that he was safe in camp. It was just possible that something had happened since or that there was some other mistake – which was why the wire of inquiry reached the Battalion on parade just before New Year.

Tim got to disentangle all of this story, with its panic and its misunderstandings and looming mortality, in camp as they waited to go back to the front line. The story was the talking point on the way to the front, as Private Jamie Nutall, of Millwall, reported: 'I expect you read that Dalrymple, Tim Coleman and MacDonald have been killed, but the statement is false as the first two are in the ranks, and MacDonald has been sent back to England.' Tim responded to the situation by putting on his cheeriest face. Tommy Gibson catches the effect in another letter home: 'Tim is in his usual happy mood and Dalrymple is as bad as ever.'

Tim also discovered news that was almost as strange as his own death. As he read his obituaries, he learnt that his old Everton colleague Sandy Young, who had moved to Australia, had been charged with murder. He was alleged to have killed his brother in a quarrel. Young was convicted of the murder but avoided the death penalty and was returned home on the grounds of mental illness. He ended his days in a secure hospital in Scotland. A little later, the newspapers revealed to the men at the front the death in a nursing home of the giant goalkeeper Willie Foulke, against whom Tim played for Northampton Town in the Cup in 1902. Tim had missed an open goal, and Foulke had gone on to win the FA Cup. The cheers of the crowd that day had been unforgettable. 'Fatty' Foulke had been reduced during the war to challenging all-comers to score penalties against him on the beach. His immense bulk brought on heart trouble and he died while the men who cheered him were marching towards the Somme.

There was also news of his old friend Leigh Richmond Roose, the closest of all his football partners. Roose had become steadily more eccentric and he had crossed the boundary between entertaining and disturbing. After more short-term stints at several clubs, he ended up at Huddersfield, where, having failed to earn a regular place in the team, he chose to insult the owners in the press, accusing them of dishonesty in bringing him to the club. They sued him and won. Roose left for the trenches rather than wait for the verdict. He went missing later in 1916, and his name is on one of the massive memorials for the Battle of the Somme. The old days seemed long ago, and many of the other great personalities of that day were wearing less well than Tim. It was as if his whole football world, the one he had fought for, was dying, while he tramped among the anonymous thousands towards the great offensive of 1916.

# The People's Footballer

The year 1916 has become synonymous with the Somme in historical memory. There had been a huge build-up of troop numbers on the Western Front. As 1916 opened, Gilbert wrote, only Britain, Australia and Canada had resisted conscription entirely and, even without it, there were still 2,675,149 British soldiers involved in the conflict at that point. It was not enough and so, on 5 January, Prime Minister Herbert Asquith brought forward the first Conscription Bill in the House of Commons. The initiative at the front lay with the Germans at the beginning of the year. They were getting ready for an assault that would include the most ferocious artillery bombardment in human history. Individual experience felt dwarfed, yet also heightened. The following few months were a time of extremes for Private Coleman. They were to be the worst days of the Footballers' war so far – and yet they also culminated in a great day, a real moment of light.

There was a short pause before the fighting resumed. Early in January, the Army on the Western Front launched what was called the Flanders Cup, an inter-battalion equivalent of the FA Cup. It was set up by Brigadier-General Kentish, once a Royal Engineers goalkeeper in the great days of the amateur side. This was official Army football, a morale-boosting strategy worked out at head-quarters. After frowning on the sport in earlier conflicts, the British Army had begun to come to terms with the popularity of football during the Boer War, and that was one of the reasons British soldiers were able to play a central role in spreading their favourite sport around the globe.

The Footballers' Battalion team was naturally the favourite to win the cup, but the players took it lightly. As Tommy Gibson said: 'The lads will walk the tourney.' They played once again, as the official team had done back home, under Buckley and Woodward, in the official white, and on properly marked out pitches. A brass band marched them to their places in successive games against an Essex battalion and then one from the South Staffordshires. Results were recorded in the Battalion Diary. Buckley's selections were once more heavily weighted towards amateurs, NCOs and officers. There were a few signs that the pros were taking a rather mocking view of proceedings. Corporal Wheelhouse, of Grimsby Town, and Corporal Bullock, of Huddersfield Town, were the full-backs. When they were trying to get stuck into their match against the South Staffordshires, Sid remarked that: 'It put me in mind of the Huddersfield ground we played on two seasons ago, when the ball would not bounce and we had to dig it out of the mud before we could kick it.' Perhaps the prospect of the trenches was getting too close for these games to stir or distract the players.

The Footballers' Battalion put six goals past the South Staffordshires. On the sidelines Tim and his mates were doing their best to get a laugh out of it. Towards the end of the game, the referee blew for a penalty to the Footballers'. The crowd began to chant their goalkeeper's name – Corporal Tommy Lonsdale, of Norwich – until he was given the job of taking the kick. He hadn't had much else to do. Up he came and obligingly struck his penalty as if it was a goal kick, sending it soaring high over the bar and into the distance to huge cheers. There were hints of a strained atmosphere at the game. Some reports observed: 'V.J. Woodward could hardly move,' because of the cold and the mud. The suggestion was indignantly denied in a follow-up letter of protest from one of his fellow officers, the Southampton amateur winger Captain Bell. It seemed as though the professionals in the ranks and their often amateur officers had contrasting views of the game – or maybe the other team were getting their own back. Either way, football clearly still mattered almost too much as the most violent war in history to that date wound towards ever greater peaks of intensity.

The next rounds of the Flanders Cup would have to wait anyway. On a subsequent Saturday soon afterwards, A and B Company 'moved into the front line at Givenchy, subsection B2'. This was a steady march south-west from Busnes, past Lillers where they had played football, towards Amiens. They were moving roughly parallel to the Channel coast and passing by locations that would acquire notoriety later in the war, such as Arras, where the bitterest battles of the late campaigns were fought. It makes one realise that Tim and his friends were to spend three years fighting in an incredibly small geographical space, packed with the bones of thousands upon thousands of soldiers as the cemeteries grew.

To get to the front line, the Footballers' marched by the side of a canal, along an old road that the British Army insisted on calling 'Harley Street'. They crossed over the canal at Pont Fixe, an old steel bridge with a deep dip in the middle. The march went past a crossroads known as Windy Corner, where a new military cemetery was growing.

Now they really were at the front line and reports of death were likely to be better founded. The biggest incident of this period occurred at around four in the morning of 23 January. They were ordered to open rapid fire as the Royal Engineers detonated mines in no man's land. In retaliation, shells flew back the other way, mainly rifle grenades, which were a German speciality. Woodward was acting as bombs officer, responsible for organising the clearing of these missiles. In the confusion of the moment he was wounded when one went off and was carried rapidly to a field hospital, where shrapnel was removed from both his legs. He was soon on the boat from Dieppe to Dover, but news reports reached home before he did: 'Vivian Woodward wounded. He has been wounded by shrapnel, his thigh being severely pierced. It has been reported that his injuries were so severe that his days of athletic activity are at an end.' Along the line, in a different regiment, H.G. Bache, West Bromwich Albion's outstanding amateur striker, was killed: football losses had started.

Meanwhile, the Footballers' Battalion had moved into an area called 'The Grouse Butts', one of the strangest places on the Western Front. The trenches here wound their way across old brick fields, covered in remnants of stone and huge kilns. There were enormous piles known as 'brick stacks' in the fields, some twenty feet high and forty feet across. The 'grouse butts' themselves were fragments of an old fortress scattered across marshy fields. It was a ghastly, night-marish place. In the memoir of the Royal Welch Fusiliers, edited by Captain Dunn and published as the classic volume called *The War the Infantry Knew*, the picture of this place and time is uniquely grim. The brick towers had 'a witching grandeur under the moon's cold light, or when a falling rocket's ghastly glare glided over their deep shadows' but they were 'terrible in the red, smoking fury of a strafe in the dark'. This was a small section of the Cuinchy sector, a further move towards the Belgian border and under even more intense assault.

Shelling was heavy and continuous at the start of February. On the fifth day of that month, the high parapet of a trench gave way, with the combination of rain and shell fire. There was a great landslide and it landed on Captain Buckley himself, forcing him to dig his way out. The reaction, as recorded in Joe Bailey's diary of the life of B Company and the Footballers', was pretty harsh: 'A laughable incident,' he noted.

Then they were caught up in Von Falkenhayn's major offensive of late February. It was in response to that that the French urged the British to move forward on the Somme as fast as possible, and as hard as they could. The lines were at breaking point. Even Paris would not be safe. On 21 February, the Germans launched the most ferocious onslaught of all, the attack on the key French fortress of Verdun. They employed their own brand of gas shells and unleashed the terrifying innovation of flamethrowers. Not to be outdone in the horror of it all, the French replied with phosgene gas shells.

For the Footballers', action was coming thick and fast. They received their first prisoners of war, who crossed no man's land with arms raised and crying, '*kamerad*'. They dug up the body of a Canadian officer from the front-line mud and buried him. At Festubert, they came upon the remains of a church, with the crucifix standing unharmed amid the rubble.

A mere private could seem lost in such vast slaughter and desolation. Many certainly felt so. Yet personality is an obstinate thing. In the midst of this series of nightmares, Tim Coleman had been in the trenches for a six-day stretch. Dragging himself away for a break, he encountered Jamie Borthwick, who had been at Everton with him. They met like any soldier friends from a more peaceful interlude amid the mud and the rubble. Borthwick asked how Tim had found the trenches and he replied that is was all 'pretty rotten', as anyone might. Still, Tim had his old sharp tongue: 'This is the worst team I ever signed for and I'm not going to sign for them again!'

Borthwick chose to send this home to the press where it became another example of Tim's supposedly cheery resilience under pressure: 'Tim's latest', 'Famed Footballer cracks a new gag with comrade', 'Tim Coleman is Irrepressible'.

The idea of a chirpy working-class footballing soldier was irresistible, even when Tim insisted on saying things that never quite fit the stereotype: 'Having come through the ordeal of being reported dead and himself denying the allegation, Tim has been having a high old time in the Footballers' Battalion and has kept the company alive with his quips and cracks.' 'Tim's Latest' became a catchphrase. His comment about signing for the Army showed that he could not suppress the old bitterness from his football days, even now. The annual ritual of signing a new contract was a central part of the life of professional footballers. No contract lasted more than a year. In the muck of the trenches, he still remembered how hard that had been. The men had now signed on 'for the duration of the conflict', which was indefinite. It was the longest contract they had ever committed to. For men of that generation of players and most workers that was the closest they ever got to 'job security'.

The Footballers' were nearing the end of this active spell at the front when Tim had another shock. Around midnight, one night in early March, his mate Sergeant Joe Mercer, of Nottingham Forest, thought he had heard something going on in no man's land. He came rushing out from a dugout to hear rifle grenades falling. Corporal Bailey joined him, and as he did so one of the grenades exploded. While Mercer and Bailey were shaken, young Percy Summers, the Grimsby goalie from that first game of 1914, was more seriously injured. It felt like a bad omen.

Then the weather, which had been mild, suddenly turned wintry. Snow fell when there should have been spring. The Colonel recorded gloomily: 'Terrible difficulty was experienced getting the transport along, the weather being extremely cold and freezing hard.' There was still 'considerable activity displayed by the enemies' artillery, the trenches being heavily shelled'. At last, the pause came: a kind of half-time interval. They marched back past Beuvry and Béthune, to Calonne-Ricouart, a chance to breathe yet no relief from that sense of being trapped. Everybody knew, by now, that there was a big push coming, a new offensive for the summer. Conscription had been introduced: vast numbers of soldiers were being accumulated for the attack. Now, just for a short time, the Footballers' Battalion had a break. In this gap on the march on the Somme, after the 'rotten' days, came Tim's most glorious ninety minutes on a foreign field. The glory of his football career seemed remote, yet this was to become his moment as the people's footballer.

The official Flanders Cup was still in progress. Major Buckley continued to run his side. On 31 March, they won a semi-final, defeating the King's Royal Rifles by six goals to nil, without Woodward but with young Jack Cock, of Huddersfield Town, Sergeant-Major Cock, as the striker. Joe Bailey managed a goal in between the big man's four goals. No one was holding their breath about the final, which would be played within the next fortnight. Results had to be sent to headquarters before arrangements could be completed. Meanwhile, as Buckley recorded in a letter that found its way into the press, they also won a parallel rugby match. The Major sent home the message that 'you can see we still keep having a game'.

The first day of April was different. That day belonged to Tim and to the real spirit of football, as it had been; one of the most powerful developments in British popular culture and everyday life in the thirty years before this horror that threatened to swallow everything. The Footballers' Battalion finally had to answer a genuine football challenge, from the Royal Garrison Artillery, which had its own proud tradition. One of its teams had lifted an important Army cup back home prior to embarkation, with a side based upon men from Bolton Wanderers, one of the old clubs of the Football League. Unlike the games in the Flanders Cup, there really was something at stake on the pitch this time, a result that might not be a foregone conclusion in deciding the best team of the Western Front. Men made their way to the match from every surrounding regiment, if they had the chance. The crowd that day in Hersen was in the thousands, even though there was no official organisation of facilities.

In the vaults of the Imperial War Museum, there are a few flickering frames of film showing soldiers trying to play football on the Western Front. Interviews accumulated since refer consistently to the importance of this largely lost experience to those involved. Even the historian Niall Ferguson, who confesses to being largely unmoved by the game, acknowledges that the men, and especially the Englishmen, played football 'obsessively' whenever there was the smallest of opportunities. Yet there are almost no proper accounts of these occasions, not surprisingly, perhaps, when you think of the circumstances at the time. Even Joe Bailey, of the Footballers' Battalion itself, recorded only the scorers, and the same is true of most diarists' records. A fair few results made their way – against the rules – into the battalion's diaries but even the most passionate fan hardly dared add details there.

This game was different, visible in the ebb and flow of personal detail, as if it were a match at home. Yet the reporter had been at the front himself since early in the war so it meant far more to him than any ordinary match could. Driver J. Nolan had been a professional soldier before the war. In fact, he was coming to the end of his Army contract, not having signed a war-time form 'for the duration'. It was hard luck indeed that conscription was going to bring him all the way back, as soon as he was freed from his contract. He was driving supplies with the Army Service Corps, close to a respite and a trip home to his native Hull. He pulled over to watch when he saw something going on and, being a true fan, he set about recording the action of that afternoon. He had evidently been an avid reader of football match reports as he got the manner and the content exactly right. He was so proud of his work – and rightly so – that he posted his report to the *Hull Sports Express* which, aware of the appeal, ran it on its front page with a suitable heading: 'Footballers' Battalion. Stirring Play On The Battlefield. Hull Driver's Description'. It was – and remains – a unique testimony, an expression of the depth of the nation's passion for football and of what the game had come to mean. These lost events, so overshadowed by the vast slaughter going on around them, were the expression of an unconscious defiance, a refusal to mourn or to die tamely.

From Nolan's entranced chronicle, it is evident that the Battalion's players themselves got to decide who would be the skipper. There was no doubt about that: Tim Coleman – F904, Private Coleman – was back in control of his life for one afternoon. He was, after all, 'an international man'. He was also the ever popular Tim, among the players as well as the pre-war fans. The team that he selected, and that Nolan registered with painstaking affection and recollection, expressed Tim's influence on every aspect of the occasion. This was his chance and he was not going to let it be wasted. There was a lot of thought and feeling behind his line-up. Not surprisingly, given the nature of the captain, there were several 'characters'. In goal was Bob Whiting, the man who faced Tim back in 1906, when Chelsea and Woolwich Arsenal met for the first time in football's First Division at Stamford Bridge. Before 60,000 fans that day, Whiting had kept him out, though Tim had been the most dangerous of his opponents. Bob was very much a man of Coleman's era, and a man after his own heart. He had come up from the roots of the southern game, making his reputation in an FA Cup-tie when his team, little Tunbridge Wells Rangers, managed to hold Norwich City and force a replay. The press that afternoon had declared that Whiting appeared to have as many arms as an octopus to repel the opposing forwards. He had kept goal successfully for Chelsea when they first reached the top division, replacing Willie Foulke, who had gone back up north. After some triumphs in the capital, Whiting had gone to Brighton to see out his career. He was still their goalie when he signed up for the Footballers' Battalion in January 1915. As ever, Corporal Whiting was one of the lads, always friendly and modest, they said. Though he had made his name in Kent, he came from East London and remained a West Ham fan. He was Tim's natural choice between the sticks.

In defence, Tim called up another of his old friends, Alf West, whom he had come across more than once during their careers. Formerly of Liverpool, West was finishing his playing days with Notts County when Tim arrived at neighbours Forest. Alf had always been a crowd favourite too wherever he went, having perfected a kind of football circus trick that they called Alf's 'double shuffle kick'. He was very much Tim's kind of player, an entertainer and a conjurer, with his roots in the old times.

A different side of Tim was expressed in finding a place for Private Billy Spittal, who had trained at Arsenal in 1913 but struggled to win a place in the team. Now he got his chance in midfield. How could Tim let an Arsenal youngster down? He knew what it felt like to struggle to make a name for himself at that club! Another young Londoner, Gallagher of Spurs, was in alongside Billy. In the front line, accompanying himself as captain, Tim put Jack Doran, of Coventry City, whose enlistment had been announced at the same time as his own. An Irishman brought up in Newcastle, Jack was a big man, strong and fast, who should really have had a place in the Battalion's official first eleven. Though Buckley valued Doran as a corporal, he didn't rate him as highly on the pitch – not yet, though he was to give him his chance back in the professional game. Tim probably knew him through Joe Bailey, with whom he had played against the Northamptonshires back in November. Doran was in Bailey's section, with Albert Holmes, also from City, whom Tim put on the wing.

Tim put his personal stamp on the selection of the team, however, with one other player in particular. On the left wing was a Liverpool lad called Jackie Sheldon. This was a real statement by Tim, recognised as such by everyone that day on and off the field. There was no question that Jackie was good enough to play in the big game. He was fast, slight and agile and his greatest moment on the field had been scoring the winning goal in an FA Cup semi-final, though he had been unable to win the final itself as Burnley beat Liverpool 1-0 in the last final to be played at Crystal Palace. Before joining Liverpool, Jackie had been at Manchester United, where Tim's friend Billy Meredith had kept him out of the team most Saturdays. Jackie had been a regular in the official Battalion eleven but he had missed out on the entire Flanders Cup campaign, just as Tim had been left out by Everton all those years ago after his defiant decision to join the Outcasts FC in the summer of 1909. Jackie, too, had become an outcast, but of a different kind.

sphere they will find a way to atone for the blot they have brought upon good old English sport.' Tim had spent his entire career fighting against the types who talked glibly of 'good old English sport', and in their own gentlemanly way conspired to rip off the players. Those outraged editors even went so far as to insist that the ban must apply to Army football: 'It has been said that it is hard that the suspended men should be debarred from Army football. Are Army football and league football so different?'

The other men involved were back home with the 2nd Footballers' Battalion, or had not yet enlisted or been conscripted. It was Jackie who was the target for criticism: 'The lads in the trenches have a bit of pride both in their football and in their regiments, and it seems to the writer that the suspensions will reach a good deal further than the limits of the British Isles should the suspended players attempt to extend their influence to football behind the firing lines.' There was even a question of whether a man such as Sheldon should be allowed to serve under the colours of the game at all: 'Is the Army a refuge for football black sheep?' The Liverpool *Football Echo* trumpeted: 'Will the Battalion take action?'

In line with official thinking as usual, Frank Buckley certainly took action. When news of the match-fixing scandal reached the front, in January, Buckley expelled Jackie, previously his regular choice on the wing, from the cup team. Despite his denials at that time, Buckley said Jackie was never to dishonour the colours of the Footballers' Battalion again. To be fair to Buckley, he was reflecting the general mood, which was one of hostility towards the guilty parties. For those who had fixed the match, it was not a good time to be in a hostile Battalion. One of the other players exposed, Tim's old Manchester Outcast friend Sandy Turnbull, applied to leave the 2nd Footballers' Battalion back home, and transferred to the East Surreys, where he was soon to be killed in the trenches. Meanwhile, Jackie was stuck with a hostile Battalion at the front.

When the papers brought news of the 'death' of Tim that January, they also carried many headlines about a great footballing scandal. Jackie had been the villain of the piece. It concerned a case of match-fixing. The game in question had been between Manchester United and Liverpool, on Good Friday, 1915. United had been struggling at the bottom of the First Division, competing with Chelsea to avoid relegation. Liverpool had had a reasonably solid season and were lying mid-table yet, against the run of form, the Merseyside team lost 2-0 and reports said that they were hopeless. Two days later they thrashed Blackburn, a top side. The result against United aroused suspicion, but general alarm was raised when a bookmaker revealed that a lot of bets had been placed on the correct score. This led to the FA launching an official inquiry, the findings of which were announced in December 1915, as the Battalion reached the front line. The newspaper reports made the outcome clear: 'J. Sheldon, the well known Liverpool winger, was among the players who have been permanently suspended for malpractice.'

Altogether nine men were found guilty and banned from the game. Sheldon, who had been at both clubs, was central to the scandal. He was widely described as 'the black sheep' and there was widespread uproar at the scandal. Some took a contrary view. 'It may be argued that these men faced great temptation because of the reduction in their wages. It could be argued in mitigation of the crime that their income was supplementary.' It was the old class-based view of professionals, gentlemen against players.

The outraged editors and writers, from their lofty positions, indulged in condemnation of Sheldon and his fellow conspirators. There was criticism of the footballers as a class, of their temptations, of the greed that is a disgrace to the national game. Some of those mentioned had joined the Footballers' Battalion.

Tim saw things rather differently. In the Easter of 1915, everyone had known that professional football was about to be suspended because of the war. The opportunity to make some money out of the game was the last chance the players would get for some time. Could they really be blamed? Tim evidently thought not, because he had Jackie back in action, on the wing, for the first time since he was condemned. He was continuing his long fight for players' rights, as he saw them, uncompromisingly, even on the Western Front. It was almost a reflex action on his part, and he was used to being out of step even with his fellow professionals. The rest of his team was made up of solid League lads, from Norwich to Stoke, from Coventry to Croydon Common. This was Tim Coleman's representative eleven, his England team and a side that embodied his football world.

The sun shone that day, 1 April, on the packed rows of soldiers as Tim's team came out to play against the Royal Garrison Artillery. The RGA were indeed a far stronger team than any the official Battalion team had played thus far. Captained by a young officer called Shields, and with some professionals in their line-up as well, these men were not here as cannon fodder. They had their own point to prove. No one needed marching bands to drum up a crowd for this occasion.

Out, in the all-white kit of the Footballers' Battalion, came Tim and his men. The pitch was set up as best as could be done, lines, goals and all. The referee was Sergeant-Major Frost, from the RGA, with two neutral linesmen to keep him in order. The atmosphere was rousing and the uproar attracted drivers from passing convoys, who pulled over to watch. This was one of the worst days on the Western Front so far. Not much more than thirty miles away, at Verdun, the German guns had launched the heaviest bombardment in human history. The French stronghold was being blown to pieces, with huge losses. Only now was the true horror of this war being revealed. Everyone at Hersen that day, in the crowd and on the pitch, knew that the big push was coming and that those German guns would soon be aimed at them. It made the game not less important, but more; for that ninety minutes nothing else seemed to matter, on the field or off it. It was like an island of life in a sea of death.

Exactly three months before the first morning of the Somme offensive, these two British Army football teams lined up and Sergeant-Major Frost blew his whistle. Some may think this was absurd, yet it was not so to the men taking part and they knew what was happening around them. Tim Coleman stood by the ball, at the centre spot with Jack Doran, and the young Irishman tapped it towards his captain. Tim watched the ball bumping towards him over the uneven surface. The moment clearly stirred Tim deeply. He was so distracted by the emotion of it all that, as the ball came towards him, he forgot to start playing. The Garrison Artillery forwards were on to him in an instant, and the ball was soon on its way towards Tim's own defenders. He pulled himself together. Turning, he saw an artillery-man rushing into the Footballers' penalty area but that man ran straight into Alf West, who was not about to let the professionals down. The young gunner went flying and the ball came back towards Tim. Gallagher, the Spurs boy, took it forward and ran straight into one of the Bolton lads, losing possession again. This was going to be a real match, nothing like the artificial exhibitions put on in the official cup games, when the Footballers' met almost no real opposition. At last, proper football had come to the Western Front.

Tim came rushing back into midfield, eager to be involved after his mistake. He got the ball at his feet and set off with a dribble that caught the imagination of Nolan particularly: 'Coleman got his men on the run with one of his old-style dribbles.' They were 'his men' indeed. Bossed around and marginalised in the official life of the Battalion, Tim was transformed here into a genuine leader. And Nolan was right in his use of 'old style' to describe Tim's style. This was not just English football coming to life, it was the best of the Edwardian game. Did Nolan exaggerate? He may or may not have been describing literally the events on that pitch, but this was how it felt to him. What could be more important or real than that? Nolan also captured the meaning of Tim Coleman for that era. If Coleman's story has subsequently been lost – and it undoubtedly has – that is because the men who stood around that field on 1 April 1916 belonged to a generation on its way to destruction, and even if individuals survived, their culture and experience did not, except for luminous fragments such as this eyewitness report, which is the football equivalent of Max Arthur's 'lost voices' of the Great War.

Back on the pitch, this was no exhibition game. The Garrison defenders were not giving anything away. They saw Tim coming. As in happier times, Tim was caught up in his own run and did not look up. They stole the ball from him and set out on a counter-attack 'checking the advance in smart fashion'. The game went back and forth in midfield after that. Then Tim saw the ball go out to his left, landing at the feet of Jackie Sheldon, 'the black sheep', the man to whom Tim had given a place in defiance not only of the critics back home but of many in the Battalion who were now watching. Jackie was famously temperamental. Even with Liverpool, in his prime, he would drive the fans mad, playing with the ball when he ought to pass it. Now he was nervous, and desperate to get a run going. The opposing winger romped away with the ball, Jackie was struggling.

Twenty minutes gone and the game remained goalless. The credit went to the Garrison boys against the professionals. Then Stuart, of Croydon Common, a decent side in the Southern First Division, took the ball forward and crashed a shot into the Garrison goal 'amidst loud applause'. This was another moment the watching Tommies had been waiting for, the chance to cheer a goal once more. It was like being back on the terraces, for an instant.

The Footballers' Battalion now stepped up their game. The ball went out to the left again, to Sheldon, an outcast even among this collection of eccentrics, outsiders and old-time heroes. The defenders were out of position, he had the goal at his mercy. Thin, fair-haired Jackie Sheldon came storming in, just as he had when Liverpool won that FA Cup semi-final against Aston Villa. This time the magic was not working, perhaps he was trying too hard. With only the goalkeeper to beat he scuffed the shot embarrassingly wide. Jeers and mockery erupted from the men gathered round, it was 'a very poor attempt at goal', as they scoffed afterwards. They all knew about the scandal too, and they were enjoying the discomfiture of the villain.

Perhaps as a result of Jackie's miss, the Garrison lads started to stir themselves again. It was nearly half-time and the Footballers' Battalion were hanging on to their single goal lead. Tim was getting heated. Even after those months in the trenches, finding corpses in the mud, hearing about injuries to his friends, he found some new energy, or the memory of old energy, and took the ball on towards the opposing goal: 'Coleman began to lead his men on the attack again.' He had shrugged off the burden of obedience, all the saluting and 'yes sir-ing'. He was a leader in his own world. He was the captain, as he had been back on Arsenal's summer tour of Europe that had ended in Belgium, not too far from where he was now. Looking up this time, he sent a long pass to young Billy Spittal, the Arsenal lad. In that moment, the ball passed from Woolwich Arsenal, all the way back in 1902, to the new club, the Arsenal of Highbury. Billy did not let his captain down. The Garrison keeper rushed off his line in a panic, but Spittal slotted the ball home.

During the interval, Tim must have insisted that the Footballers' start playing differently. He wanted to bring the game to life, to play it the way he knew and believed it should be played. When the whistle blew for the restart, Stuart and Tim were passing the ball back and forward between them, in 'some smart movements'. This was Tim's instinctive way of playing, right back to his Woolwich and even Northampton Town days. All along, plenty of critics had disapproved of this sort of passing style, but he had stuck to it. And now he wanted to show the fans what football could really be, that footballers were the true source of football as entertainment – for nothing as well, not even their four pounds a week. He was still fighting against all those 'anonymous' experts back to his Arsenal days, who wanted to abandon the passing game and go for route-one football, 'the long swinging ball'.

The Garrison men showed that they were also 'up for it' after a break. Tim watched as the shots flew in and Bob Whiting was called into action again, deflecting the best one round a post for a corner, and then rushing out to punch that cross clear. For Tim, and for those in the crowd, it was like going back a decade and seeing a First Division game of the high Edwardian days. Eventually, the opposition did get a shot past Whiting. Two-one: was there going to be a twist in the tale of the game? The passes continued to flow until Jack Doran had the ball at his feet. He went round several defenders with 'a neat dribble' and fired home to make it 3-1. The honour of the Footballers' was safe. Coleman and Doran provided some more neat passes to entertain the spectators before the end, and the Garrison men managed a couple more attacks. Then the whistle blew and Tim's team had won. Even the outcast Sheldon was swept up in the cheering and the enthusiasm. It was the start of a long road back for him, but at least it was a beginning.

When Tim talked about football on the Western Front, in a later interview, he expressed his attitude with his characteristic bittersweet tone: 'As you may guess, we enjoyed playing football as we never did at home. Our games made life endurable.' He implied again here that there were harder sides to a football life back home. But you can tell from these words – and feel from the game just recounted – that for Coleman, football was a way of life, a way of living. And here he was, staring death in the face.

The clock was ticking towards the trenches but, on 11 April, the official Footballers' Battalion team still had to play in the final of the Flanders Cup, at Hersen. This was the Army's official football day behind the lines but it was a very different occasion to Coleman's free-flowing play only a fortnight previously. Today the game had to be just so. Everything had been planned to perfection. Yet little detail has survived of the game or the occasion, even in the Battalion Diary. It was not first and foremost a football occasion, which probably explains the lack of letters in the papers, other than the bare facts (and some more colourful incidents after the game too).

Major Buckley was in charge, of the football and also of the Battalion. The Colonel was on leave. Buckley would leave nothing to chance: he was already preparing for his post-war career as a manager. It was the perfect opportunity to show off his credentials. He was also a compulsive organiser, and an extremely good one too. It was a good thing because Brigadier-General Daley would be in attendance. He would present the medals to the winners and losers, and the cup. This meant that nothing could be allowed to go wrong. The weather was fine but still there had to be a proper seated area, with covering, for the Brigadier-General and his party. No groups of men could be permitted to surge in a rush around the touchline to take their positions to watch the game. Battalion bands were supposed to lead the marching soldiers into the ground for such official occasions. Military order would remain throughout. You could not have a Brigadier-General watching an uproar.

There had to be changing areas for the teams. If there were no outhouses still standing at the venue, then there had to be tents. Above all, the pitch had to be marked out as if it were the Crystal Palace. The Brigadier-General would have welcomed the officials and players, hands would be shaken, anthems played. For referees, let alone players, these were great occasions. It was at this time that a young lieutenant called Stanley Rous, who was stationed in Egypt, spent several afternoons a month refereeing any Army match he could find, and he especially loved cup games. These were the occasions that, as he later said, prepared him for a career as an international referee, and, subsequently, as the secretary of the FA and president of FIFA, the world game's governing body.

On the pitch the official Battalion forward line, led by the tall, striking figure of Sergeant-Major Jack Cock, was unstoppable. Before the war, Jack had only just got into the Huddersfield Town first team. He had headed north from his London home in order to become a professional and was hanging on to the game by his fingertips. By the time he got back from the war, he was on a different path to success. In the first post-war season, he would play only a few games for Huddersfield before he got his first England cap. He was to score England's first goal after the war. Then he was off to Chelsea and, down the Kings Road, he became a symbol of the new era. This cup final behind the lines was the turning point for Jack. It was also a springboard for Major Buckley, carefully hosting the visiting dignitaries and making sure that everything was correct. He too would return to new possibilities. He had come to the end of his playing days and he was just beginning his managerial career.

For Tim, cheering or joking alongside Jack Doran and Alf West in the crowd, it was merely another afternoon off. The players actually enjoyed playing the parts of spectators for once: they chanted their friends' names and annoyed each other with a continual stream of banter, comparing their respective home grounds to that dug-up field.

In the event, the game was a non-event and the Footballers' Battalion took the cup by winning 11-0. Brigadier-General Daley presented the medals and the trophy. All was as expected. Even Joe Bailey, medallist though he was, did not linger over the game sufficiently to record the goal-scorers. This was someone else's triumph, perhaps Brigadier-General Kentish, who had founded the Flanders Cup. A triumph it was, but of organisation and planning, rather than of football, as the game against the Royal Garrison Artillery had been.

There was some drama associated with the game, but it surfaced months later in the columns of the *Athletic News*, as had so many details of this strange tour of duty. The formalities of the occasion had been completed. Percy Barnfather, winger for Barnsley and Croydon Common, and now a Battalion sergeant, let his military discipline lapse for a moment and slipped back into his old football self. He grabbed the battered leather ball and headed back towards his quarters. That ball would be a different kind of war souvenir. He had played in every match of the Flanders Cup and if anyone deserved the souvenir it was surely Percy. He was not the most talented player in the Footballers' Battalion and he had maybe earned his place more because he was a sergeant than because of his ability as a winger. Still, this was something to send back to his parents in Barnsley. Even he, rising in the ranks as he was, waited for no orders about what to do with the ball.

The Major was too sharp for him though: Buckley had his own plans for that ball. It was to be his publicity master stroke. The Battalion had authorised a proper celebration of its Flanders Cup success. The match ball was to be signed not only by the eleven who played but also by many of the best-known players back home. Altogether forty-two men signed the Flanders Cup ball: there was the Nottingham Forest group of Coleman, Mercer and Gibson; Jack Cock and Fred Bullock, of Huddersfield Town; Alf West was there for Liverpool and Notts County; and there too were Sid Wheelhouse, of Grimsby Town, and Alan Foster, of Reading. Sid was from football's older generation, his club's skipper and a pro since the early Edwardian time. Alan had been a star at Reading, where he had gone from his native Rotherham to start a football career. He scored the winner in a famous Cup-tie against the giants of Aston Villa, who asked to sign him that day. The Reading directors refused. Instead, he got to sign this ball to testify that he was in football's elite. Sid and Alan did not have long to revel in their triumph. Both were to die in the carnage that followed.

Frank Buckley sent the ball home to his friend Frank Shields, a well-known actor on stage and screen. Shields auctioned it for charity just before Christmas 1916. It was conceived in a moment of victory, but that celebrity ball had by then become a symbol not of the Flanders Cup but of the Somme. When the *Athletic News* reported the auction, they called it 'the historic ball bearing signatures of many good lads. Some alas will take the field no more.' Tim had become part of the official squad, after all. His was a name well worth adding to the auction.

# Into the Darkness

The last days of April 1916 were dominated by waves of German gas attacks after their failure to take Verdun. A war that had seemed already to be as grim as possible on the ground was about to get worse. This spring of 1916 also brought the introduction of two new medals: 'the Military Cross, for officers, and the Military Medal, open to men and women. The Military Medal was intended principally for private soldiers.' It seemed unlikely that either of these innovations would concern Private Coleman, who was hanging on in the ranks and waiting for the next football match.

The nadir was approaching. The Footballers' Battalion spent most of May in what the Colonel called the support area of 'Cité Calonne'. Then, on 1 June 1916, exactly two months after the match against the Royal Garrison Artillery, a huge series of explosions went off in no man's land, beyond the positions occupied by the Battalion. It was the build-up to the big push. The tactic that day was to make craters beyond the front line and then to advance and occupy them. The Germans understood this tactic perfectly and attempted, in turn, to seize the holes for themselves. That evening, from about nine o'clock, the players, mainly in B Company, flowed out into no man's land for a fight.

All around, men fell to the ground: young Tetley of 7th Platoon had a stomach wound, Jack Harvey was blown to pieces. The young officers who had held the company together were suffering badly: Skerry was dead and so was Bradstreet, along with many of the boys who cheered the players on in their last matches. Into the small hours they carried on, until they had 'consolidated' the craters. The Battalion lost seventy-five men that one night, including a young winger, Blades, who had played for Walthamstow Avenue before the war, and had been advancing his career in the Battalion itself, in the hope of better days to come. Buckley, as brave as he was ambitious, himself got the DSO.

Having been delayed by bad weather for a week, 1 July became day one of the Somme offensive. At 7.28 a.m., ten mines were exploded under the German trenches. Eyewitness reports in the Imperial War Museum collection speak of 'The whole village actually lifted up out of the earth.' Then: 'When the whistle went everyone climbed up the scaling ladders and through holes in the trench.' At an agonisingly slow pace, the long-planned advance began. Slowly, the British forces emerged into the light. The German machine-gunners were supposed to have been put out of action by a week-long barrage. In fact, they were ready and taking aim.

Among the East Surreys, Captain Nevill famously asked, in Gilbert's words, 'if he could furnish each platoon with a football and allow them to kick it forward and follow it'. The commanding officer assented but warned that when 'a man came across the football, he could kick it forward but mustn't chase after it.' They did not get far enough for it to matter. The 2nd Footballers' Battalion was in the initial advance and included several friends of Tim's, especially Wilf Nixon, the old Fulham goalie. Wilf made sure that he stayed as safe as possible, 'going casual' as he said afterwards. Fred Parker, of the Orient, was in that advance too. Soon the Battalion started to lose men, such as Oscar Linkson, a Manchester United defender, who was one of the few who had not joined the Outcasts that summer of 1909. All along the front line footballers fell among their fans: the Heart of Midlothian club suffered particularly bad losses, since its entire squad had signed up in C Company of the 16th Royal Scots.

Meanwhile, the 1st Footballers' were among the reserves moving forward that terrible day and reached the front line on the evening of 2 July, with the sound of heavy artillery in the background. They had their first action at midnight on 3 July, losing three men in the process as they fought in support of the King's Royal Rifles. Then they had a pause, shuttling back and forward on trains and in forced marches, as the offensive stalled and tactics became indecisive. They found themselves at Cabaret Rouge, about fifty kilometres from Albert and the Somme River. It was still a dangerous time. Tim's Grimsby opponents from that game in 1914 were suffering badly: Sid Wheelhouse was hurt, along with the forward Alf Gregson and the midfielder Frank Martin.

The marches got tougher as they got into position. On 18 July, the 17th Middlesex were on a forced march, filling in the gaps at the front as so many other units were doing. Everyone knew what was coming next: another assault. Then, along the battered road, one of the men fell: F904, Private Coleman was down, injured. He had not been hit, though, he had merely turned an ankle, according to his medical record deep in the National Archives files. It was an old football injury, probably the one that kept him out back in February 1915, the weekend he decided to enlist. Now, on his way to the front line, he could not walk any more. They carried him until they could get him to a field hospital. And for Tim and the war, that was that for the moment – just in time perhaps. His life had its lucky side too, whatever his tendency to see the dark side of things.

He spent the next fortnight in a field hospital. It was only a short break, and it did not enable him to avoid the Battle of the Somme completely, but he did miss one particularly bad moment, as bad as any. When Tim returned to his company, on 3 August, they were resting near Waterlot Farm. The weather was warm. The guns were not far away, but this was the closest they had come to a break for a while. Tim's mates had plenty to tell him, and there were gaps in their ranks for him to see for himself.

The Footballers' Battalion had been part of the famous – or infamous – advance into Delville Wood, one of the most murderous of the whole offensive. This all took place in the tightly compressed arena of the conflict, only an hour and a half or so in modern travelling time from the coast at Boulogne and no more than seventy kilometres from Béthune, where the Battalion had been based at the start of their deployment. They had got effectively nowhere, from their own point of view, whatever the wider strategy implied. In the woodland advance, they had scrambled along tangled pathways littered with bodies from previous assaults. The Germans had machine-gun nests around the edges of this dense wood, and they had been firing for days and nights on British and South African forces trying to break through. A reporter for *The Times* sent back a dispatch headed: 'What Wood Fighting Means'. His words leave no room for any doubt of the experience towards which the Footballers' Battalion were now travelling: 'It is difficult to convey to anyone at a distance the desperate character of the fighting which goes on in these woods. It is perhaps worst in the dark, but whether in the dark, in broad daylight, when the twilight of dawn, it is always terrible.'

When the Battalion's attack began, the situation was particularly bad. One of the first to go was young Willie Jonas, who had scored for Clapton Orient against Tim's Nottingham Forest in April 1915, when they were all new recruits together. Jonas's death was relayed by his friend Richard McFadden, who had been with him. The whole situation became too much for Jonas and, despite his friend's efforts, he simply got up from the crater in which he was sheltering and walked into opposing fire. Frank Buckley had disappeared into the same inferno, taking Tim's favourite centre-forward, Jack Doran, with him. Jack was still there to tell Tim the story. The two of them had become cut off and had no idea which way to go amid the gunfire. Then, through the smoke, had come, like the cavalry in a cowboy story, Richard McFadden to guide them home. Buckley was wounded soon afterwards and taken out of the fight for the moment, though he had done enough to get mentioned in dispatches. Doran was still standing, and would win a medal for his efforts. So too would McFadden, although the Orient centre-forward, who had been just behind Tim in the list of Second Division scorers that final season, had himself been wounded by shrapnel.

Among the other casualties was Fred Bullock, the Huddersfield defender whom Tim had pitted his wits against for Fulham and Forest: he was shot through the shoulder. Tommy Barber, of Aston Villa, who had played with Tim for Clapton Orient in that on-off season in the autumn of 1915, had a leg shattered, running messages through the woods. Those who had seen him said that he was sure he would never play again. Ted Hanney, the Manchester City captain, was wounded, and Norman Wood, who had played for Stockport, was killed: he had been part of the group of young players around Tim's friend Joe Bailey. Altogether, in that woodland offensive, the Footballers' Battalion had reported 35 dead and nearly 200 wounded, out of a total of just over 1,300 servicemen. The official record read: 'All ranks behaved with great gallantry. The devotion to duty was magnificent. The division has been thanked by GHQ for capturing the wood. On that same day, 31 July, the official stamp 'Killed in Action' was put on Private William Jonas's service record.

Tim had gained only a short respite and was soon in the thick of the action. Three days after Tim returned, the Battalion were involved in another major offensive. This was the massive Waterlot Farm onslaught, a new attempt to break through the German lines. It was reported in weary tones in the official diary: 'Although all ranks have had a very trying time in Delville Wood, they were called out to attack Z.Z. trench.' They had progressed, in fact, less than a kilometre from the wood. It was effectively another part of the same battle.

Tim and B Company set off at half past four in the morning, once a flare had blazed above the German lines. The advance guard was sent to occupy the first German trench, but they were bombed out of it. Several more waves of British troops moved forward and all were driven back. Promised reinforcements and machine-guns did not arrive. By contrast, the Germans had well-prepared gun emplacements. Just after seven o'clock it emerged 'that practically the whole of the party who entered the German trench was killed, wounded or captured.' The confusion worsened and in the end the Battalion lost twenty-nine men on the day; another nine died later of their wounds, one hundred and fifteen more were wounded and forty-five further men were missing. Altogether, that was more than 10 per cent of the Battalion killed or hurt in three hours of fighting. B Company suffered especially. The symbolic loss of the day was Alan Foster, the lad from Rotherham who had been a Reading forward. In all he scored fifty-three goals in one hundred and forty-six League matches for Reading: not a bad record.

As the terrible September went on, Tim's football landscape was being shattered. Jackie Sheldon was badly hurt and sent home to hospital. Tim's close friend, and now Company Sergeant-Major, Tommy Gibson, of Nottingham Forest, who had enjoyed Tim's denial of his death, was also sent home suffering from shell shock. Alf West, who had played so well in that game against the Artillery, was 'wounded in action'. Harold Iremonger, the Forest goalkeeper, was shot through the thigh. Sergeant H. Gibson, one of the men who played with Tim for Clapton Orient, was badly wounded.

Even during the Somme offensive a week of leave was still possible, and Tim got his break after nearly two months of fighting. On Saturday, 23 September, in the midst of the battle, the little red-headed player who had been 'Forest's popular signing' of 1914 was back in their ground in Nottingham for an afternoon. He had seven days' leave and he was going to spend one afternoon at the football, even though there was only a Midlands regional game to see. He needed the crowd, and the press, and the people from the club, after all the things he had seen. He was certainly recognised: everyone knew who he was, and where he had been. An item in the *Athletic News* conveyed the warmth of the whole occasion. Yet there was also a sense of unease, not surprisingly considering what he had just come from, and where he was shortly to return. The poet Edmund Blunden reflected on going home during the Battle of the Somme: 'I became increasingly uncertain of the value of returning home to England for periods of leave. Of course being welcomed back and sitting down again with one's own, and going for a little trot, and seeing a few people left whom one knew, that was a great thing. Yet not being able to discourse about the things which were at the forefront of one's feelings, that was difficult.'

By this stage of his war Tim knew all there was to know about life and death at the front: after Waterlot Farm, there was nothing hidden. He had advanced past trenches full of dead bodies, he had known what it meant to lose young men in the prime of their life, men whose football promise made the loss of their futures all the more poignant. Even before that, he thought the Army was the 'worst team' he had ever signed for. But, as Blunden said, it was impossible to bridge the gulf that separated the experience of the front from the world of those at home. 'He is one of the soldiers of the Footballers' Battalion who have escaped injury after being in the midst of the fighting for over a year.' The best you could do was to look as if you were managing. But, like others who returned home for a brief visit, Tim's mind was on those he had left behind.

Another of his former colleagues, John Hunter, of Woolwich Arsenal, wrote home to report an encounter with the Footballers' Battalion and Tim: 'Tim Coleman is A1, and he's still keeping things cheery by his wit and his repertoire of jokes.' That letter, of course, made its way into the press, as it was meant to do, adding to the positive impression Tim had left in person.

When he returned from home leave, Tim found yet more gaps in the old line-up. The squad was shrinking and his old football world was collapsing fast. Rain had been falling heavily at the front. A party of volunteers had been out to try to repair the parapet protecting the trench, which was slipping in the mud. Among them was Corporal Wheelhouse, of Grimsby Town. While they were working, gas shells landed, and all eleven men in the working party died. Wheelhouse even managed to walk to the field station, but he did not make it any farther. By the end of September, it was reported that 'the Footballers' have had about 500 casualties and possibly 100 in all ranks have been killed.' The *Football Post* added: 'Those are facts for the critics to put in their pipes – if they smoke.' (The critics were those who still persisted in thinking of footballers as somehow less patriotic than other men because they had carried on playing in 1914.) These casualties now totalled half of the Battalion's total number.

They carried on advancing and during the build-up to the second big push, at the end of October 1916, they were marching up a busy road, mixed in with many other units. In the confusion, German shells began to rain upon them. Among those killed that day was Richard McFadden, and the Plymouth Argyle midfielder Baker. The men who had played in that game between Forest and Orient in April 1915 were becoming fewer and fewer.

Eventually the advance came to an end, as the winter of 1916-17 closed in. After the harrowing and horrific experience of the Somme, the mood among the football soldiers, as in the Army generally, was subdued. The losses were too fresh. They did their best, though, to keep their spirits up. Private Dodds, of Millwall, wrote home proudly to his club about himself and his fellow players, enclosing a photograph: 'Accept this picture as a souvenir of the war from a few of the old pros that are left with the Battalion.' It was hardly cheerful. The losses were overwhelming. Dodds felt as though he was one of only a small group of surviving players, but football did still provide some hope, even in these circumstances: 'Every player on the photograph has been out here for two years,' said Dodds, 'and although we have had some rough times, we still retain very good form when we have an opportunity for a game.' They were still trying to get a game wherever they could: 'We arrive at some village for a few days and of course our first thought after a day or so of rest is to fix a game up,' he said. These men had been shuttled around, by train and route march, from place to place until none of them really knew where he was any more. But the moment there was any opportunity at all, what mattered was to get a team together once more.

Even then, this was harder to achieve than it had been the previous year. As Dodds said: 'Very often a suitable ground is hard to find, and to give you an idea, the worst grounds at home are very often croquet lawns [compared] to where we play!' In earlier days, Army matches, such as Tim's game with the Royal Artillery, had managed almost to recreate the feeling of home. Now, if anything, these games emphasised the distance from their familiar environment. Dodds and his friends had to wander about trying to find a flat space to play. Their weariness spills over into his account. Then he catches himself and strikes the enthusiastic tone he has been trying to maintain: 'However, our keenness overcomes this and then we play for four or five days.' To young Dodds, it sometimes seemed as if the rest of the British Army was queueing up to vie for the honour of being the ones to defeat the Footballers' Battalion: 'Sometimes we have teams waiting for us as we come out of the line to try and lower our colours.' Exhaustion and pride are hard to tell apart in these words that catch the declining phase of the Battalion, which extended over another hard year before they came to an end as a unit, denuded still further by the next wave of battles.

One of Tim's friends seemed to have missed all this action, on the battlefield and on what passed for the football pitch. Corporal Bob Whiting was conspicuous by his absence from the Battalion. As the fighting on the Somme came to a close, there was another shock for Tim: Whiting was brought back from Brighton as a prisoner. He had been staying with his family since the summer, having simply not come back from leave. He had been kept in the notorious prison section of the Bull Ring camp near Étaples in France, and then brought back to the Battalion. He was due to be tried by a tribunal for desertion. It had been altogether a bad autumn for Tim's chosen team. Now the most popular goalkeeper in the League from Coleman's London was about to face disgrace and execution.

As recorded carefully in his service record, kept in the National Archives in Kew, south-west London, it was February before the tribunal met. The venue was Albert, one of the key points in the Somme offensive. After much argument on both sides, Bob Whiting was inevitably found guilty of desertion. Against the grain of such tribunals, he was sentenced to a year in military prison and demotion to private. All of that in turn was translated into a conditional return to his unit. Had his popularity had any influence in his treatment? If so, it did not help him for long.

For these bitter months, Tim was carried along in the tide of the vast conflict, as so many men were. April 1917 was the hardest time since the Battle of the Somme ended. It began with the Battle of Arras on 9 April, which cost nearly 36,000 British lives. Immediately after that came Vimy Ridge, where the Canadians suffered huge losses. The whole offensive, organised by the French General Nivelle, was another failure. In late April, as the Germans pushed back against the faltering French forces, the British tried to launch counter-attacks. It was in one of these that the Footballers' took some of their worst losses.

On the evening of 27 April 1917, the Footballers' Battalion formed up for battle opposite a wood and next to a small village. This was to be the ill-fated battle of Oppy Wood. They were no more than five kilometres from the Vimy Ridge itself, where the vast cemetery and memorial now stand. All this time, since the serious fighting began for them in February 1916, they had come about ten kilometres from Givenchy to be here at Oppy.

Once more, they set off around 4.30 in the morning, under a barrage from British guns. It took them only ten minutes to occupy the front-line German trench – because it had been deliberately abandoned. As the Footballers' Battalion advanced, the German retreat stopped. It was a trap. The German soldiers who had left their trenches were waiting for them.

D Company, to which Bob Whiting had been returned, were ordered to 'consolidate' a village that was occupied by the Germans. By eight o'clock the Battalion commander reported 'that the enemy is working round both flanks'. The men in that village had been abandoned. Machine-guns had been waiting prepared for their arrival. Communication broke down. When a runner eventually appeared, 'his evidence made it clear that these troops had been practically exterminated by the superior pressure of the enemy. The few survivors probably surrendered.' Bob Whiting was one of those men who had been 'exterminated' – later reports said that he had been killed going to the aid of a friend. There were rumours that he had been shot as a deserter, rumours that his wife rightly denied, as Kemp and Riddoch report. Tim had lost another of his football generation, and one of his great football friends.

This day was also effectively the end for the 'famous Footballers' Battalion'. Into the autumn, on the way to the Battle of Cambrai, the Battalion trooped back past Lillers, where they played that third round cup-tie in January 1916, and then on to Isbergues, the scene of the first camp and opening match. As November went on, they headed deeper into the territory of the old Somme offensive. All the villages through which they passed had, their new Colonel, Stafford, noted gloomily, been systematically razed to the ground, and when they got to Bapaume, the first objective of the Somme campaign, there was nothing standing at all. They took up their position along the road between Bapaume and Cambrai, and the enemy shells started to rain down. It was even worse than usual. The safe places turned out to be traps: 'all dugouts seemed to be well-known and several had direct hits.'

These terrible days were the beginning of the third offensive, which reduced the entire British army to breaking point. Between 30 November and 3 December 1917, the 1st Footballers' Battalion was on the receiving end of a full-scale German counter-attack on this front, south of Cambrai. On the night of 29 November, their last commanding officer, Colonel Stafford, reported laconically that 'a certain number of mustard shells' had fallen on them. The following day, it felt as though the entire German army was on top of them. D Company was led into battle by Captain McReady-Diarmid, and Tim's B Company by Captain Stansfield, who had been particularly popular with the players. For his actions over the next three days, McReady-Diarmid won the Victoria Cross, at the cost of his own life. Stansfield was hurt, forty soldiers died and one hundred and thirty-eight were wounded. When the Colonel inspected the trenches that they eventually regained, he counted one hundred and fifty German corpses. His pride in his men's achievement was coloured by a tinge of sheer human horror. Even by the standards of the Great War, these were dark days.

Early in January 1918, the 1st Footballers' were resting in a camp of Nissen huts. The weather was terrible: cold and wet. In the evening of 10 January, they marched over to Bapaume where, amid the wreckage, they saw a performance of Cinderella. Bapaume was the original objective of the big push in the summer of 1916; now it hosted Cinderella for the remnants to watch. The next week the first reinforcements for a long time began to arrive. There were forty ordinary soldiers, and two Non-Commissioned Officers. Colonel Stafford recorded with touching amazement and gloom: 'a large percentage just 19 [years old].' It was as if the supply of men had simply dried up; it was in such contrast to the days when the Battalion was formed, when there had seemed such a surplus of young bodies in all those football crowds.

In February 1918, the men of the Footballers' Battalion were formed up once more on parade, in the mist of a winter morning. They were at Metz, still on the Western Front, around fifteen kilometres from Bapaume and the landscape of the Somme. It was a Thursday, the eleventh. Fifteen officers and three hundred 'other ranks' were waiting before their commanding officer. This was the last day of the 'Famous Footballers'. There were not enough men left to sustain a separate Battalion and no more reinforcements were due. Among those depleted ranks there was still F904, Private Coleman, the charmed man according to the notices he had received back home.

Around Tim in that cold morning mist gathered several of his favourite players: Corporal John Doran was one of them. Another was F1695, Private J. Sheldon. He had returned from his injury and had been fighting his own battle on two fronts. There had been a High Court hearing about that match-fixing scandal, a result of an action brought against the FA by one of the other players. Jackie Sheldon turned star witness for the football authorities, against his former friend. He saved the day for the FA and now he was hopeful for the future. It may not have been Tim's way of doing things but here they were still together. Along with them was F708, Private Albert Holmes, previously Holmes of Coventry City, another of that April team. And further along there was F804, Lance Corporal West, of Liverpool and Notts County. Sergeant-Major Gibson had also recovered from shell shock to take his place in the ranks. These were the remnants of the Battalion and, with them, the remnants of Tim Coleman's football life. Private Nutall, of Millwall, who had recorded Tim's goings-on back in January 1916, was still there. They were well supplied with goalkeepers, including Tommy Lonsdale, of Grimsby and Norwich, or S314, Private Webster, of West Ham. They had some good strikers: Lamb, of Sheffield Wednesday, and Woodhouse, of Brighton, among them.

The *Athletic News* counted the roll call of their war: 'Among the actions fought by the famous Footballers' Battalion which went out in

1915 were: Ypres, Festubert [where Woodward was wounded], Vimy Ridge, Delville Wood and Beaumont Hamel.' Now the British Army and their French allies were awaiting the arrival of the Americans on the Western Front. Meanwhile, the remaining forces were being reorganised into more sustainable units. Three years after this Battalion was assembled to defend the honour of the game, they boarded buses to see out the war under new colours. Tim and most of his friends were bound for the 13th Battalion of the Middlesex Regiment that February morning. In fact, one more great crisis of his war was yet to come. So far he had been football's lucky charm, unscathed among the many who had fallen, dead and wounded. But his fighting was far from done and the greatest dangers were yet to be faced.

Meanwhile, the spring of 1918 was the darkest point since the Somme. The Germans launched a huge offensive across the Western Front and came close to breaking through the Allied lines. Losses were immense. For football, the most symbolic was the death of Walter Tull, the game's black officer, the man who the fans may have jeered out of Tottenham Hotspur in 1908 but who had made good with Northampton Town later on. His Battalion commander, Alan Haig-Brown, had also played for Spurs – and he too fell in that onslaught. Captain Eddie Bell, of Southampton, who had been the adjutant for the Footballers' Battalion before joining the General Staff, was another who did not make it.

In the end the Americans did arrive, and the lines held. A brief stalemate followed. The 13th Middlesex carried out a successful raid across the lines. Over the summer, the main loss was the full-back, Fred Bullock, who injured his knee playing one last match behind the lines. He was sent to Tipperary in Ireland to recover. Tim and the rest of the football lads who had transferred to the 13th Middlesex kept going. They were almost at full-time.

# Double Medal Winner

October 1918 was the climax of the fighting and Tim came face to face with the surprising truth about himself as a soldier. The journey to that last month was a hard trek, for the 13th and for all the surviving men in the British forces on the Western Front. By that late summer, as John Terraine quotes in his account of the last year of the conflict, 'There was not only a shortage of experienced officers and NCOs, but the ranks of the infantry units had been filled up with young recruits from home.' Yet, at this low ebb, the Allies launched a great assault on 8 August 1918, which Ludendorff, the German commander-in-chief, recognised was 'the black day of the German army in the history of the war'. It was the real beginning of the end, because it started the process of German withdrawal.

In the Battle of Amiens that followed, tanks had become a key weapon and air forces were more important than before. The Hindenburg Line, to which the Germans had retreated, was their next objective. By 21 August, the Allied advance was sweeping across the old fields of the Somme and in late August *The Times* was proclaiming the 'fall of the Somme strongholds'. On 27 August they advanced through Delville Wood, where so many of the Footballers' had fallen in 1916. By 8 September a Scottish sergeant, observed by Terraine, was able to record his impression of the battered enemy: 'They are marked with the sign of the defeated.'

And then there was the attack on the Hindenburg Line itself. This was decisive, both symbolically and strategically. Captain Hart's memoir of the experiences of the Royal Welch Fusiliers includes vivid testimony to the British awe at this fortification: 'The Hindenburg Line was a truly wonderful piece of engineering. It consisted of two trenches, two hundred or more yards apart . . . here and there timbered steps led to front and rear, also to concrete machine-gun emplacements along the parapet.' The fortification ran by the Héninel-Croisilles road, not far from Arras and still that hundred or so kilometres from Boulogne and the Channel coast.

Now, though, British awe at German strength was fading. The successful assault began on 18 September and by 28 September the Allies were achieving advances of more than five miles in a single day. In nine days they broke the Hindenburg Line and by 5 October the fate of the war was swinging decisively in the Allies' favour.

In the bigger picture, meanwhile, America's President Wilson had turned down a German attempt to make peace at the start of October. He demanded that they withdraw from all the lands they had occupied. On 8 October, the British Army launched an attack along a twenty-mile front, which became the Second Battle of Cambrai. Things began to move fast. American forces broke the German lines on 10 October. These were the days when the 13th Battalion of the Middlesex Regiment found their lives changing too. After all the years of almost static struggle, punctuated by frantic offensives, they were at last called upon to make an old-fashioned military charge and pursuit. It was almost as if the warfare of Waterloo had returned.

On 8 October 1918, with the Allies advancing rapidly and the German army pulling back towards the border, the 13th Battalion, with Private Coleman in B Company, was moving with the 73rd Brigade through Belgium. They had paused in camp to sort out their equipment and ammunition, but the nights there were far from peaceful. Although in daylight the enemy were retreating, by night they were fighting: 'several casualties were caused by shellfire', according to the

Battalion diary. At five o'clock in the afternoon, they headed out of camp and tramped into what are described as 'old trenches': there they remained as the darkness closed in. Just under four years before Tim had first reached the front line with the 17th Battalion. Now victory was inevitable, but that did not mean that anyone was safe that night.

Having huddled through the darkness, listening out for shells, they continued to follow the Germans as far as the town of Awoingt. This was about thirty kilometres from Bapaume and the Somme. Surely this war was finished in all but name and there would not be a return to the terrors of those recent days. The closer they came to the end, the more men who had given themselves up for lost thought about getting back home. But now, at the finishing line, the enemy turned and fought, and the whole of the brigade was needed for action. Just like that terrible day in April 1917 outside Oppy Wood, the Germans had not really retreated. On the contrary, they were ready and waiting. The line was being held up ahead. The German command was uncertain how to handle the situation. Some wondered whether they might yet withstand the Allied advance at least until winter closed in. Heavy shelling and machine-gun fire opened up.

The Second Battle of Cambrai began on 8 October with machine-guns remaining as the last great German weapon, as they had been on that first day on the Somme. Now the balance had altered. Soon Haig himself was across the Hindenburg Line and was unleashing cavalry charges in his eagerness to press ahead.

On 9 October battle was joined in earnest. This was no longer the familiar ritual of trench warfare, endured over years. An older game of charge and counter-charge was being played. Tim and his companions in B Company, including some other players such as Whittaker, the Millwall winger, and Lamb, a striker from Sheffield Wednesday, were close enough to hear the uproar as the forward-most parts of the Brigade engaged the enemy. Sergeant-Major Tommy Gibson, the Forest full-back, was now a section commander. He always had strong nerves; he was a natural penalty-taker. He had been the first Forest player to enlist, in February 1915, and it had been to uphold the honour of the forwards that Tim had explained his own trip to the Trent Bridge recruiting office. Darkness returned and they scrambled into a railway cutting for shelter.

When they stared into the dawn of 10 October, the situation had changed. The Germans were nowhere to be seen, or heard. They had gone, leaving a kind of question mark behind. The Sussex Regiment, close by, was ordered to find them. Reports soon came back to the officers of the 13th, indicating that they had got as far as the town of Rieux. There the enemy had dug themselves in. It was about ten kilometres from Awoingt where this episode began and about the same journey from Cambria itself, the epicentre of the storm.

The pursuers moved quickly through shattered villages. In the distance, as if in a dream, they could see a group of cavalry, according to the Battalion War Diary. There was also a posse of cyclists up front. These were the advance forces, checking out the lie of the land as they had done for centuries. The atmosphere, which pervades the detailed operations report, was tense and full of foreboding. From the bicycling scouts, a messenger rumbled back to report. The news was bad, a dispatch telling the men of the 13th that they would lead the action against the occupied town. C and D Company moved on ahead, with B Company, footballers and all, 'in close support'. The village was well fortified.

After a restless interval, the unlucky men of the 13th began to climb a hill above the town. From there they could attempt to drive the enemy from their stronghold. There was another pause while the arrangements were sorted out. No one really knew what was going on in these unstable clashes. The Germans could have hurried in reinforcements or they might have pulled back in numbers, leaving a decoy force behind. The British would soon find out. Tim and his mates in B Company watched as the rest of the Battalion headed down the road. After another short wait, they began to tramp behind. For a while, it was quiet. The Germans were waiting to see what would happen next. As they filed up the slope overlooking the occupied town, the shellfire began. Tim and his companions were out of range but they could see the other companies of their Battalion taking the brunt of the attack. They kept on moving forward. Amid the shellfire, several machine-guns opened up. There were nests left in place targeting that hill. The Germans had guessed the Allied strategy. B Company was drawn into action earlier than the plan had specified.

All of this action was part of a wider engagement that now sits sharply defined in the history books as the Second Battle of Cambrai. At the time nothing was so clear. What was happening to Tim and his colleagues was typical of the British experience. They were running into the most stubborn of the German gun positions. Terraine quotes one vivid eyewitness account: 'High explosive shells came with the shrapnel, and where they fell geysers of torn earth and black smoke roared up . . . a foul murky cloud of dust and smoke formed . . . the silent ridge to the left awoke with machine-guns and rifles . . . the raw smell of blood was in men's nostrils.'

Such military actions were usually recorded in separate operations notes. For that particular sector, the notes are far more critical than the largely deferential comments regarding earlier operations: 'Intense machine-gun fire. Not sufficient depth to press home the attack until it was successful. Lack of preliminary reconnaissance. Tanks would have been of the most value.' A hundred men and more from the 13th Battalion were testimony to the relevance and accuracy of such criticisms. It was a bitter battle for those on the ground: 'Headquarters were too far back to get information quickly and act on it. A brigade forwards station with Battalion headquarters just in front would have been of great value.' The lines of communication that had developed out of the years of trench fighting broke down as the war became faster moving and more volatile.

Tim had been in open combat before but, given the chaos and the extent of what was at stake on both sides, this was the fiercest he had known. The screaming of shells and bullets was incessant. You could do nothing except hope. The smoke and dust of battle made it ever harder to get a clear picture, and afterwards no one really knew the shape of what had happened. That is the reality of those last clashes, which have almost slipped from the recognised story of the war, where the image of the trenches and 'going over the top' shape our collective memory. These last days were almost the opposite: frantic and unpredictable, but no less dangerous. Within a short time, the British had lost dozens. None of the footballers around Tim had yet been hit: lucky men. No longer ranged 'in support' of the other companies, B was now right at the front. In the growing chaos, the different parts of the Battalion were merging.

In this embattled corner, the triumphant British pursuit of Germans and of victory, which had been full of high spirits the previous days, was threatening to break down. The light faded. The bombardment continued into the evening, as the Germans attempted to dislodge their enemy. By now, men were lying all around. It was a sheer struggle for survival between men reduced to their basic, primitive selves, with the possibility of a future flickering in the air before them. Many would not make it. Under this fire stretchers could not collect men and the best that could be done was to leave them in human 'dumps'. The night sky was ominous, giving enough light for the German gunners. The men of B Company were trapped on the slope that they had been sent to occupy. There was not much shelter. They could not return fire: rifles were useless at that range. The machine-guns fired on in bursts into the night.

The soldiers had become hypersensitive to light and darkness, sensing the moods of the sky. As the first streaks of light appeared, there was relief at reaching another day. Captain Clark, the Company commander, was on his feet. Looking around, they knew they were right in the middle of the British line. The Captain called out the dawn's first command: 'Advance!' He was calling the entire Allied army forward, but at this moment his order was addressed directly to them. They had had no refreshment and were unable to reach their wounded comrades. This added to the hellish atmosphere.

Yet, as morning began to break, B Company was determined to renew the advance. This was their moment in the wider story, in history. For many men that autumn the urge to win last-minute glory eclipsed the wish to survive. The hill was still the objective. They surged up on to the attack. What else could a man do? Tim had been called a 'star of the front line' back in the days of Woolwich Arsenal; now the phrase was about to become true in a different kind of front line. Captain Clark and his second-in-command, Lieutenant Early, led the way. In the air was that strange war fever. Suddenly, officers and soldiers who had made their way carefully and quietly through the war were feeling that they could not go home without the ultimate honour, a medal for valour. Men who had been wary throughout the trench years now raced towards enemy machine-guns. Captain Clark took that spirit to heart and the line of bullets cut him down. Lieutenant Early was in charge and he did not last much longer. The company was leaderless, as happened to many on this final surge. In these crises, soldiers who had followed commands and routines for years suddenly found themselves with a choice. There was nobody looking, not out there. As the day broke, and the guns still sputtered, it was literally every man for himself. The 'command and control' that had kept the whole rhythm of military life so rigid now collapsed. Each man made his decision, knowing it might be his last.

The situation was still unclear. The Colonel came out to inspect them and see the lie of the land. He was cut down before their eyes by a last stray machine-gun bullet. Still they went forward, however. B Company rallied and drove on around F904, Private J.G. Coleman. They found themselves in one of the classic landscapes of the war: a sunken road, overhung with the remains of earth walls and bushes. Even in the gathering light, it was gloomy. These were typical places to hold a last stand and this was where Coleman's Company decided to fight.

The sequence of events was concealed from those involved. A snatch of a letter that he wrote home afterwards, and that eventually surfaced in a later *Athletic News* of early 1919, shows how Tim had felt, as well as revealing the outcome: 'Tell Walter White that Tim can win a medal at this game as well as at the other.' White had been Tim's team-mate at Everton, and again at Fulham. He was the man whom Tim accused of talking a foreign language, with his Scottish accent, and whom he tormented at cards. They had always been competitive friends. When he decided to fight as never before, Tim was thinking of football and his football friends: he had turned at last back into the man who wanted, more than anything else, to win, to show that he was better than the others, to get the goal himself. It was the same Tim Coleman who, having missed that penalty in his debut for Woolwich Arsenal, kept going until he got a really stunning goal. In that last fight on the Western Front, he was in touch with the man he had been in front of goal.

On that sunken road, without their official commanders to take the decisions, the men had to work it out for themselves. Through the morning, as the October sun rose, they began their resistance, isolated from the general flow of Allied victory. Gradually, the British barrage opened up and they were less alone. By the middle of the day, as the report put it, 'the line was established'. In a famous telegram to Haig, the British Prime Minister, David Lloyd George, defined that moment: 'The courage and tenacity with which the troops of the empire, after withstanding the terrific enemy onslaught of the spring of this year, have again resumed the offensive with such decisive results is the greatest chapter in our military history.' Those scrappy, vicious events involving the 13th Middlesex were also, in the larger picture, part of this definitive offensive. Eventually, further reinforcements arrived and the attack swept on around them. They remained on the hillside, as another night wrapped around them and the shells came down. One more morning and they were pulled back.

The official report reduced the story to the bare bones. The Germans had continued to resist them: 'Considerable opposition was met with.' The Company Commander, Captain Clark, was lost and then his replacement was killed. Battle raged into the morning and in the end the objective was achieved. It had been a bitter fight, 'under heavy shellfire all night and the following morning'.

The officers who survived were full of the same complaints and expressions of alarm as a result of this kind of situation, which arose repeatedly in the final exchanges of the war: 'By the time these two trenches had been dealt with our troops had lost touch with the barrage and the left company came under most intense machine-gun fire from the flanks inflicting severe casualties and making further advance impossible.' As in that fight outside Rieux, it was usually the machine-guns that were the most dangerous of the enemy's weapons because they were so unpredictable: 'Further machine-guns were encountered east of the trench. These . . . trickled back and prevented further advance.'

The account of the heroic stand was representative of those final days: 'The Battalion went to ground in the sunken portion of the road. Orders were issued in the expectation of the division taking part in a wide sweep forward, but as yet the leading battalions were unable to get better battle patrols through the villages in front. The Germans were making good use of cycle machine-guns, and were shelling the brigade position continuously and fairly heavily. The companies had casualties.' They lost more than 100 men, killed, wounded or missing, and six officers. It was to be the last big encounter of the Footballers' war. After the turmoil, Rieux fell to the Allied advance. The men of the 13th moved into town and took over. It was about five o'clock on the evening of 13 October. It seemed like years since those long evenings in camp, when occasional shellfire had felt so menacing. Now the odd blast would have felt like the whispering of the wind.

Many recent accounts of the Great War have put victory down to factors other than the Allies' eventual superiority on the battlefields of France and Belgium. Terraine's recent work agrees with the old official history which declared that 'the collapse of Germany began not in the Navy, not in the homeland, not in any of the sideshows, but on the Western Front in consequence of defeat in the field.' He remarks a touch acerbically that: 'It is strange how generations of clever men have failed to notice this.' Tim's role in this was one tiny part, as were those of countless others. He had won his medal on a day when the wider picture of the Great War also shifted decisively. As Gilbert wrote: 'On 10 October Serb forces entered Nis . . . the city had been defended by German troops . . . Every nation in the allied line was moving forward. On 10 October, the American First Army under Pershing finally succeeded in driving the Germans out of the Argonne forest.'

This was the day of destiny after all. It had been a long, agonising wait since the carnage of 1 July 1916, which was supposed to have been the turning point. Tim had been lucky enough to be among the reserves that day. Now he was in the front line of the truly decisive day's action: 'On 11 October, German forces began a systematic withdrawal from the Western Front.'

After the fury, a pause. On 21 October 1918 three private soldiers were called out of the Battalion parade. Private Coleman of B Company, Private Park of A Company and Sergeant Reynolds of C Company stand to attention, waiting to receive the Military Medal, the common soldier's award for extreme valour in combat. These are the men who were at the centre of their respective companies' battles on that hillside, in one more desperate night and morning of the war. The leading spirit from D Company, Private Moxham, was awarded his medal posthumously. Finally, the bureaucratic world recognised the long-time rebel. The Battalion Diary of the 13th Middlesex recorded in careful pencil script that '904 Private J.G. Coleman of B Company' had received his due, for once, as he would have said. That last fight under the shellfire through the night and the morning had finally turned Tim into a front-line fighter here too.

In the early days of the war, the official propaganda described the fighting as 'the greater game' in contrast presumably to the lesser sports of football and cricket. Tim felt that he had had the last word: he had won his medal at what, he defiantly suggested to Walter White, was certainly not a greater game than the real one, football. How could a man who was good at football not succeed at this game too? It was characteristic of Tim that in announcing the fact that he had been awarded his medal he did so by claiming that it showed how a footballer could also win at soldiering, and he somehow managed to imply that he, or maybe all players, had been unjustly talked down in the past. The tang of bitterness remained, even in the moment of triumph.

The last weeks of the war loosened the Army system. As the war moved faster, there emerged a more mobile kind of society – Tim's kind of world, where, for a short interlude at least, the rigid procedures of trench life were replaced by a shifting and spontaneous flow of events. He was not a hero from the Somme, the steady advance with slow steps; he was a hero from a different kind of war, his kind of war.

He never did like doing what the bosses said. The old joke at his clubs was that, when the manager was away, he would greet visitors with the announcement that Mr Coleman was available in his office to see them. Eventually, his wish had come true: out on that hillside, under the shells, he had had his moment in charge, or at least at the centre of things, making decisions for himself. He was also always seemingly at his best just after plans had gone wrong, in a match or in a strike. In that first game for Woolwich Arsenal, back in 1903, when he missed the penalty against Port Vale, it served only to make him play better, until he got his debut goal after all.

The 13th Middlesex continued to advance, crossing into Belgium. They were following the Germans all the way now. The Western Front was over: this was injury-time. The last of their football casualties died on 4 November 1918. Rudd was an amateur full-back with Clapton Orient. He played alongside Tim in the autumn of 1915. He even got a game for one of the Battalion sides at Christmas of 1915. He died in the last skirmish that this group of men ever fought. It was a ridiculous incident in which they came under belated shellfire trying to ford a river. Clapton Orient had been proud of their many enlisted players; they paid a high price for that pride. Further along the front, George Lake, a Chelsea midfielder, also fell with a week to go to the armistice that everyone knew was coming.

When 11 November came, Tim was in Belgium at Le Louvain, or Leuven, with the 13th Middlesex. They had crossed the border pushing the Germans back the way they had first come, through Mons, scene of the Allied retreat, and then they had gone close by Waterloo. He was surrounded by the usual group of players: Sergeant-Major Gibson, Private Sheldon, men from Millwall and Sheffield Wednesday, Brighton and West Ham. On that day Percy Barnfather, who played on the wing for Croydon, was formally promoted to the rank of captain.

On 16 November 1918, the first Chelsea programme after the Armistice included a tribute to Tim: 'Hearty congrats to happy Tim Coleman, once so popular a member of the Cottagers, on his being awarded the Military Medal.' The old image was back again: he was 'happy' and 'popular' and, more than that, he was football's final star of the whole war. There had been other footballing medallists, and more distinguished medals. Two players had won the VC: Donald Bell, who played, albeit briefly, for Crystal Palace and Newcastle

United, and Willie Angus, of Celtic. Angus survived, although he was severely disabled; Bell had fallen on the Somme. Frank Buckley won the DSO, the officers' gallantry medal, and Jack Cock, of Huddersfield, was awarded the Military Medal, the gallantry award for 'other ranks', also on the Somme.

Still Tim's award had a special ring to it. When he returned to London after demobilisation, in the early spring of 1919, he agreed to meet a journalist and tell him the story of these, his last days in the Army. In the published interview, the *Athletic News* featured that remark about medal-winning, addressed to Walter White, as if it were the last word not only on Tim but on football's fight at the front. For that short time, immediately the fighting finished, it was as if Tim had scored the winning goal in the sport's battle against those critics who had been hostile since that obstinately completed season in 1914-15. Then the players had been, according to the Poet Laureate, Robert Bridges, 'more dangerous than the Germans', because they under-mined the nation's dedication. To anybody who still thought that, here was their answer – Tim Coleman, the little Gunner, MM. There had been plenty of others, of course: it was timing that gave Tim his brief moment back in the spotlight.

As his interview in the *Athletic News* also recorded, he still had one other medal to win too, before he left the Army. The 13th Middlesex remained in camp into the New Year of 1919. Some troops had moved into Germany, others waited to go home. Tim was back in Belgium where, years before, he noticed how the border officials reacted to that German eagle embroidered on his cushion, and wondered about the Woolwich boys and a European war. To keep the troops busy, the Army continued to stage football tournaments. In that part of the old battlefield, as 1919 dawned, the big competition was for the 24th Divisional Cup, contested by all the Battalions in the region. Effectively, it was a Belgian Cup for the British Army. It was the last military football of the war – for it still seemed like the war, until the troops reached home. The 13th possessed the core of the Footballers' Battalion and there was fierce competition for places but there could be only one skipper: Tim Coleman was up for one last contest before the end of this Continental tour.

The weather was freezing, which did not stop him, or his friends. He had alongside him in the final front line of the Great War Woodhouse, of Brighton, on one wing, Lamb, of Sheffield Wednesday, in the centre, and Whittaker, of Millwall, on his own flank outside him. Woodhouse was supported at inside-forward by Dick Upex, of Croydon. The whole saga made another great tale, which Tim told to that interviewer in March 1919: 'A jolly fine side it was,' said Tim. Even Sergeant-Major Tommy Gibson got a game, though he was not playing up front as he preferred. It was defence for him.

They went sailing through their first round on 19 January, and four days later they defeated a team raised from a whole brigade of the Royal Field Artillery. On 25 January, they came up against the 7th Battalion of the Northamptonshire Regiment. It was one of those strange coincidences. In his first firing-line match, reported by the press in the Christmas of 1915, Tim had played against a Northamptonshire Regiment side. Now, he met more of the Kettering and Wellingborough lads, the men against whom he had started way back, or perhaps against their fathers and uncles. This January, they were no match for him: Tim's 13th Battalion team marched on by five goals to one, though that was two less than he recorded against them at the start of this expedition.

Snow then fell and there was a hard frost but it made no difference. In the final of that last Divisional Army cup, Tim's last wartime eleven defeated the Fusiliers 6-0. Tim was wound up to breaking point and he scored a hat-trick with which to finish his war. He had won a last Military Medal for football and now he won a last Army cup. The two medals summed up his victory over the war: Tim made that clear by making them the highlight of his post-match, post-war interview. He also had an eye on the future that cold January. While in Brussels, he was picked for a British Army side that defeated a Belgian team. As the press put it: 'Thus allies in war return to the recreations of peace.' Tim was more interested in whether he could use these last Army games to re-establish his football career, even in his late thirties and after everything he had been through. There was a moment of hope: 'I was chosen to play in an Army trial match, which should have taken place at Valenciennes . . . But the weather was so bad that the game was postponed.' If only it had gone ahead; perhaps that would have reminded people of his true calibre. There were other chances: 'Before I came away I was told there might be a representative Army team sent over from France to play in England and I was asked if I would be agreeable to take part in it if I were selected.' In looking back, he described his reply as if he were a character in Dickens: 'I consented.' As if he had any choice! The grand language contrasted with the threadbare possibilities of life, and he intended the bitter contrast; it was one he had used before.

That was what the aftermath of the war felt like for Tim, despite his double triumph. He brought masses of invention to a situation that was actually bleak and bare, not funny at all, as well he knew. In an anecdote that effectively, and consciously, rounded off the stories of football at war, he told his *Athletic News* interviewer how he went to his demobilisation interview in February. He was handed the application form for demob. One of the categories was 'Occupation', and Tim wrote in that box: 'Agricultural labourer'. It was his way of dramatising how few options he had. He then told the episode so as to allow his interviewer to record it as if it were almost a funny story:

'Is this correct, Coleman?'

'Yes, sir!' Tim then, as he reported, saluted calmly.

The officer was not convinced, apparently: 'What branch of agriculture were you engaged in before you joined up?'

'Thresher, sir.'

The reply was accepted: 'Ah, just so. I understand.'

The interviewer tried to portray the dialogue as a funny Coleman story: 'You have read and heard many yarns about the funny things he has said and done. The most recent story concerns what happened when Coleman was about to leave France for good.' Tim's original point shows through: what opportunity *did* he have, if not labouring? It might not be in the fields . . .

In fact, ahead of things as ever, Tim had foreseen a hard world not only for himself but for the whole generation of briefly acclaimed heroes. Nevertheless, he allowed the anecdote to have a happy ending, knowing what the audience wanted: 'It happened however that the form had to undergo scrutiny by an Army Captain who knew his men. He sent for the man who had specialised in things that grow out of *the ground*.' He knew Tim was an old Woolwich icon: 'Look here, Coleman, I just want to tell you that I have known you to be a professional footballer for ever so long. Are you not the Tim Coleman who played for Woolwich when a lad, 16 or 17 years ago?'

*Part Four*

The Future

# The Last Goals

A glimpse of Tim's life back from the war came in the scene-setting details of an interview he gave to the *Athletic News* in March: 'In a quiet London thoroughfare this week I met Tim Coleman. "Just giving the bulldog an airing," he remarked by way of salutation. A black spaniel, no bigger than a football boot, wagged the tiniest of tails and glanced appealing to its master as if in protest at the stoppage to the outing.'

Though most of the article was used to tell the story of the end of the war, Tim also had a gesture towards the future. 'Here I am, fit as ever,' he said. No club appeared to be listening, though. Forest had no vacancies in their front line, though they did give Tommy Gibson a chance in defence. Fulham gave his mate Wilf Nixon, back from the 2nd Footballers', another try in goal. Clapton Orient put up a brass plaque to commemorate Willie Jonas and Richard McFadden, and they let Tim's comrade Bob Dalrymple back into the attack. Fred Bullock won the London Combination with Brentford in the spring of 1919 and was Huddersfield captain that September, for the resumption of the Football League. Jackie Sheldon ran down the Anfield tunnel again in the sunshine that greeted the 1919-20 season, pardoned by the committee men. Frank Buckley was no longer playing but he became manager at Norwich, where he gave Jack Doran a new start. For Tim it was a hard search. He was that bit older and he also personified the old world, as he always had done. Cult figures can date suddenly.

Eventually, though, his persistence paid off, up to a point. He did find a home for the new season, on the edge of the game, but still one of the professionals. Times were hard that September in the valleys of South Wales. Still, as the local paper said: 'King Football has come again to Ebbw Vale after being asleep for many years. The signs are not wanting that he will awake to a renewed life, and there seems to be tremendous optimism present that football will be played by greater numbers and witnessed by vaster crowds than ever before.' The Ebbw Vale Football Club were to take part in the Second Division of the Southern League, the First Division of the Welsh League and the English FA Cup. Spirits were high: 'Everybody is enthusiastic – players, committee and spectators.' There was not much money, though: 'Will the committee provide boots which enable the players to keep their feet from slipping?' Many of the team were amateurs. They had a pro in charge, a small, curly-haired inside-right. The fans still appreciated him: 'Isn't Tim Coleman an artist? Passes the leather at the right time to the right place.'

Professor Timothy was back on his travels. This was not really where he had hoped to be when he gave that interview to the *Athletic News* back in March, with all those ideas of playing for the Army team still alive. In the hard world of September 1919, a former international in his late thirties was lucky to find a job at all: many of the returning men were still waiting, in football and other walks of life. That charm, though, remained powerful. He always could win over any football crowd in the land, from the Welsh valleys to Merseyside, from Northampton to south London – where Arsenal began – and from the Thames towpath to the banks of the Trent. The message was loud and clear: it would take more than nearly four years on the Western Front to cut the artistry out of Tim Coleman. This was the positive side of his personality, throwing himself into the life of a team and a town, leaving behind for the moment all the anger and sense of exclusion that still appeared in his remarks.

On 13 September 1919, Coleman, of Woolwich Arsenal, Everton, Sunderland, Fulham and Nottingham Forest, took the field for Ebbw Vale's home match against Porth in the Southern League. Military Medals and Battalion Cups were now a world away. First of all, with everybody in the ground waiting for the kick-off, news arrived that 'the visitors had had a breakdown on their way'. Hundreds of fans left the ground after waiting for an hour. Finally, Porth arrived in their bus at 'about six o'clock'. Tim won the toss, when they eventually got going as the September evening gathered. After a few minutes' play, he was on the attack and dribbling into the opponents' penalty area. Out of his depth, one of the defenders pulled him down: penalty. Naturally, Tim was up for it, as he had been back in 1902 – and this time he crashed the ball against the crossbar. An ordinary man's head might have gone down. Instead, a few minutes later he hit a tremendous shot, which the goalie just managed to push out for a corner. At half-time it was 0-0 but Tim was fighting the good fight.

It was getting dark by the time they began the second half. The home side went ahead and then the visitors equalised. It was proving a ding-dong battle after all. With only a minute to go, Woodford, of Ebbw Vale, managed to put in a cross and there on the end of it, inevitably, was Tim Coleman. He trapped the ball neatly and fired an unstoppable shot. It was his day, like so many other Saturdays. No single moment expresses more powerfully what it meant to return from the Western Front. Little material reward awaited any of them: poverty dripped from this scene, even boots being in short supply. Yet, in the centre of the picture, the old talent was inextinguishable and so was the old response to his 'art'. As the light faded across the valley, Tim was keeping the faith, with himself and with his fans, at least those who had the patience to stay until the visitors' bus arrived.

Tim kept his flag flying in the valleys. He was trying to take on more of a managerial role, going off to see 'how the second team shaped', as he told the press. Into October and Ebbw Vale had to prepare for a tie in the first round of the FA Cup. They were up against Mid-Rhondda, whose star player was Joe Bache as their star – a recruit to the England front line with Tim as long ago as 1907. There was to be no magical Cup run this year – Rhondda were too strong for them. Tim was as resourceful as ever, he just did not have the team around him to make the most of his talents. 'Coleman placed accurately to Woodford, and the latter did not get possession.' One minute he was trying to set up his team-mates in attack and the next he was back in desperate defence. Rhondda 'forced a corner and Coleman cleared'. Then, to add injury to frustration, 'immediately after the resumption Coleman received a hard drive in the stomach and was winded.' The final defeat was more than just another game: it felt as though the breath really had been knocked out of him.

Tim's return to football was not as strange as that of some players. On Saturday, 27 December 1919, a match was scheduled on the ground belonging to the Culver Iron and Steelworks in Colchester. It was the first round of the Worthington Evans Cup, an Essex competition. The host side were Mumford's, an eleven made up of workers from the foundry. The visitors were Clacton Town and it was a needle game. However, the crowd was far out of proportion even to that local excitement. Most of them had come to see a man rather than a match. Across the country there had been strikes in the iron and steel industry that autumn. This little ground, without a grandstand of any kind, belonged to a bitter world. And on to this pitch there came a ghostly figure from the past: V.J. Woodward, England skipper and Spurs legend. The last of the great amateurs was back home in Essex football. 'Jack' was back at Clacton Town, where he began as a teenage prodigy before even the Boer War. Evidently, the holiday and his fortieth birthday had not been enough to keep Vivian John Woodward from having one more go at the game, despite the predictions of those papers back in 1916.

The crowd was waiting as he came on to that field: 'The entry of

Vivian Woodward was the signal for considerable applause, his reception paying eloquent testimony to his popularity with Essex sportsmen.' But the body was simply failing: 'A lessening of speed was, as only to be expected, noticeable. Generally he kept well up-field, and when the ball was sent to him transferred it without delay just where it was wanted.' Coleman and Woodward, the personification of professional and amateur football in Edwardian London, now had far more in common: they were both still fighting to hang on to the game.

By the end of the 1919-20 season, Tim knew he was going to have to move on. He had come to the end of yet another one-year contract, and there was no renewal – Ebbw Vale could not afford him any longer. He was not the only one. His old commander, Frank Buckley, had ended his first season in management by having to resign. He had had to sell John Doran – and got only £400 for him from Brighton. The critics were gathering: why had Norwich not taken an offer of thousands of pounds back in the autumn? It was not the last of the Major's transfer dealings to excite suspicion among the fans and the press. For the moment, he was a travelling salesman.

Tim was proving as resourceful as ever, a hard man to put down. On Saturday, 28 August 1920 the great footballing journeyman began a new journey. Out on to a small, military ground at Chatham, Kent, trotted Tunbridge Wells Rangers. Fifteen years previously, Bob Whiting had been in this line-up, on the verge of his breakthrough into the big time. This Saturday afternoon they were led out by a man who was travelling the other way. The new star down in Tunbridge Wells was Tim Coleman, having found another one-year contract to keep his show on the road. The local paper announced with excitement prior to the game that: 'Coleman is the Arsenal international forward who has signed on since last week.' It was a last-minute deal. He must have felt that he had got to the end of the line but suddenly there came the chance to earn what hardly amounted to a living in the Kent League. Back then the dominant side in the county was Charlton Athletic, though they were soon headed for better things in the Football League. Ten years previously, he was coming down the tunnel at Roker Park, the new star in the Sunderland firmament. The problem for the survivors from the Footballers' Battalion was that they were five years older than they ought to be in football terms: those missing years made life after the war so much more difficult.

Tim had declared himself to be 'fit' after the war. The question was what that meant, for him and for his friends. Many of the men simply found their footballing lives ebbing away. Jimmy Hugall was a tough Glaswegian goalkeeper, a friend of Tim's mate Dalrymple at Orient. He had become a lieutenant, hurt his leg but kept going. He returned to keep goal for Clapton again. On good days he made fine saves but those war injuries never really healed. Hugall died in 1925, his football career barely over. Often these footballing veterans collapsed when they had to give up playing. Joe Mercer, a close friend of Tim's at Forest, became the Tranmere skipper for a few seasons. His breath grew shorter, he left the sport and within a year he too was dead. (His young son, also Joe, became an Arsenal star of the Thirties and then a famous manager and television pundit.) Tom Barber, of Aston Villa who played with Tim for Orient at Chelsea before they went to the trenches, managed a series of one-year deals, ending up at Walsall. He too died in 1925, a few months after his career had ended.

Colin Veitch had been the other great hope of England's front line in 1907. He was another great Players' Union man. He objected to the war at the beginning but finished up as a lieutenant in the Siege Artillery. At the end of the war, he had the chance to run for Parliament. Another life hovered before his eyes, but he could not take the opportunity. He was shattered by the war. Veitch became a coach and a football writer, but died in 1938 aged fifty, in a sanatorium in Switzerland, as if his health was all used up.

Yet all the while Tim marched on. People rightly talk about the triumphs of the human spirit over the trenches. Tim's 1920-21 season was one long refusal to surrender. In the week before Christmas the headlines were ablaze with admiration: 'Coleman's Brilliance. Rangers play splendid football at Chatham.' They had hammered the Royal Engineers by five goals to one. He was only a local hero these days but the flavour was the same: 'The big feature of the game being the perfect work of Tim Coleman, who secured four of the Rangers goals, performing his hat-trick in about 10 minutes.' The Royal Engineers had gone on to the attack from the kick-off and the Rangers goalkeeper had been forced to make a great save. Tim had come back to help the defence. He took the ball from his own goalkeeper and 'ran right through'. He went the whole way up the pitch, past the entire Engineers team, before 'sending a crashing shot' that left the keeper stranded, as amazed as everyone else. The Engineers kicked off, Tim seized the ball and went all the way through to score again. They kicked off again and 'from the kick-off, Coleman yet again secured and with a sensational run broke through, and a further goal was only just prevented'.

On Christmas Day 1920, Rangers completed the double over the Engineers, winning again by five goals to one in front of 1,500 people: 'Carrick passed the ball to Todd, who sent the ball goalwards, and Coleman getting his foot to it, sent in a terrific shot, which crashed into the net.' The goals and the style was still there but, in reality, the strength and power was not. Defiance made good the deficit but by the end of that season it was clear that the legs had nothing more to give.

By September, Tim had surfaced at Maidstone United. He hoped to begin a managerial career at the Kent club. He did some coaching and ended up being responsible for the reserves, with whom he also played. By February T. Coleman had eight goals for the reserves. Their leading scorer had twenty-two. His name was A. Coleman. It was Tim's son Arthur, who had been standing so awkwardly in that front-page picture as a teenager when the family received the telegram telling them that Tim was alive and well. Now he was the star of his dad's team. On 4 February 1922, six years on from that famous newspaper picture, Tim and Arthur lined up in the forward line for Maidstone United Reserves against Sittingbourne Paper Mills and they provided a family goal feast. The game finished 11-0. Arthur led 2-1 in the Colemans' private battle in the first half and added two more in the second. After that success, he graduated to the first team. At the end of the season a club photograph was taken, with father and son lining up together, Tim standing behind a seated Arthur. It was a nice touch, a neat conclusion perhaps. Yet in fact this was far from the end of Tim Coleman's football life.

# Another Time

The Dutch town of Enschede is right on the border with Germany, in the far east of Holland. By the 1920s it had a well-established textile industry, founded in part by a factory-owner from Oldham. Like those mill towns in the north of England, Enschede was a football town. In 1910 its main team, Sporting Club (SC) Enschede, was formed by the merger of the two rival sides, Hercules and Phoenix, and they attracted crowds of several thousand to their tree-lined stadium, with its neat wooden grandstands. The players were all amateurs: professional football did not arrive in Holland until the Fifties. The heart of the club, on and off the field, was in the factories.

Though the players were not paid, Dutch clubs had a different approach when it came to coaches. It was a sign of ambition in a Dutch club to employ a British coach, often a former player. The most famous, Jack Reynolds, had been a lesser-known player in England to put it politely. He turned out around thirty times for Grimsby Town as a full-back. This was while Tim was getting established at Woolwich Arsenal. Reynolds was born the same year as Tim, 1881. Realising that his playing career was leading nowhere, he turned to coaching instead, initially in Switzerland and then in Holland. His main job was with a young club in Amsterdam called Ajax. They became a footballing institution and had various English connections, a story that has been richly told by Simon Kuper. Reynolds took over at Ajax from Jack Kirwan, an Irishman who had played for Spurs and Chelsea around the time that

Tim was playing in the capital. Kirwan and Reynolds, especially the latter, helped to set on its way one of the world's greatest football clubs.

After the Great War, Ajax began to win the Dutch championship, which at that time was contested by the winners of regional competitions. Among their main rivals were Sparta Rotterdam, who were also helped on their way by a British manager, Edgar Chadwick, fresh from success running the Dutch national team. Chadwick had a solid professional career, most notably at Blackburn Rovers.

SC Enschede were not at the level of Ajax and Sparta Rotterdam, the rising powers of the Dutch game. Still, in 1925, the town of Enschede was celebrating its six-hundredth anniversary, according to Wiegman's town chronicle. At the end of August, the town held a festival, including horse racing events, which attracted a crowd of 10,000. The People's Park had exhibitions to which 100,000 people came over the subsequent months. This was a community in buoyant mood. The economy was doing well, undamaged as it was by the war in which the country had stayed neutral. That was why a club such as SC Enschede could afford to hire an English coach and, after all, the club wanted to do their bit for the town in its celebratory year.

It had always been something of a joke in the past when Tim had pretended to be the manager. 'Mr Coleman is in' he would announce when Phil Kelso was absent and visitors arrived at Craven Cottage. His only time as a club skipper in the professional game was on Woolwich Arsenal's continental tour. The only other time he captained a side was the day in 1916 when he brought the game to life to the joy of Driver Nolan and some thousands of other soldiers. His impersonation of Percy Sands, the real Woolwich Arsenal captain, was another famous jape – at least it was for everyone else. His Dutch adventure confirmed that for Tim the idea of coaching had never been merely a joke. He had seen no real reason why he should not play those roles, and his humour had always had a vein of bitterness at what he felt was his exclusion from them.

Back in England, in 1926, Herbert Chapman had been lured south to Arsenal after guiding Huddersfield Town to three League titles in a row. But only the biggest clubs had any cash. The country was plunging towards the General Strike, with high unemployment and wages looking likely to be cut. No wonder Tim tried to look elsewhere. He had evidently been inspired by the success of some of his contemporaries in Holland and had, in the words of a future British politician, Norman Tebbit, whom he would have loathed, 'got on his bike'. He was back in continental Europe, close to the border with the nation against whom he had fought for nearly four years. Enschede must have struck Tim as being very German in character: that was the second language spoken in the town, not English, and the nearest big cities were over the border in Germany. Dortmund was much closer than Amsterdam. After all he had gone through, being there must have brought back memories.

The Dutch football season was split into two phases. The first involved the regional leagues. The winners of the five regions played together in a kind of national league, and the winners of that competition were crowned champions. This structure remained until the professional game arrived in Holland in 1954. The strongest club in the eastern league at the time was FC Heracles, near neighbours and rivals of Enschede. The two sides were pretty evenly matched but for once this was to be Enschede's year, to go with the civic celebrations. The coverage in the *Nieuwe Rotterdamsche Courant* or NRC, the leading liberal paper of the day, showed a fierce battle for supremacy between Enschede and Heracles for the eastern title. Heracles won at Enschede in a spectacular match by four goals to three, and their return meeting was drawn 1-1. Over the season, though, Enschede edged out their rivals to win the title, finishing two points ahead. Enschede outscored Heracles too, by fifty-six goals to fifty-four, but the real difference came in defence. Tim's side conceded only nineteen goals in eighteen games, four of which came in that one home defeat. Apart from that slip against Heracles, they won all their home matches, including several runaway victories by five and six goals. They were hard to beat away from home as well, clocking up 4-2 and 4-1 wins at Hengelo and Vitesse.

The NRC picked out their tactical precision and the swiftness of their play as the key factors in their success. This was a Coleman outfit, playing the game as he had learnt it at Woolwich Arsenal under Phil Kelso and also as he described it in his columns for the *Weekly News*, in which he emphasised the importance of players knowing each other's 'little ways'. This was the team-based footballing philosophy he valued and yet there was something else too. SC Enschede's great strength, as you would expect from a team coached by Tim, was said by NRC to be the pairing of winger and inside-right, Nagels and Frohlich. So he was able to pass on some of the secrets of his successful partnerships with Lawrence and Briercliffe, Shanks and Sharp, and the rest over the years. His experience contributed directly to the success of these Dutch forwards.

Having won the regional title, there came a real challenge, the contest for the national crown. This brought Tim's team up against Feyenoord of Rotterdam, one of the great names of European football history and already a dominant side in the Dutch game. The others were MVV of Maastricht, Stormvogels, and the wonderfully titled Be Quick Groningen. The real threat was from the Rotterdam side but Enschede hammered them 4-1 at home and, even more impressively, they beat them 3-2 at Feyenoord's ground. Tim's tight and tactically sharp side were unbeaten in their eight games, chalking up six victories, and they finished four points clear of Maastricht and six ahead of the mighty Feyenoord. Again, their goal difference spoke volumes about the strength of the team: twenty-five to eleven making them by far the meanest defence as well as the most potent attack.

The NRC reported that the players and officials returned home with the trophy, to be met by the mayor, Mr Bergsma, and a civic celebration. In the People's Park, where the town had been commemorating its six-hundredth year, the residents now acclaimed a modern success. There were flags everywhere. The other football clubs from Enschede brought flowers to crown the victory of their rivals. It was a success, in other words, for the whole town.

It was a strange turn of events for Tim Coleman. Back in England, he had failed to make an impression as a sort of player-coach of the reserves at Maidstone. Yet here he was, with the flags flying and the crowds cheering, winning the championship in Holland and being congratulated by the mayor and at the centre of a town's celebration of its history. His team had been acclaimed not only for their unprecedented success – Enschede had never done anything of this sort before – but also for their tactical superiority. He was the man who had made this town and team into national champions – ten years after he was thought to have died, twenty years after his best days at Woolwich Arsenal. Now he was back at the centre of another football explosion.

Holland was fast evolving into the football power that we know today. In 1901, according to the standard history by C. Niermans, there had been 80 clubs in the country. Ten years later there were 340 and by 1921 the total had risen to almost 1,200. Another thousand or so clubs were formed in the 1920s, making that the decade when the game really took hold in the consciousness of the nation. The number of players rose from 48,000 to 98,000 in the decade. Amateur it may have remained on the pitch, but this was becoming a formidable football nation. This was also the decade when the game really won over the working people, who now provided the majority of the players in what had previously been a more middle-class sport. Tim had won the title for Enschede in the middle of the decade that really created Dutch football. He had now experienced the birth of two football nations, the English and the Dutch: one as a rebel player, a great and difficult talent, and the second as a victorious professional coach.

The success of the season is embodied in two photographs. They both feature a triumphant team, showing off the spoils of their victory. One shows the eleven players, with a substitute, standing proudly with folded arms and a shining shield in front of them. Behind them is their home ground, with its two small, neat stands against a backdrop of tall trees. The other picture shows the same men, grouped differently and with club officials in smart jackets and ties. Once again, the background is beautifully green. Next to his players stands their trainer. He is on the short side, solidly built and with a neat moustache and a slightly receding hairline. Tim Coleman has won another medal after all.

The football brain that shone through his writing about the game turned out to be capable of organising a winning team. Naturally it was against the odds – for that too was a Coleman speciality. He was a natural pioneer, who, given less than half a chance, but more than none, would have made his way as a manager, as later generations of players did. He was ready for the future, which was not quite ready for him back home. His anger and resentment were partly a streak of his complex personality. They were also understandable when you consider what he was indeed capable of achieving.

Sporting Club Enschede never won the Dutch title again. They later became one of the teams that merged in the 1960s to form the regional side FC Twente, currently a strong competitor in the Dutch league and in Europe. FC Twente lay claim to that 1925-26 title as if it were their own but they have never quite managed to attain such heights, not yet. They have been showing promising signs under the direction of Steve McClaren, the former England manager, who is, in this way, aiming to rival the success of Tim Coleman back in the Twenties.

As was so often the case with Tim, a period of success was almost inevitably followed by one of contrasting fortunes. A letter from his son, John Victor, published in the Kettering press much later, suggested that Tim did spend more than one season in Holland but he did not stay permanently in the country, unlike Jack Reynolds, the most established of the English coaches there. It might have been Tim's restless or even self-destructive streak that caused him to move on again, or it might have been simply the worsening conditions. Holland, having remained neutral in the war, enjoyed an initial advantage in the 1920s but that relative prosperity did not last and when difficulties hit, they struck hard, as Van Zanden's economic history of the country makes clear. The opportunities dried up here too, but Tim had had his day of acclaim, at the centre of a new football nation.

# Journey's End

The great years in Dutch football did not last, in the economic and political chill of the late Twenties and early Thirties, and Tim returned to England soon after Enschede's triumph. If a modern-day player had had such a long career, taking in clubs such as Arsenal, Everton, Sunderland and Fulham, he would be made for life financially. If he had Coleman's intelligence and articulacy, and his already proven journalistic flair, he would have a second career in the world of punditry and as a media personality. If he had enjoyed coaching success as well, he would also have the choice of a career in management, which would be highly lucrative if insecure! Tim had neither the security of accumulated wealth nor the prospect of further opportunity in the game. He had, in fact, next to nothing to come back to.

Tim's home was in London. He went back to the area that was his home when he was at Fulham and where the family had still been in 1916, West London near Craven Cottage. His younger son, John Victor, stayed near by, while Arthur remained for a time in Kent, although he never managed to get beyond Maidstone's reserves and an occasional foray with the first team. It is hard to believe now, when retiring players have so many ways in which to remain in the game, but there was no way of continuing any kind of football life for Tim, and in the bitter cold of the depression he had no qualifications or formal education to fall back on. London and the south-east did see an economic revival of sorts, one based especially in house-building, the legacy of which includes many of the capital's outer suburbs. Tim worked as a labourer, at least that is what he was by the time the Second World War erupted.

By November of 1940, London and Tim were in the midst of the Blitz. According to *The Times*, 150 tons of bombs had fallen on the capital on the night of Tuesday, 14 November. Westminster Abbey had been hit and so had St Paul's Cathedral. On the sixteenth, the London Hospital took a direct hit. Later in the week a welfare centre sheltering children was destroyed. West London was taking a heavy toll in the Blitz. In places, whole rows of terraced homes were reduced virtually to rubble.

It was from one such terraced street, Buer Road in Fulham, that Tim Coleman emerged early on the morning of 20 November. He had his bag of labouring tools, and a workman's cap against the rain. This had been Tim's life through most of his fifties, the life of a workman hanging on in rocky times. On this particular day his destination lay within walking distance of his home. Along the route he passed signs of the previous week's damage: houses nearly falling down, shop fronts collapsing, great holes in the ground. Everyone was talking about the new German bomb, which they called 'Satan'. A week earlier it had practically destroyed the main Post Office depot at Mount Pleasant and had even hit Euston Station. Bombs lay in the streets, waiting for the overworked teams to try to defuse them. As he tramped on, smoke was still rising from dozens of sites. The scene may well have taken men such as Tim back to their marches through another battered landscape.

But this was home. It was hardly more than a week since the Prime Minister had made one of his darkest and most memorable speeches, to the House of Commons. 'History with its flickering lamp stumbles along the shell of the past trying to reconstruct its scenes, to revive its echoes, and kindle with pale gleams the passion of former days.' Those words could have been written for Tim, the former footballer supreme as he picked his way through the rubble of London's streets.

But, at such moments of crisis, as Churchill told the nation, the only thing to do was to live in the present, according to one's own lights: 'The only guide to a man is his conscience; the shield to his memory is the rectitude and sincerity of his actions.' Then came some of his great words: 'However long the struggle may last, or however dark be the clouds which overhang us, no future generation of English-speaking folk – for that is the tribunal to which we appeal – will doubt that, even at a great cost to ourselves in technical preparation, we were guiltless of the bloodshed, terror and misery which have engulfed so many lands and peoples.' The response was clear: 'Long, hard and hazardous years lie before us but at least we embarked upon them united and with clean hearts.' These words were in all the papers, all the headlines and in every memory.

As Tim walked that morning, nobody recognised him, at least nobody outside of neighbours, family and friends. He was no longer a famous face. After that last season trying to coach the Maidstone reserves and helping his son Arthur into the first team, his English career had run dry. He had had his success elsewhere but in that era a victory in Holland was like a triumph on another planet. There were no films or television replays to preserve his fame as a player, and the age of the pundits was still decades away. At most, there were memories and conversations, but people had not wanted to look back to the pre-war times, where his fame had been at its brightest.

He turned into a grander road, Prince Consort Road, leading towards Kensington and the Albert Memorial. This street had some fine buildings in it, including the Royal College of Music. It was a patriotic symbol on such mornings. That was not Coleman's destination, though. He was making his way to a far more mundane location. At this point in the war, however, it was far more important. There was a more functional building than a music college – an electricity generating station. It reached up above him into the rainy London sky.

Tim reported for duty on the site. He went over to the foreman, a mate of his by now, Henry McCormick. Tim's job that day was to repair the damaged glass on the roof. It had not suffered a direct hit, though such installations were often targeted. A bomb landing near by had done the damage. After all these years, he was back in the war again. It was not quite propping up the trench parapets but, as he said then, navvying was the main thing that ordinary folk did in a war.

It was almost exactly forty years since his football career began. Just over twenty years ago, he had come out of the smoke of that fight on the sunken road above Rieux to claim his, and football's, medal. Nearly two hundred top-flight goals, the Military Medal, crowds singing his name, and now one more journey ending in this slow ascent into the London drizzle. He climbed a ladder to the roof and made his way out to inspect the damage. From up there he could see the battered city. Down below, Henry was watching him. He made his way over the uneven surface. There were sharp daggers of glass everywhere. The rain was still coming down. Back in his Woolwich Arsenal days, the papers often said he was better when the pitch was dry and the ball lighter. In the wet, it was his feet that finally let him down, the feet that had been so balanced and agile all those years ago. Now, all on his own, with no one marking him, he lost his footing.

Before Henry's eyes, Coleman toppled over the parapet. It all happened in a flash: 'I saw him fall and at that speed I don't think there was any chance he would survive,' said the foreman. The incident was put on record as an industrial accident, but really Tim Coleman was as much a victim of the Blitz as if he had been blown up by a bomb. This man's career began before electricity lit up the great football grounds and that morning he ended his life battling against the elements to secure a small part of London's power supply. He was really a figure of the last great age of steam, when teams travelled to matches by train, and electricity was a strange fluid needed by Mr Marconi's new fangled gadgetry, as the journalist had remarked all those decades ago trying to capture the excitement at the Manor Ground the night Woolwich Arsenal gained promotion.

The hospital was not far away and Tim was carried there. Technically, therefore, Tim Coleman died at St Mary Abbot's Hospital in Kensington. In fact, his life ended on the pavement beneath the generating station where he fell, his lungs punctured and his ribs broken. In the West London papers, the incident received the brief coverage usually devoted to such accidents. The *West London Observer*, the *Kensington News and West London Times*, the *West London Press, Westminster and Chelsea News* and the *West London and Fulham Gazette* all recorded the fall from the roof of the generating station of 'J.G. Coleman, 59 – labourer', as witnessed by his foreman. It made a stark contrast with the announcements of his death back in 1916. Then, he had been defiantly 'Tim' Coleman, whatever they wrote on his Army enlistment form. Now he was only J.G. Coleman, an unknown workman.

This was not the case for one man in his early thirties, who lived in Burlington Road, another terraced street around the corner from Buer Road. There Mr John Victor Coleman still knew all about Tim Coleman, his father. At the age of six, he had been photographed looking at his dad's picture, on the day his mother opened the telegram telling her that he was still alive: 'The Welcome News in Tim Coleman's Home', a headline had called it. He had not believed it when the Kettering and Northampton papers began running the story of his father's death back then, according to the *Athletic News*. Now, seeking to keep the memory of 'Tim' alive, at least in people's minds, he wrote back home, to the *Kettering Leader and Guardian*.

He sent the letter on the day of his father's death and two days later, on Friday, 22 November, amid the reporting of another war, the only real obituary of Tim Coleman appeared: 'Memories of the old pre-Great War team will flood back into the minds of Kettering football fans with the death of John George "Tim" Coleman – one of the finest forwards of his day.' With that name 'Tim', the past flashed back into life. In its way, this was as much of a rebirth as the story in that New Year of 1916: 'Mr Albert Peters described him as "the best Kettering ever produced". Tim – short, dark, thickset and a clever inside-left – was universally popular with the crowd.' All those rumours, stories and counter-stories had faded to leave this one local memorial. Yet the keynote was still there: 'universally popular with the crowd'. It was the same old Tim Coleman as ever. November 1915 had claimed his life the first time; now November 1940 completed the job. But the essence of him lingered: 'popular Tim Coleman'.

Ninety years after the 1902-03 season, the one that brought Tim Coleman to Woolwich Arsenal and set him on the road to football fame, a new revolution began in English football when the old First Division of the Football League became The Premiership. The Arsenal kicked off the new era by facing, and losing to, Norwich City, ninety years after Tim began his first season with them by scoring against Burslem Port Vale. The frustrations of the Highbury fans as their side were embarrassed by Norwich were much the same as those felt by the supporters at the Manor Ground when they watched Tim miss that early penalty.

An even more dramatic revolution was to follow at the end of September 1996 when the former Monaco coach Arsène Wenger took over as manager. This was ninety years after Tim's most successful season with Woolwich, when they managed to lead the First Division for some time against the big clubs of the North and Midlands, with a line-up far stronger than any Woolwich had boasted before. The 1996-97 season also saw a new wave of players at the club, including the arrival of Patrick Vieira, from Milan, and then of Nicolas Anelka, an 18-year-old from Paris St Germain. The following season the club won the Premiership and the FA Cup, ninety years on from the financial crisis that nearly destroyed the old Woolwich club and produced all Tim's financial problems and his angry departure. Another season later and Wenger added the most iconic of all of Arsenal's famous imports, Thierry Henry. Eight decades earlier, Private Coleman, himself a star import at the time, was fighting the final battles of his war in France and Belgium.

Modernisation and expansion continued apace in the first decade of the twenty-first century. Arsenal moved into their state-of-the-art Emirates Stadium, a stone's throw from their old Highbury home, in 2006-07. Outside there are two cannons from the Royal Arsenal at Woolwich, a proud link with the era when Tim took the field for the first time.

On 28 October 2006, Arsenal had a hard-fought 1-1 home draw against Everton, the club Tim left for and the one against whom he had scored his first top-flight goal, all those years ago in the Plumstead fog. The home team featured Lehmann, Fabregas, Gilberto and Adebayor, a global galaxy of talents, and their goal was scored by Van Persie, a descendant in his way of the Dutch footballers whom Tim and others had developed in the 1920s.

For all the symbolism, though, there is something deeper still connecting the two eras. On 20 October 1906, the nearest equivalent day at the old Manor Ground, Tim Coleman's Woolwich Arsenal hosted, and beat, Notts County, and the *Plumstead News* was full of the passion and uproar around the game, and around the player. 'When Neave [of Arsenal] placed the corner, the ball was headed in to Iremonger, who fisted out slightly. It was then kicked on to McEachrane, who returned it. As it dropped, Coleman shot on the run and the ball flew into the net. Mad cheers! . . . Tim Coleman was the star of the field.' The *Morning Leader's* description could apply to football throughout the ages. 'There was then a scene of enthusiasm which beggars description . . . Coleman was the star artist of the front line.' That was true of his whole football life.

# Select Bibliography

Max Arthur, *Forgotten Voices of the Great War*, Ebury, 2003

Charles Buchan, *A Lifetime in Football*, Phoenix House 1955

Bryon Butler, *The Football League 1888-1988: The Official Illustrated History*, Queen Anne Press, 1987

Richard Cox, Dave Russell and Wray Vamplew (eds), *Encyclopedia of British Football*, Frank Cass, 2002

Martin Gilbert, *First World War*, HarperCollins, 1995

David Goldblatt, *The Ball Is Round*, Penguin, 2007

John Harding, *For the Good of the Game,* Robson Books, 1991

Michael Joyce, *Football League Players' Records,* Soccerdata, 2002

Simon Kuper, *Ajax, The Dutch, The War*, Orion, 2003

Clive Leatherdale (ed) *The Book of Football (1906)*, Desert Island Books, 1997

Tony Mason, *Association Football and English Society*, Harvester, 1980

*Men Famous in Football* (1905 edition, reprinted), Bedford Publishing, 1988

Andrew Riddoch and John Kemp, *When the Whistle Blows*, JH Haynes Publishing, 2008

Sir Stanley Rous, *Football Worlds,* Faber, 1978

D.J. Taylor, *On the Corinthian Spirit*, Yellow Jersey Press, 2006

John Tennant, *Football – The Golden Age: Extraordinary Images 1900-1985*

John Terraine, *To Win a War: 1918, The Year of Victory*, Cassell, 2000

Phil Vassili, *Colouring over the White Line: The History of Black Footballers in Britain*, Mainstream Publishing, 2000

Sir Frederick Wall, *Fifty Years of Football 1884-1934*, Cassell, 1935

James Walvin, *The People's Game: The History of Football Revisited*, Mainstream Publishing, 1994

Jonathan Wilson, *Inverting the Pyramid: A History of Football Tactics*, Orion 2008

# Index

Vimy Ridge 189, 193

Walden, Harold 155
Wall, Frederick 32, 61, 134, 138
Wall, George 99, 103
Walsall 218
Walthamstow Avenue 181
Walvin, James xiv, 29–30, 90, 104
War Office 134, 157
Watford 48–49
Weldon, Harry 143
Wellingborough 7, 13, 207
West, Alf 141, 167, 172, 176, 178, 185, 192
West Bromwich Albion 162
West Ham 7, 15, 17, 26, 41, 167, 192
White, Walter 'Wattie' 116, 125, 143, 201, 204, 206
Whiting, Bob 74, 141, 167, 175, 188–9, 217
Wheelhouse, Sid 146, 160, 178, 182, 187

Wolverhampton Wanderers 27, 31, 40, 126, 128
Wood, Norman 184
Woodward, Vivian John 'Jack' 63–4, 66, 136, 141, 145, 149, 150, 160, 161–2, 165, 193, 216–17
Woolwich Arsenal FC x, xi, xiii, xiv, 3–42, 46, 48–57, 58–62, 64–79, 81–3, 87, 91, 110, 113, 115, 121, 122, 124, 125, 126, 127, 135, 137, 141, 143, 151, 167, 168, 174, 175, 186, 200, 201, 205, 206, 209, 214, 215, 217, 218, 221, 222, 223, 224, 225, 228, 231, 232, 233, 234
Workman's Compensation Act 91
Worthington Evans Cup 216

Young, Sandy 31, 33, 36–7, 88, 109, 116, 157